WILD IRISH WOMEN

D0031950

'A rollicking read'
Books Ireland

'Before reading this I hadn't heard of half the women,
now I will dip into this book to read again and
again about the remarkable women
who helped to shape Éire'
Women's News

'Marian Broderick should take a bow for resurrecting
an eclectic body of Irish women's history –
the good, the bad and the ugly, as well as
the international beauties'
Justine McCarthy, *Irish Independent*

'After reading this book, one can never again
ignore the role of Irishwomen'
Dublin Historical Record

'Broderick's prose is simple and accessible, and her fascination with
her two favourite subjects - Irish history and women's studies -
jumps out from every page'
Sunday Business Post

MARIAN BRODERICK is a writer and editor who lives and works in London. She is second-generation Irish; her parents are from Limerick and Donegal. She spent every summer of her childhood in Ireland and has developed strong links with the place and the people. This is her first book.

Wild Irish Women

EXTRAORDINARY LIVES
FROM HISTORY

MARIAN BRODERICK

The University of
Wisconsin Press

The University of Wisconsin Press
1930 Monroe Street
Madison, Wisconsin 53711

www.wisc.edu/wisconsinpress/

A Cataloging-in-Publication record for this book is available from the Library of Congress
ISBN 0-299-19584-8 (paper)

First published by The O'Brien Press Ltd, Dublin, Ireland

Editing, typesetting, layout and design: The O'Brien Press Ltd
Printing: Nørhaven Paperback A/S, Denmark

PICTURE CREDITS

The author and publisher would like to thank the following for permission to reproduce visual material: Catherine McAuley courtesy of the Mercy International Centre; Sarah Curran reproduced courtesy of the Caine family, late of Ardee, County Louth; Nano Nagle courtesy of the Presentation Sisters, Monasterevin; Máire Rua O'Brien courtesy of a private collection; Lola Montez courtesy of Schloss Nymphenburg, Munich. Bayerische Verwaltung der staatlichen Schlosser, Garten und Seen; Lady Gregory and Lady Mary Heath courtesy of An Post; Peig Sayers courtesy of An Roinn Béaloideasa, UCD; Maud Gonne courtesy of the National Gallery of Ireland; Constance Markievicz courtesy of the National Museum of Ireland; Mary Ann McCracken courtesy of the Ulster Museum; Mother Jones courtesy of the Library of Congress, Washington; Mary Reid & Anne Bonny, and Grace O'Malley courtesy of the Mary Evans Picture Library, Siobh«n McKenna courtesy of C Carson; Kathleen Clarke courtesy of E Clarke. The following are all reproduced by kind permission of the National Library of Ireland: Maria Edgeworth; Lady Sydney Morgan; Countess Blessington; Somerville and Ross; the Ladies of Llangollen; Charlotte Despard; Hanna Sheehy Skeffington; Lady Wilde; the Yeats sisters; Delia Larkin; Peg Woffington; Sara Allgood; Dorothy Jordan; Kitty Kiernan; Grace Gifford. Cover painting by Sarah Purser, *The Blue Hat* (1923), by permission of the copyright holders.

Dedication

To Mary Clement Broderick and Pat Broderick,
with love and thanks to you both for
all that you have given me.

Acknowledgements

My grateful thanks for help and encouragement to: Tom Rainsford; Dr Maria Luddy, University of Warwick; Rosemary Raughter of UCD; Terry Wogan at the Civic Museum, Dublin; Ciara McKenna, the National Council for Women, Ireland; Rena at the Gregory/Kiltartan Museum; staff at the National Library, Dublin; Dublin Corporation Public Libraries; Liz Broderick and Frank Cormack; Maeve Broderick and Nigel Kane; Pearse Broderick and Clair Evans; Aidan Byrne; Anne Conaghan; Charlotte Lochhead; Amanda Brace; Carol Cooper; Suzy Fotheringham; staff at the British Library, London; and all at The O'Brien Press, especially editor Rachel Pierce and designer Emma Byrne. The author and publisher also wish to acknowledge the kind help of Douglas Sealy, Dr and Mrs Michael Purser, Mr Brian Caine, Dr Hugh Weir and The Hon. Mrs Grania Weir, Joanna Finegan, Gráinne Mac Lochlainn, Sr Agnes Gleeson, the Estate of Eilís Dillon for permission to reproduce 'The Lament for Arthur O'Leary' (www.eilisdillon.com), and Mairéad Ashe FitzGerald.

Contents

AHEAD OF THEIR TIME

POLITICAL ANIMALS

SAINTS AND SINNERS

TOUGH COOKIES

INTREPID TRAVELLERS

STARS OF STAGE AND SCREEN

ARTISTIC TEMPERAMENTS

INTRODUCTION

With all the presumption of the truly underqualified, I decided to write this book because I felt that my two favourite subjects – Irish history and women's studies – did not meet up often enough. The place of Irish women in history, or any women in any history for that matter, has been largely ignored. My intention is that this collection should go some small way to redress the balance.

There are three criteria for inclusion in this collection. The first is that these women are all fascinating. Although not necessarily the 'wild Irish girls' of Sydney Owenson's famous novel, to which the title of this book refers, they are certainly women who broke the rules in days when rule-breaking was riskier than it is today. Most were unselfconscious about this, the very last thing on their minds a desire to be seen as 'pioneering women'. Some, however, were unashamed limelight-lovers who, far from being mugged by Fate, were only too aware of their moments of destiny – and enjoyed them to the full.

The second criterion is an Irish connection, and as one might expect from a London-Irish author, this can be pretty tenuous. Though most of the women in the book are Irish-born and bred, there are those, like myself, who merely limp in with an Irish background. The Irishness of my women is variously and liberally mixed and diluted with the cultures of Europe, the USA, South America, the Caribbean, Japan and Australasia. (Then there's Katherine Parnell, who's just plain English!)

Lastly, it should be obvious that, since this is a historical collection, none of the women in this book is living – although the redoubtable Old Countess of Desmond might well be had she not fallen out of a tree at age 140. Although cynics might suggest that my decision to write only about dead women is not entirely unconnected with libel law, it would be more accurate to cite the calibre of the increasing number of women alive today that are represented in politics, public life, arts and entertainment. Once started on some of these women, it would be difficult to know when to stop – and this would be a completely different book.

The women in this collection enjoy varying degrees of fame, or notoriety. Some, such as Countess Markiewicz and Sarah Purser, are famous in their own right. Others bear household names, such as Yeats, Wilde and Parnell, yet remain shadowy figures. Who would think of the artistic sisters Lily and Lolly Yeats before their genius brother William Butler, even though WB's early poems would never have been written without his sisters' financial support? Similarly, who would think of the brilliant and deeply eccentric Lady Jane Wilde instead of Oscar, even though his celebrated style and wit was based largely on hers?

I have balanced the famous names in the book with the inclusion of some little-known but colourful characters. These include Biddy Early, animal-healer and poteen-drinker extraordinaire; 'Lady Betty', murderer and public executioner; the cross-dressing soldier Kit Cavanagh; and Ireland's last 'changeling', Bridget Cleary.

The response to the first edition showed that the stories of these and all the other women in the book still have the power to engage. *Wild Irish Women* is a book of stories – heroic, farcical, shocking, inspiring and tragic – and at the centre of each is a real, breathing, living woman. Alexander Pope held the view that 'most women have no characters at all', but I hope these stories demonstrate the opposite.

Marian Broderick
August 2002

WOMEN OF LETTERS

*'I am ambitious, yet the strongest point of my
ambition is to be every inch a woman.'*
Lady Sydney Morgan

Maria Edgeworth

1767–1849

*Novelist, best known for her children's stories and her novels of Irish life,
such as* Castle Rackrent *(1800) and* The Absentee *(1812)*

Maria Edgeworth was the second of the twenty-two children of
the extraordinary Richard Lovell Edgeworth, who was a liberal
thinker of enormous energy, author, inventor, educationalist,
magistrate and, as heir to a family estate in County Longford,
pillar of Ireland's Anglo-Irish landed gentry. Maria was born in
her mother's home at Blackbourton, Oxfordshire, on New Year's
Day 1767, the product of an unhappy first marriage between
Richard and Anna Maria Elers. When Maria was six years old her
mother died as a result of that common occupational hazard:
childbirth. Her father married the beautiful Honora Sneyd within
a few months and moved the whole family home to Ireland.

Two years later, at the age of eight, Maria was sent away from
Edgeworthstown to be educated in England. She did not return
for seven years. When Maria came back in 1782, Honora had died
of consumption and had been quickly replaced as the mistress of
Edgeworthstown by her sister, Elizabeth Sneyd.

Maria's home was now an Irish estate where her father was a
mini-king. Surrounded by his children, extended family (including two more unmarried Sneyd sisters), servants and tenants,
Maria's father ruled as a benevolent dictator. In sharp contrast to
the attitudes of most Anglo-Irish landlords of the day, however,
Richard felt a responsibility toward his tenants. He ignored the
Penal Laws to grant security of tenure to tenants who improved

their land. Equally unconventionally, he adhered to the principles of the French philosopher Jean Jacques Rousseau in relation to the education of his family. This involved encouraging the child to enjoy his or her learning experiences, and teaching the child to be self-sufficient and resourceful. Richard was universally adored by the locals, by his wife and children, but most of all by Maria, who spent her life striving to live up to his high expectations.

In this, Maria made a good start. Although shy, very short and so plain that she avoided mirrors, Maria's personal qualities were fine. She was intelligent, capable, energetic, generous, very keen to do good and, above all, dutiful. She had plenty of initiative, but was also willing to be guided by her incurably didactic father. By the age of just fifteen, Maria was managing the accounts at Edge-worthstown House and acting as her father's secretary in his many improving and inventive projects. In a house where there was a seemingly never-ending procession of stepmothers, Maria became the most reliable mother figure of all.

If working for her father was Maria's day job, her night-time occupation and real passion was always writing. Apart from completing compositions that her father set and corrected for her, she also wrote incessantly for the amusement and edification of her ever-increasing tribe of half-siblings – stories with a simple moral, such as 'Simple Susan' and 'Lazy Lawrence'. Her work always had to pass muster with her father – it had to carry the right Edgewor-thian message, demonstrating the beauties of industry, economy and punctuality.

For Maria the 1790s were a busy time. When she was twenty-eight she published her first work, *Letters for Literary Ladies*

(1795), which, startlingly, advocated education for girls. Maria's next book, *The Parent's Assistant* (1796), was directly lifted from those night-time scribblings of her teens and twenties. Following this she collaborated with her father on *Practical Education* (1798), a treatise on education based on Rousseau's writings, which explored modern childcare methods, such as the relevance of play and the importance of the natural impulses of the child. It was her work on educational issues that made Maria's name in the USA, a rare feat for a female writer at that time.

The year of rebellion, 1798, was traumatic and financially devastating for many landowning families, but the Edgeworths emerged totally unscathed. Maria later described it as 'a mixture of the ridiculous and the horrid'. True, they had to flee their house as the rebels marched on Edgeworthstown, and true, they narrowly escaped being part of a party that was subsequently blown to pieces, but their popularity with the locals stood them in good stead and the rebels left their property alone. Amazingly, the only damage sustained was a few broken windows.

A more important event in the family circle was the death of stepmother, Elizabeth Sneyd, of consumption; she left nine children. Maria's father responded to this tragedy by making a speedy fourth marriage, this time to the daughter of a County Louth clergyman. Maria, who was older than her new stepmother, took on the jobs of caring for her many orphaned siblings, continuing estate business – and writing prolifically.

Maria's fame grew in the years between 1800 and 1814. She published thirteen major works in some twenty-two volumes, including novels, plays for children and collections of essays and moral tales. Her most popular novel, *Castle Rackrent*, published the same year as the Act of Union (1800), dealt with the mismanagement of estates by Ascendancy landlords. Maria had an eye for detail and had witnessed first-hand the abuses of the landlord system, which compared unfavourably with her father's way of doing business. *Castle Rackrent* was original – Maria was the first to choose this subject matter and she was the first to report 'Irishness' accurately in terms of speech and habits. Based as it was on her personal knowledge of the Edgeworthstown tenants and locals, it had the ring of authenticity about it. *Castle Rackrent* is more humorous and less didactic than most of her other work; it is no surprise that she published it independently, anonymously and without the collaboration – or interference – of her beloved 'critic, partner, father, friend'.

In 1802 Maria travelled to England, France, Belgium and Scotland. The author of seven highly regarded and widely read books, she was now a celebrated woman of letters. Her name became a byword for intelligent conversation, yet she charmed everyone she met with her total lack of egotism. At this time, at the age of thirty-five, she also received what appears to have been her only marriage proposal – from a Swedish count and attaché to Stockholm's royal court, a man by the name of Edelcrantz. According to the fourth and final Mrs Edgeworth, Maria loved the count but turned him down. She knew that she was essential to the family and that they simply couldn't manage without her. So, like one of her own heroines, she put duty before love and never saw Edelcrantz again. The spurned count returned to Sweden and never married.

Back at Edgeworthstown, Maria continued to write. *Irish Bulls* (1802) was followed by *Popular Tales* (1804), *Modern Griselda*

(1804), *Leonora* (1806), the first series of *Tales of Fashionable Life* (1809), the second series of *Tales of Fashionable Life* (1812) and *Patronage* (1814). As her fame grew steadily, she counted among her admirers Jane Austen, Lord Byron, John Ruskin and Sir Walter Scott.

In 1817 Maria's idolised father died. Feeling that she had 'lost more than ever daughter lost before', she threw herself into editing his memoirs (published 1820). Her younger brother, Lovell, inherited the estate on the death of his father, but proved to be so inept that he came close to ruining the family fortune. Maria bought him out in 1826 with the money she had earned from her books and ran the estate full-time herself.

Edgeworthstown became a Mecca for visitors. Maria's celebrity brought celebrities to see her – William Wordsworth, Sir William Herschel, Sir Humphrey Davy, William Wilberforce, all came to Edgeworthstown. In 1825 Maria received the man who was a kindred spirit and a friend until his death: Sir Walter Scott. Scott was conscious of his debt to Maria's work on the 'regional' novel, and to him she was a 'very remarkable person … the great Maria'. Lord Byron was another guest. It is difficult to know what the cheerful little middle-aged spinster and the young brooding romantic hero would have had to say to each other, but the visit was a mark of the esteem in which she was held by the literary world, not to mention by Byron himself, who did not bestow his approval lightly.

From 1834 to 1849, Maria's published output decreased as she concentrated on running the estate, tactfully pretending all the while that her useless brother was still in charge. She rented out village houses, oversaw repairs, built a market house and modernised the local sewerage system. In 1845 the Great Famine (1845–1849) ravaged Ireland, and Maria worked strenuously to help the local peasantry. She obtained flour from American admirers and distributed food herself, soliciting her many friends and acquaintances for funds. In 1848 she came out of retirement to publish a children's story, *Orlandino*, the proceeds of which went to famine relief.

On 22 May 1849, at the age of eighty-two, Maria Edgeworth died peacefully at Edgeworthstown, outliving sixteen of her twenty-one brothers and sisters. Though famous all over Europe and America, in her lifetime she earned approximately £11,000 from her writing, while her 'brother spirit' Sir Walter Scott made this amount in just one successful year. Maria is buried in the cemetery of St John's Church in Edgeworthstown, which is now usually known by its older and less colonial name of Mostrim. Edgeworthstown House is now a nursing home run by the Sisters of Mercy.

Lady Sydney Morgan
c.1776–1859

Novelist

Sydney Owenson always claimed she was born on a ship crossing the Irish Sea on Christmas Day in 1776. Her father was the actor Robert Owenson (originally MacOwen) of Tirawley, County Mayo. Robert was an Irish-speaking Catholic, but at a time when Catholics couldn't vote, stand for Parliament, go into professions, buy or inherit land, or teach or study at university, Robert turned

Protestant and anglicised his name to advance himself in his chosen career.

After marrying Sydney's mother, Jane Hill, a middle-class Wesleyan from Shropshire, and producing Sydney and her younger sister, Olivia, Robert settled in Dublin and tried to run a theatre in Fishamble Street. But he was extravagant and unpredictable and the Owensons were always poor. Worse, the authorities took a dim view of Robert's theatre – a nationalistic effort where Wolfe Tone once trod the boards – and quickly closed it down. Shortly afterwards, Sydney's mother died and Sydney and Olivia were packed off to a Huguenot boarding school in Clontarf for three years while their father toured the provinces trying to make ends meet.

When she finished school, Sydney went into the usual respectable profession for impecunious middle-class girls – she became a governess, first in Westmeath and then in Tipperary. Contrary to what one might expect, governessing was a happy experience for Sydney. Using her considerable charm to make herself popular with her families, she consequently did hardly any work and instead spent her time improving her mind in their well-stocked libraries. She studied poetry, philosophy and chemistry and, in the evenings, still found time to play and dance jigs for 'the quality'. She also had leisure enough to write for pleasure, and in 1801 her first book, *Poems* – a book of forty poems – was published. Her first novel, a romance called *St Clair, or the Heiress of Desmond* was published in 1803, giving Sydney Owenson her 'bluestocking' entrée into the world of letters. Her payment was four copies of her own novel – not much even for the standards of the day – but the book itself was reasonably successful in Ireland and in

England. It was at this point that Sydney decided she had had enough of governessing and took herself and her intellectual aspirations to Dublin to break into society.

Sydney had all the necessary accomplishments to achieve her aim: she could write, she spoke French fluently and played the harp beautifully. She was lively and intelligent company with plenty to say. She was mischievous and spirited and, perhaps surprisingly for one who was brought up so closely connected with the less successful end of the theatre world, she had managed to stay out of trouble with unscrupulous men, so she was 'respectable'. Sydney was not beautiful – her looks were marred by a slight squint and a dropped shoulder – but she knew how to make the best of herself. After all, she had been watching the most famous actresses of the day, Mrs Siddons and Mrs Jordan, since she was a child. 'I am ambitious,' she later admitted to Richard Brinsley Sheridan's sister, Alicia Le Fanu, 'yet the strongest point of my ambition is to be every inch a *woman*.' So she painted her face, cut her hair into the latest fashion, knocked several years off her age (she was already twenty-five) and threw herself at Dublin.

Sydney was an immediate success. She got into a circle that included Le Fanu, Mary Tighe and other notable literary women, and continued writing and learning, immersing herself in a study of old Irish music. She quickly produced another romantic novel, *The Novice of St Dominick,* and travelled to London for the first time to pitch it personally to Richard Phillips, the publisher. Her direct approach worked and the novel was published in 1805.

A nationalist sympathiser like her father, the trip to England made Sydney realise just how much contempt was levelled at

Ireland by its prosperous neighbour. After the Act of Union in 1800, which did away with the Irish Parliament, English opinion of Ireland and the Irish was at an all-time low and English newspapers invariably depicted the Irish as apes. At the same time, having taken on Napoleon, English opinion of England was at an all-time high: national arrogance was the order of the day.

It was against this background that Sydney wrote her most famous novel, *The Wild Irish Girl* (1806). Ostensibly a romance, the story dealt with the question of national Irish identity, emancipation and the richness and antiquity of the indigenous culture. No Dublin publisher would touch the manuscript as it was considered dangerously anti-English. Eventually, it was published by Richard Phillips of London. The book was a runaway success and made Sydney Owenson a literary star. The drubbing it received at the hands of the Tory Establishment was outweighed by the admiration of such heavyweight intellectual critics as Maria Edgeworth. Sydney had achieved her dream – she lived for praise and now she had success, attention and, with her harp and her singing of old Irish songs, she was universally seen as the embodiment of her novel's heroine, Glorvina, and a symbol of all things Irish.

On the strength of *The Wild Irish Girl*, Sydney quickly knocked out a successful comic opera featuring her adored father and called *The First Attempt or Whim of a Moment*. Flawed though he was, Robert Owenson had continued to be a towering male figure in Sydney's life, and most of her efforts were aimed at bailing him out. Around this time she also showed her more intellectual side by publishing a serious polemic, *Patriotic Sketches*, which discussed the social and political problems of the day.

In 1808, fresh from Dublin success, Sydney presented herself to Regency London and was a success there too. She may have had little money but she did have the best Dublin contacts, and through them she met many of the leading names of the day, including Lord Byron, the actor Richard Kemble and the eccentric Ladies of Llangollen. The following year she completed another novel – this time set in Greece, a place she had never even visited – called *Ida of Athens* (1809).

Sydney left London and returned home to Ireland, where she was taken up by the fashionable marquis and marchioness of Abercorn. They installed her in their grand home, Baron's Court in County Tyrone, as a writer-in-residence, and she obliged them by churning out *The Missionary* (1811). Soon it became clear that the Abercorns wanted to set Sydney up in more ways than one – they introduced her to their new family physician, Charles Morgan, who just happened to be a young eligible widower.

Sydney was a flirt and had been all her life. She had an army of suitors and one on-off long-term lover, Sir Charles Ormsby, a widowed barrister old enough to be her father. She had finally broken off with Sir Charles at the beginning of her tenure with the Abercorns and, by now in her mid-thirties (although she would never have admitted it), her patrons were pressing her to settle down. Sydney, however, was a feisty soul who had struggled a long time to become an overnight success. Naturally she looked askance at the sacrifices that marriage to Charles Morgan would entail – being continually in the orbit of the fabulously wealthy Abercorns, for example, who, although kind, had an annoying tendency to refer to her as 'little Owenson' and treat her as an exotic pet.

Despite these objections, and after some prevarication and an extended break away from the Abercorns, Sydney Owenson and the recently knighted Sir Charles Morgan were married quietly in January 1812 at Baron's Court.

The marriage was a great success. Sydney's father's death shortly afterwards removed a major impediment to a committed and mature relationship with her husband, whom she later described as her 'most dear and true friend'. Sydney and Sir Charles extricated themselves from the Abercorns and established a home in fashionable Kildare Street, Dublin, where they started a popular literary salon – the only one in Ireland at that time.

In 1814 Sydney published *O'Donnel*, another novel with a strong female lead and a barely veiled argument for Catholic emancipation. This book estranged her from some members of the Ascendancy who did not appreciate the views of their one-time pet, nevertheless *O'Donnel* was another bestseller. In terms of the wider campaign for religious emancipation and national independence, Sydney was later to downplay her writing as merely 'the nibbling of the mouse at the lion's net', but, in fact, as the author and academic Maria Luddy points out, her novels formed part of the 'propaganda war of the [emancipation] campaign'.

In 1816, with encouragement from her new publisher, Henry Colburn, Sydney went to France to research a new book, *France*. This was to be a journalistic work reporting on life in the country after the restoration of Louis XVIII to the monarchy. *France* was published in 1817 and its liberalism, anticlericalism and disparagement of the sovereign caused an uproar. The following year Colburn published *Florence Macarthy*, a nationalist and feminist novel of contemporary Ireland, and after that Sydney and Sir Charles went travelling to research her next book, *Italy*.

Stationed *en route* in a fashionable part of Paris, Sydney spent every Wednesday hosting her now-famous literary salons, then it was off across the Alps to Italy. After two years of travel and research, the Morgans returned to Dublin to write the book. When it was published in 1821 it provoked more of an uproar than *France*, albeit for the same reasons. Not for nothing did Lord Byron call this book 'fearless'; this time it was banned by the Pope himself.

Sydney spent the 1820s as Dublin's main literary hostess in what she called her 'snuggery' in Kildare Street. When she was not travelling or developing her reputation as a brilliant and witty conversationalist, she was still producing bestsellers, including *The O'Briens and the O'Flaherties* (1827). Sydney welcomed Catholic emancipation in 1829, but she became disillusioned with Daniel O'Connell, whom she regarded less as a liberator and more as an opportunist.

In 1837 Sydney was granted a government literary pension of £300 per year, the first of its kind offered to a woman (nearly fifty years later, Lady Wilde would receive only £100 per year). However, she and her husband had become disenchanted with Dublin and in the same year they moved permanently to Belgravia, London.

Sydney enjoyed London, but she fell prey to all the afflictions of the elderly, such as a fast-shrinking social circle. In 1843 she suffered the greatest blow of all when she lost her darling husband and co-writer to heart disease: 'So ends my life,' she wrote despairingly. Just two years later, in 1845, Olivia, her only sister, died.

Alone again, Sydney resolutely re-entered society, kept busy and was welcomed everywhere. A popular old celebrity to the last, she threw her own St Patrick's Day party in 1851, at which she caught a cold. Maintaining that for her the world 'had been a good world', she died a month later and was buried in Brompton cemetery, London.

Marguerite, Countess of Blessington
1789–1849

Society beauty, salon hostess and successful writer

Marguerite Power was born at Knockbrit near Clonmel, County Tipperary. She was one of the many children of the dashing Francis 'Buck' Power, an unsuccessful merchant. According to one of Marguerite's earliest biographers, Buck was a 'typical Irishman' – quick-tempered, extravagant and fond of gambling. Marguerite, already a precocious storyteller, was delicate but pretty. When she was fifteen years old, the charming Buck effectively sold her into marriage to pay off his debts.

Marguerite's husband, an army officer named Maurice St Leger Farmer, was a sadist and a bully. Marriage for Marguerite consisted of punches, starvation and imprisonment in her own home. When, finally, Farmer was posted to India on duty, she refused to follow him and instead moved to London. Still only a teenager, her status as a separated woman lent her an air of scandal.

Over the next few years, Marguerite became famous as one of London's foremost beauties – a darling of society, celebrated for her looks, wit and beautiful speaking voice. She discreetly took as her lover the wealthy (and married) Charles Gardiner, viscount Mountjoy and earl of Blessington. When Blessington's and Marguerite's spouses died in 1814 and 1817 respectively (Marguerite's husband got drunk and fell out of a window), the two were married.

The Blessingtons had famously extravagant lifestyles, even by late Georgian standards. Happy and rich, Marguerite shared her good fortune by helping out her many siblings and cousins in Ireland and England. But soon after the marriage the flighty Marguerite decided she was bored in fashionable St James's Square and persuaded her adoring husband to take her on a Grand Tour of Europe. They stayed away for several years, carrying so much luggage that they were known as the Blessington Circus. In one of his less bright moments, Blessington also invited 'le beau d'Orsay', reputedly the handsomest man in Europe, to accompany them on their tour.

Count d'Orsay was tall and dark with brilliant white teeth and no money. He was an artist, sculptor, swordsman, horseman and a crack shot. He was also such a dandy that it took two men to lift his dressing case. As the party travelled through Europe together, sharing living quarters, what is known as 'the inevitable' soon happened: d'Orsay and Marguerite started an affair.

The manipulative Marguerite looked at her hale and hearty husband and, realising he had years to live, knew she had no hope of marrying le beau d'Orsay. So she persuaded Blessington to arrange a marriage between his daughter, Lady Harriet, and d'Orsay. Blessington thought it a splendid idea and the match was made. Marguerite and d'Orsay were then able to be together continually without causing any gossip, while the unfortunate Harriet sat on the sidelines and Blessington was none the wiser. However, Marguerite's timing was off, for just a few months later, in 1829, Blessington suffered a stroke and died suddenly in Paris.

Blessington left Marguerite well provided for, with jewels, a carriage and £2,000 a year. She moved back to London and persuaded Lady Harriet – with her husband, of course – to move in with her in St James's Square. This was a big mistake. In 1831, after three years of this ridiculous arrangement, the mild-mannered Lady Harriet had had all she could take of her step-mother's appropriation of her husband and moved out, leaving Marguerite and d'Orsay to face social opprobrium.

For the sake of appearances, Marguerite and d'Orsay ran separate homes, but d'Orsay acted as host at Marguerite's salons and the whole world knew they were lovers. Predictably, society rejected her but not him, even though he was the one who was still married – after all, he was a man of fashion and he had the all-important title. At the same time, Marguerite started writing for money to support both herself and d'Orsay. Her first books were thinly disguised satires on the society that had rejected her. They were without much literary merit but, due to her phenomenal networking abilities, she made a success out of them.

In 1836 Marguerite moved to Gore House, Kensington, which became famous as a bohemian salon 'outside' society and entirely populated by men. Such diverse characters as Charles Dickens,

Benjamin d'Israeli and his father, and Prince Louis Napoleon frequented the salon meetings. Despite appearances, Marguerite was getting poorer and continued to support herself and d'Orsay by her writing. She could churn out anything from a light novel (*Grace Cassidy* in 1834; *The Fatal Error* in 1847) to travel books (*The Idler in Italy* in 1839; *The Idler in France* in 1841) to gossipy columns in London's newspapers. Although extravagant and permanently in debt, she was famously shrewd in business, maximising her earnings by making clever publishing deals: she was one of the first writers to get her work serialised in the *Sunday Times*.

By 1849 Marguerite had totally lost the knack of living within her means and creditors all over London were baying for her blood. The Great Famine in Ireland and the subsequent lack of revenue from her lands there meant she and d'Orsay had to decamp to Paris to avoid prosecution. A month later she died of a stroke, just as her husband had twenty years earlier. She is buried in St Germain, Paris.

Lady Jane Wilde
c.1821–1896

A popular nationalist poet, a gifted translator in German, French, Danish, Italian and Swedish, and the mother of Oscar Wilde

Jane Francesca Elgee was born in County Wexford into a solidly middle-class, Protestant family. Young Jane was surrounded by the Catholic poor, yet hardly ever came into contact with them and was therefore indifferent to their plight. Yet in early adulthood she would develop her own unique brand of nationalism and become a figurehead for the disenfranchised majority.

One of the worst aspects of 1820s rural Ireland was the curse of absenteeism, the system by which English settlers lived in what they regarded as 'home', that is, England, while at the same time collecting high rents from their tenants in Ireland. These same tenants were prevented by law from ever owning the land on which they lived and worked. By the 1840s, opposition to such injustice was led by a radical group of Protestants and Catholics, known as the Young Irelanders, whose objective was the repeal of the Act of Union (1800), which had largely contributed to absenteeism. In 1842 three members of the group, Thomas Davis, Charles Gavan Duffy and John Blake Dillon, founded a patriotic weekly paper, the *Nation*. One day the strong-minded Jane Elgee came across a copy of the *Nation* with its fiery rhetoric and impassioned poetry. She experienced something of an epiphany and, as she later said, 'turned nationalist' on the spot.

Tall and articulate, idealistic and immensely pushy, once Jane's patriotism had been kindled there was no stopping her. Flying in the face of her family's predictably pro-Union politics, she started writing for the *Nation* in 1846, the second year of the Great Famine.

There was certainly plenty for Jane to write about. All over the black, fungus-ridden countryside people were starving to death on the roadsides, their bodies rotting where they fell. Orphans – usually covered in the fine hair (lanugo) that indicates the last stages of starvation – filled the workhouses. Famine-related diseases, including typhus and cholera, crept into the towns and killed indiscriminately. Where any small monetary relief was granted by the authorities, it was given only on completion of pointless manual tasks, lest the ungrateful recipients think they were getting something for nothing. During the five years of the Hunger, about a million Irish people died, while at least another million emigrated on the dreaded coffin ships. Jane wrote about all this and more in a style that captured the hearts of her readers, although it is considered overly melodramatic today.

> *'Weary men, what reap ye?–*
> *Golden corn for the stranger.*
> *What sow ye?–*
> *Human corses that*
> *wait for the avenger.*
> *Fainting forms, hunger-stricken,*
> *what see you in the offing?*
> *Stately ships to bear our food away,*
> *amid the stranger's scoffing.'*

from 'The Famine Year'

Jane signed her poetry 'Speranza' (Hope), and it was by this name, still only in her early twenties, that she achieved national and international fame.

Jane laid the blame for the evictions, the starvation and the emigration squarely at the door of the English government. In 1848 – the year of revolution in Europe and of failed revolution in Ireland – she penned an anonymous leader for the *Nation* that amounted to a call to arms. The piece landed the paper and its editor, Charles Gavan Duffy, in court on a charge of sedition. Realising that Duffy would go to jail rather than reveal her name, Jane attended the hearing and at the crucial moment stood up in the public gallery and proudly proclaimed her authorship of the piece with the words: 'I am the criminal who, as the author of the article that has just been read, should be in the dock. Any blame ... belongs to me.' She was not prosecuted and the charges against Duffy were eventually dropped. Once circulated, the story of this grand gesture made Jane a nationalist heroine.

In 1851 the fiery young poetess married Dr William Wilde, a successful eye and ear doctor, antiquary, workaholic and woman-iser from the west of Ireland. It was a happy marriage – Jane was too high-minded and lofty to bother about his many affairs – and it produced three children, Willie, Oscar and a beloved only daughter, Isola. The family lived in palatial splendour at number 1 Merrion Square, Dublin, where Jane spent the mornings reading in bed and the afternoons talking at visitors. She made the most of her past fame as a poet, maintained strong opinions on everything under the sun and saw herself as a cultural icon, a leader of the intellectual set. Every week she held a salon, or 'At Home', for the literary, the artistic, the scientific and any celebrity she could get her hands on. She made a strong impression on everyone who met her with her combination of 'nonsense with a sprinkling of gen-ius', as one of her guests so eloquently phrased it.

The Merrion Square years were probably the happiest period of Jane's life. As she grew fat and middle-aged, she developed a cast-iron sense of her own importance. Her translations were doing well and she was surrounded by interesting people. When, in

1864, William was knighted and Jane became Lady Wilde, her happiness seemed complete. But then something went wrong. By the end of that year Jane found herself in court being sued by what we would nowadays call a stalker.

Mary Travers was an unbalanced young woman with whom Sir William had been having an on-off affair. Jane had welcomed Mary into the family home as a regular visitor. However, Mary perceived insults of some real or imagined kind from Jane and William and decided to take it out on the whole family. She avenged herself on the Wildes by harassing Jane and accusing Sir William of rape. The harassment included following Jane, shouting at her, posting offensive items and impersonating her.

Buoyed by her own healthy self-esteem, Jane tolerated this for some time. Then the girl decided to pay newspaper boys to distribute pamphlets criticising Jane, and Jane made a grave mistake: instead of visiting Mary's father to complain in person, she wrote to him. Mary found the letter and immediately sued Jane for libel (an eerie foreshadowing of the circumstances that would later see her son, Oscar, publicly disgraced). At a sensational trial, which was the talk of Dublin, Mary won her case against the Wildes. However, damages were a nominal and humiliating one farthing; Mary retreated in disgrace and a dignified Jane claimed the defeat as a moral victory.

In 1867 life changed irrevocably for Jane when her daughter, Isola, aged just nine years old, suddenly died. The whole family was traumatised by this loss, and Jane, a devoted mother, never got over it. Previously a popular and gregarious socialite, she stopped going out, preferring instead to keep to the house and write poetry. She continued hosting her salons, however, which saw up to 100 people attending every week. Perhaps the fact that she was now known as the best hostess in Dublin soothed Jane's grief a little.

During the late 1860s and 1870s, Jane wrote little for publication. The Fenian Brotherhood was becoming more active, but Jane, once the outspoken revolutionary, disapproved of them. Although she was a supporter of Home Rule and of the Land League, she was no republican; Lady Wilde had made the middle-aged journey away from radicalism and wanted to keep her own place at the top of Irish society. 'Heaven keep us from a Fenian republic!' she wrote feelingly. She completely missed the point about the real causes of sporadic famine in Ireland, and later she wrote that emigration to Australia was the perfect answer for Ireland's young men: instead of 'eating the bread of compulsory idleness at the expense of taxpayers,' she wrote, 'they could [be] of immense use, if only tending sheep and growing corn for the Empire on the broad plains of the southern continent.'

On a personal level, Jane could be more generous-spirited. In 1876, Sir William died. Oscar later recalled how his mother allowed one of Sir William's mistresses to sit with him while he was dying. Perhaps she would have been less magnanimous if she had realised that in order to pay for his lifestyle, Sir William had mortgaged everything in sight and on his death Jane would be thrown into a poverty that would grow steadily worse for the rest of her life.

For now, though, Jane was a larger-than-life figure, a huge, veiled, stately widow in her fifties. She became eccentric in her dress, wearing ballgowns in the middle of the day and a vast array of ribbons and trinkets pinned on her person. She was also provocative in her conversation: 'Paradox,' she wrote, 'is the very essence of social wit and brilliancy.' People either loved her or laughed at her, but her son Oscar took note and the pithy epigrams for which he later became famous resembled closely his mother's conversational style. Three years after Sir William's death, Jane and her elder son, Willie, moved to Chelsea, London, to start a new life. Oscar followed them, and soon began his own meteoric social ascent. The Wildes never lived in Ireland again.

A severe lack of money meant that Jane was writing for publication once more, but unfortunately, Willie always drank whatever few pounds the work earned. A book on Irish independence for the American market and a memoir of the antiquarian Gabriel Beranger (based on her husband's notes) were supplemented by regular contributions to London's *Burlington* magazine. She also published *Driftwood from Scandinavia* (1884), *Ancient Legends* (1886), *Ancient Cures* (1890) and *Social Studies* (1893). Meanwhile she successfully restarted her weekly salons, always in darkened rooms – 'veiled light is indispensable to conversation' – wherein she could hold forth to her heart's content. Her grandson, Vyvyan Holland, remembers her at this point in her life as a 'terrifying and severe old lady ... dressed like a tragedy queen, her bosom covered in brooches and cameos.'

Just as Jane had blinded herself to the sexual shenanigans of her husband all their married life, now in old age she blinded herself to the faults of both her 'boys', seeing only their talent, their potential and their love for her. But in reality, Willie was a feckless, lazy drunk who couldn't or wouldn't hold down a job. As for Oscar, by the late 1880s he was experiencing great success with his lecture tours and plays and was earning a fortune, but still he failed to organise either a pension for his mother or steady maintenance for his wife and two children – although he always cleared their debts. Instead, throughout the late 1880s and early 1890s, Oscar irresponsibly spent a vast amount on the man he loved and who proved to be his downfall – his darling Bosie, better known as Lord Alfred Douglas.

As Jane got older, she got poorer and her health began to fail. She rented ever smaller and shabbier houses in the bohemian parts of London, and she rarely ventured out. She never saw any of Oscar's plays. She also seems to have been completely unaware that Oscar had decided to flout narrow-minded, Victorian convention by coming out as a homosexual. Such things were never discussed by her visitors or indeed by anyone in polite society. However, when Bosie's father, the marquess of Queensberry, libelled Oscar, Jane finally saw the storm clouds gathering over her beloved son. She responded with the bravado of a woman who believed herself and her family to be 'above respectability'. She strongly encouraged him to sue.

As we know, Oscar's was a love that dared not speak its name in the nineteenth century. Losing the disastrous libel case resulted in his own trial for 'indecent acts'. While waiting for his case to come to court, Oscar was offered a chance to escape to Europe. Again, Jane gave him typical advice: she told him in no uncertain terms that if he fled, she would never speak to him again. To Jane, he was, above all, an Irish gentleman – honour came first, always.

In May 1895 Jane was given the devastating news that Oscar had been found guilty of indecency and sentenced to two years' hard labour. She never saw or heard from him again. She died of bronchitis on 3 February 1896 and was buried in Kensal Green cemetery, west London. Oscar was released in 1897 and moved to France. By 1900 both he and his brother Willie were dead.

Lady Augusta Gregory
1852–1932

Playwright and a significant participant in the Irish Literary Revival

Lady Augusta Gregory is most famous for her co-directorship of the Abbey Theatre, Dublin, alongside WB Yeats. Although the 'Old Lady', as she was universally known, generally worked behind the scenes, she played a major part in the resurgence of native culture that is now called the Irish Literary Revival. Without her practical and creative input, the work of some of Ireland's greatest writers, such as WB Yeats, JM Synge, James Joyce, Sean O'Casey and George Bernard Shaw, might never have seen the light of day. Augusta was a hard worker all her life: she spent her youth dutifully looking after her brothers, her thirties as a high-caste social hostess, her forties as a folklorist and translator, and her fifties and sixties as a playwright and theatre director.

She was born Isabella Augusta Persse at Roxborough House, Loughrea, County Galway, the twelfth of her father's sixteen children. She was the youngest and, according to her mother, the plainest daughter of the house. A family story tells how Mrs Persse, disappointed that the child was not a boy, threw a blanket over the new-born and proceeded to forget all about her until a servant noticed she was suffocating and rescued her.

The Persses were Anglo-Irish Ascendancy through and through, and Augusta's family tree was bowing under the weight of lord lieutenants, sheriffs and viscounts. Despite this, Augusta, from her relatively lowly position on the edges of the household, acquired a mixed cultural identity. Virtually ignored by her own mother, Augusta's real mother figure was her nurse, Mary Sheridan, who worked at Roxborough for forty years. In a house saturated with Orangeism, Unionism and strict Protestantism, young Augusta was reared by an Irish-speaking, folktale-telling, staunchly Catholic nationalist with rebel tendencies.

A quiet and dutiful little girl, Augusta was small and brown-eyed, shy and something of a loner. She tried to overcome this tendency in order to help Roxborough's tenants; her biographer Elizabeth Coxhead noted that from her teens onwards she acted as a 'voluntary social worker' on the estate, doing what she could for the sick and the poor. Augusta was not interested in hunting, shooting and fishing and, in typical Big House style, she received schooling insufficient to fit her for anything else, so she tried to educate herself by reading widely. Her philanthropic and educational efforts were regarded by everyone – including herself – as subsidiary to her real job, which was to be available at all times to nurse the tubercular and alcoholic young men of the family.

Throughout her twenties, while her more beautiful sisters married and moved away, Augusta unstintingly and uncomplainingly did her duty: teaching Sunday school, helping local girls to sell embroidery, nursing first one brother then another. Then, at the relatively late age of twenty-eight, Augusta landed a marital catch that surprised everybody. In 1880 she met and married Sir William Gregory of Coole Park, thirty-five years her senior and seriously rich. The bride gained the security, status and independence she could never hope for at home, while the bridegroom gained a housekeeper for his homes in London and Coole, a companion who would not baulk at being a nurse, and 'a good listener'.

Overnight, the short, dumpy, shy Augusta was transformed into the lady of the manor, with all the responsibilities that entailed. She immediately reverted to the most deeply ingrained habit of her life – service to the men around her. She merely replaced her brothers with her husband. In the future, she would replace her husband with her son, her nephew, the Abbey Theatre and all the greatest playwrights in Ireland.

The Gregory marriage was happy and produced a child, Robert, in May 1881. In 1892, after just twelve years together, Lady Gregory was widowed at the age of thirty-nine. She never remarried and wore black for the rest of her life. After her husband's death she threw herself into the work of editing his memoirs.

Possibly the most important non-familial relationship of Lady Gregory's life was with WB Yeats, whom she met in London in 1894 when the young poet had nothing to his name. The maternal Lady Gregory spotted Yeats' genius straightaway and decided to help him. Yeats was grateful though somewhat nonplussed by her attentions, and saw her as 'kind and able ... but to what measure?'

Lady Gregory recognised what he did not: that creativity needed a place to flourish. Accordingly, she created a haven for Yeats at Coole Park every summer for many years. She looked after his health, gave him the best rooms in the house, took him for nature rambles, sent him nourishing soup to give him strength to come to breakfast, lent him money so he could give up his day job and offered valuable constructive advice on his work.

Many people cattily thought that the forty-three-year-old widow was looking for a handsome thirty-year-old husband, but this was never the case. She was a woman more passionate about Irish literature than about physical love, and Yeats, who described her as 'mother, friend, sister and brother', grew to depend on her advice regarding both his work and his problematic love life. 'I doubt if I should have done much with my life,' he wrote, 'except for her firmness and care.' 'It is impossible to overestimate her influence on Yeats,' wrote Micheál mac Liammóir, 'she was his friend and counsellor, an understanding eye in the tumultuous and haunted places of his mind.' Lady Gregory would never let him down.

One summer day in 1897, while visiting their friend, the landowner Edward Martyn, Lady Gregory and Yeats were inspired by the idea of setting up a national theatre to showcase new Irish drama. Lady Gregory immediately set about getting funding and publicity for the new venture, and Yeats started writing for it. The first incarnation of their brainchild was the Irish Literary Theatre, which produced plays from 1899 to 1901. The Irish Literary Theatre was replaced by the Irish National Theatre Society, which performed various works in different venues, including the unforgettable *Cathleen ni Houlihan* of 1902 with Maud Gonne in the lead role. The following year an English heiress named Miss Horniman agreed to subsidise the Society and refurbish a building for it. Accordingly, in late 1904 the Abbey Theatre opened on central Dublin's Abbey Street. Lady Gregory, WB Yeats and JM Synge were the first directors.

Apart from Yeats' friendship and the love of her son, Lady Gregory always cut a lonely figure, especially at the Abbey. One of her most exhausting and thankless tasks was fund-raising for the company, which put her in the invidious position of having to balance the nationalist elements in the Abbey with the mainly Unionist funders. She was always caught in the middle: nationalists distrusted her because of her background and title, while unionists distrusted her because they could see she was, in fact, a nationalist.

Although Lady Gregory's personal qualities were sterling – she was unfailingly kind, courteous and committed – her manner was frequently off-putting. It was as if she were aware that there was an unbridgeable gap between herself and almost everyone she met through the Abbey. 'She had a queenly way with her,' said Gerard Fay; the 'frosty dignity' never left her manner, said Micheál mac Liammóir; she had a 'Protestant high-school air,' said George Moore; 'she was a pleasant if rather condescending person, who treated us all rather as children,' said leading lady Máire nic Shiubhlaigh. Yet Lady Gregory worked and worked for the people who thought she looked down on them. 'She acted the part of a charwoman,' wrote the notoriously difficult Sean O'Casey, one of the few working-class people who genuinely liked her, 'but one with a star on her breast.'

As a consolation for her loneliness – and to make money – Lady

Gregory wrote. Ever since her nursery days with Mary Sheridan she had been fascinated by Ireland's folklore, and since the 1890s she had been actively researching her local area, Kiltarten, for stories. She published folklore collections – *Cuchulainn of Muirthemne* in 1902 and *Gods and Fighting Men* in 1904 – and then, to furnish the Abbey repertory company with material, she turned to writing plays.

Between 1900 and 1928 Lady Gregory experienced the most creative period of her life. In total she published some forty works of poetry and prose, including more than twenty plays, and she invented a dialect, Kiltartenese, that was to influence Irish playwrights for years to come. Her plays, both comedies and tragedies and all nationalist in tone, were successful, particularly *Spreading the News* (1904), *The Rising of the Moon* (1907) and *The Workhouse Ward* (1908). Despite their popularity, she was never considered to be in the first order of playwrights.

In 1911 Lady Gregory stepped out from behind Yeats and into the limelight when she alone took the Abbey company on tour to the USA. Nervously, she forced herself to complete public-speaking engagements, meet President Theodore Roosevelt and deal with the continuing controversy surrounding JM Synge's play, *The Playboy of the Western World*. The furore around the play was such that there were riots in New York and Philadelphia. As one actress recalled, the 'rotund, thin-lipped and very determined-looking' fifty-nine-year-old widow used to conceal herself in parts of the set and hiss at the actors to 'keep playing!' One night she made the company perform the whole play again from the beginning because it could not be heard the first time due to the shouts of hecklers. Despite these hostile scenes the tour was a success, and Lady Gregory returned to Dublin in triumph.

But grief was just around the corner. With the outbreak of World War I, her only son, Robert, immediately joined the airforce. Against all the odds he survived until 1918, when his mother finally received the telegram she had been dreading for so long. Robert had been killed in action over France, leaving a wife and three children. Comparing herself to a machine, a heartbroken Lady Gregory did the only thing she could – she carried on working.

The post-war years were troubled times for Ireland. Avowedly anti-Home Rule in her youth, Lady Gregory moved toward what Micheál mac Liammóir called a 'gently fervent patriotism'. The reprisal executions of fifteen rebel leaders after the Easter Rising of 1916 strengthened her nationalism. During the War of Independence and the Civil War, Lady Gregory was ostracised by her grander Galway neighbours and by her extended family because of her political inclinations – even though she made it plain she did not believe in violence and never allowed the Abbey to be used for propaganda plays. Meanwhile, she had to stand by as the IRA killed one of her own nephews and burnt down her beloved childhood home, Roxborough.

While others were bent on destruction, Lady Gregory strove to preserve Ireland's cultural heritage for the Irish. She fought a bitter struggle to retrieve from London's National Gallery an important collection of modern Irish paintings, known as the Lane Pictures, and have them housed in a new Dublin gallery. (The paintings are now co-owned by the Hugh Lane Municipal Gallery at

Charlemont House, Dublin, and the National Portrait Gallery, London.) In the 1920s her best success revolved around working with Sean O'Casey, whom she encouraged as she had Yeats thirty years earlier. Controversial as his plays were, she threw her weight behind them and *Shadow of a Gunman* (1923), *Juno and the Paycock* (1924) and *The Plough and the Stars* (1926) proved to be modern classics. She published her own last batch of plays in 1928, and then retired from the Abbey.

By now the energy of the seventy-six-year-old was failing. She had an operation for breast cancer in 1926, but lived on at Coole Park another six years. She died peacefully in her bed on 22 May 1932 at the age of eighty. Her house was demolished in 1941, but the grounds were preserved and visitors can still see the famous autograph tree, which bears the initials of some of those who visited and were indebted to Lady Gregory: George Bernard Shaw, JM Synge, Jack B Yeats, Sara Allgood, George Russell (Æ) and Sean O'Casey, among others.

Somerville, 1858–1949
and Ross, 1862–1915

One of Ireland's most successful literary partnerships

Edith Somerville and Violet Martin, who was better known as Martin Ross, had a hugely successful comic-writing partnership lasting twenty-six years. They produced more than thirty books, including the very popular *Irish RM* series.

Both women were born into the decadent world of the Anglo-Irish Ascendancy, a world where only hunting and dancing were taken seriously and where both money and the locals were treated with humorous disdain. This world was eccentric, incestuous, self-contained, arrogant – and already dying when the two started working together. Their books provide an insightful caricature of a rarefied society that will never be seen again.

Somerville was born into the Somervilles of Castletownshend, County Cork. The family had migrated to Cork from Scotland in 1690 and, over the next century and a half, had become well-to-do merchants and estate farmers who married their relations with monotonous regularity. Ross was from a much grander and older family, the Martins of Ross, County Galway. The Martins were one of the ancient 'Tribes' of Galway and had been the feudal masters of a massive Connemara estate since Elizabethan times. The two girls were second cousins, but they didn't meet until 1886 when Ross and her mother visited Somerville's mother at Drishane House, Castletownshend.

Somerville and Ross had very different personalities. Somerville was the eldest child in her family, and was an active, outgoing, affectionate, matriarchal multitasker. Ross, in contrast, was the baby of her family and was a delicate, reserved, quiet, somewhat detached aristocrat. However, as their acquaintance developed they discovered they shared much in common: they were both creative (Somerville was a trained artist and Ross had had articles published), they had phenomenally retentive memories for stories, and they enjoyed poking fun in a sardonic, rather cruel manner. Ross soon became a regular visitor to the madcap world of the

Somervilles with its swarms of dogs, continual fox-hunting and fancy-dress parties. She also became permanently enamoured of her soulmate's company.

Their first collaboration arose from the sneaking pride both felt in the glorious barminess of their extended family. They produced a dictionary of 'Buddh' – an invented Anglo-Irish lingo used only by the well-heeled inhabitants of Drishane. In Buddh, a 'spladge' was a hand, a 'gommawn' was an idiot and a 'blort' was a temperamental outburst. This effort was so enjoyable that – in spite of the derision of their families – they embarked on a full-length novel, aptly named *An Irish Cousin* (1889). The book was a success, family objections fell away in the face of financial gain and a literary partnership was born.

The books of Somerville and Ross were praised for their deflating depiction of the gentry class and for their comic accounts of the native Irish, though in recent times some of their work has come to be seen as patronising and politically incorrect. The 1890s were their most creative period, even though much of their time was occupied by family duties, such as maintaining their respective ancestral homes. Despite their enforced separation, their writing appeared seamless: one of them would have an idea, which would then be posted back and forth for rewriting until both were satisfied.

The secret of their success as writers was that they complemented each other perfectly. The energetic Somerville was a fast, slapdash writer, bursting with ideas; she provided the impetus to drive Ross's creativity. As a professional artist she also provided illustrations to accompany the text. The less motivated Ross – a 'lazy slut', according to her partner, because of her slatterliness –

was nevertheless a clever and subtle writer with an eye for minute detail, and she provided the best and blackest humour in the books. She was also a better business woman than Somerville and acted as their agent. Between 1889 and 1915 the two published sixteen books, including novels, travel books and short stories. Their best novel is thought to be *The Real Charlotte* (1894).

Although Somerville and Ross were both suffragists, and became president and vice-president respectively of the Munster Women's Franchise League in 1913, they differed in other areas of politics. Somerville had nationalist leanings, and in May 1916 she sent letters to the newspapers begging for clemency for the leaders of the Easter Rising. Ross, on the other hand, was a conservative Unionist who witnessed the changing relationship between her family and 'their people' on the estate, and resented it.

In November 1898 Ross had a serious accident while out hunting, chronically damaging her spine and leaving her a semi-invalid for the rest of her life. Despite this, she and Somerville continued their work and the first of the *Irish RM* series was published the year after the accident. On the death of her brother and her mother, Ross finally closed up the decaying Ross House and moved into Drishane with Somerville in 1906. To Somerville's intense admiration she even got back in the saddle, but she couldn't keep this up for long and spent most of her time lying on a sofa, writing.

The last years of the partnership were spent happily and productively. Then, in December 1915, Ross was taken ill and died suddenly of a brain tumour. Somerville, devastated at the loss of what she called her 'share of the world', mourned for a year for her friend and partner. She had always known people who believed in spiritualism and who contacted the dead; after Ross's death, Somerville embraced this idea wholeheartedly. She became convinced that Ross's presence was still with her. At the end of her mourning she began to write again and, for the rest of her life, she believed Ross was helping her. She published fifteen of her next sixteen titles under both their names.

In 1932, Edith Somerville received an honorary doctorate from Trinity College, Dublin, in the name of the literary partnership of Somerville and Ross. She published her last book in 1946 and died in Castletownshend three years later. Somerville and Ross are buried side by side in the local churchyard at nearby St Barrahane.

Peig Sayers
1873–1958

One of the last of the traditional storytellers and a major contributor to Ireland's folklore archive

Peig Sayers was born in Dunquin (Dún Chaoin) on the Dingle Peninsula in the Kerry Gaeltacht. Her father, Tomás Sayers (Mac an tSaoir), was a gifted storyteller. He and his wife, Peig Brosnan (Ní Bhrosnacháin), were survivors of the Great Famine (1845–1849) and they were never far from hardship and bereavement. Peig's mother gave birth to thirteen children, but buried no fewer than nine of them in infancy. Peig was the youngest of the four survivors.

Ironically for a woman whose work is used in the curriculum to teach Irish, there is confusion about Peig's level of literacy in Irish. Some tourist literature claims that she spoke Irish as a first language but could write and read only in English (as was often the case at a time when speaking *only* Irish was regarded as something of a liability). However, in her autobiography, Peig herself states that she learned to read and write both English and Irish while at school.

At fourteen, Peig was a tall, strapping girl and she went to work at one of the two jobs poor country girls were qualified to do: domestic service. Her employers, the Currens, were based in Dingle town and were relations of her father's. They were kind and she was happy enough in her work, but like all young people Peig wanted to better her circumstances: she wanted to emigrate.

In the 1890s emigration was the most successful business in Ireland. In the years of the Great Famine, emigration had claimed more people than death – about one million – most of whom were young men. After the Famine, emigration continued apace and Ireland became known as a land of the very old and the very young. (This pattern was broken only in the early 1990s when Ireland's economy began to improve.) People from Dunquin tended to emigrate to the USA, which was seen as the land of opportunity, but this was only possible if a family member or friend sent passage money. Young Peig was full of life and the desire to go, and her oldest friend, Cáit-Jim, promised to send her the fare. However, after months of hopes and plans it became clear that no money was forthcoming. Peig's door of opportunity had slammed shut in her face.

But another opportunity was about to present itself. At nineteen, she was offered the chance to do the other job country girls were equipped for: the job of marriage. The custom in rural areas was for matches to be arranged by a young woman's male relatives, usually her father. There was no romance involved, rather the opposite. It was a social and economic contract. The criteria included solvency, reputation, kinship, religion and land, all of which were far more important than love. When Peig was told that a suitable match had been arranged for her, she saw her bridegroom just once before their wedding day when he paid a formal visit to her family home. As she herself said afterwards, when he arrived that day with two other men she was not even sure which of them it was she was marrying.

Peig's husband-to-be was thirty-year-old Pádraig Ó Guithín from the Great Blasket Island. He married Peig in February 1892 in the church in Dunquin. In an echo of an old Gaelic custom, Peig retained her own family name after her wedding. With the island penchant for nicknames, the tall young woman became known as Peig Mhór (Big Peig).

When she married Pádraig, Peig committed to the lot of a typical islandwoman. If the weather did not make the crossing impassable, as it frequently did, she would sail three miles by curragh to get to the mainland. She would then travel a further twelve miles to attend a wedding or funeral, go to hospital or visit a shop.

On the treeless Great Blasket, Peig's days would be spent loading turf onto a creel on a donkey's back and bringing it home, while she carried bundles of heather on her own back. She would scavenge the beach for driftwood to be used as fuel for the hearth.

She would cook – mainly fish and potatoes – bake bread and hand-churn milk for her husband, his parents and his two brothers in the family home. She would fetch water from the well, wash clothes, spin, knit and mend. She would do all her indoor tasks by the light of a paraffin lamp because, in the age of atomic power, electricity still hadn't reached Great Blasket. She would give birth to ten children on the island with only the local women to help her. In a sad echo of her mother's experience, five of Peig's children would die in infancy. The surviving five would emigrate to the USA.

However, there was something that lifted the spirits of Peig and the other islanders on the long, dark winter nights: storytelling. This important form of entertainment was part of the old Irish oral tradition. A dáil, or assembly, would meet at night in a house, and a comedy, mystery or tragedy would slowly unfold. Peig, with her pure Irish and her beautiful embellishments and turns of phrase, was an acknowledged master of the art. She kept hundreds of stories in her phenomenal memory, and she was able to memorise a story that would take a week in the telling after hearing it just once.

In the early years of the twentieth century, as part of the Gaelic Revival, visitors from abroad and the mainland started to arrive on Great Blasket, interested in its culture and in the purity of the Irish spoken there. The visitors included people who saw a stay on the unspoilt island as a necessary part of the Revival, for example, JM Synge, who came in 1905 before visiting the Irish-speaking Aran Islands in Galway. (He wrote *Playboy of the Western World* as a result of his island experiences.) By 1914, Great Blasket was experiencing an unexpected literary blossoming as its poetry and folklore was written down for the first time. Ironically, it was three English scholars who pioneered the island's literary renaissance: Robin Flower (known to islanders as Bláithín, or Little Flower), Kenneth Jackson and George Thomson (also known as Seoirse Mac Thomáis).

In 1917 Tomás Ó Criomhthain, another Blasket-dweller, encouraged by the Kerry scholar Brian Ó Ceallaigh, wrote the classic *An tOileánach* (*The Islandman*), and paved the way for Peig Sayers. Encouraged by the scholars who recognised her talent, Peig agreed to have some of her stories written down. Peig's son, known locally as Maidhc File (Mike the Poet), returned from the USA and committed her stories to paper directly as she told them in Irish. Her polished style and skill were such that they were composed perfectly and needed little editing. Jackson and Flower then published them in journals (*An Lóchrann* and *An Claidheamh Soluis*), and subsequently released a book called *Scéalta ón mBlascaod* (*Stories from the Blasket*).

After years of storytelling, a constant stream of visitors and a steadily growing fame, Peig was persuaded by the Irish scholar Máire Ní Chinnéide and the student Léan Ní Chonalláin to write her autobiography. *Peig: Tuairisc a thug Peig Sayers ar imeachtaí a beatha féin* (*Peig: An account given by Peig Sayers on the events of her own life)* was released in 1936, and in 1937 it won the prestigious Douglas Hyde prize.

In 1942 Peig, now nearly seventy years old, and Maidhc File returned to Dunquin, to the townland of Vicarstown (Baile Bhiocáire) where she had been born. Nearly blind, but still receiving visitors, Peig lived to the ripe old age of eighty-five. She is buried in the churchyard in Dunquin. Five years before her death, in 1953, the people of the Great Blasket Island finally admitted that island life was too hard for their ageing population. They evacuated to the mainland and the way of life that Peig had known came to an end forever.

Kate O'Brien
1897–1974
Novelist and playwright

Kate O'Brien was born into a middle-class Catholic family in Limerick. She lost her mother at six years old and was sent to board at a strict school, Laurel Hill Convent School, in Limerick City. She then won a scholarship to University College, Dublin. After university she took time off to go travelling. She worked on a newspaper in Manchester and worked in the USA as a secretary to her uncle. She also worked as a governess in Spain and formed a lifelong interest in the country and its culture. In 1923 she married a Dutch journalist, Gustaaf Renier, but they divorced within a year. She settled in London in 1926 and became a full-time writer.

Although best known for her twelve novels, Kate started off as a playwright and produced three plays. The first of these, *Distinguished Villas* (1926), enjoyed a three-month run in London's West End. Her first novel, *Without My Cloak* (1931), won two prestigious prizes – the Hawthornden and the James Tait Black –

establishing her as a top-class novelist. She was one of the first to write about middle-class Catholics in small Irish towns. Her themes included the moral and sexual dilemmas facing young women in provincial Ireland and the importance of equal education opportunities.

Kate O'Brien became notorious in Ireland when her second and fourth novels, *Mary Lavelle* (1936) and *The Land of Spices* (1941), were banned by Free State legislation called the Censorship of Publications Act (1929). The offending points were the coded treatment of homosexuality and a psychological exploration into the mind of a nun. Since most good Irish authors had works banned by this overzealous censorship board at some point, the ban did not impede Kate's career and her work continued to be successful.

That Lady (1946), the story of the discarded mistress of Philip II of Spain, is considered Kate O'Brien's best novel. It was adapted for the New York stage, then, in 1955, was made into a film starring Olivia de Havilland, which its author hated. The book's unfavourable portrait of Philip II caused it to be banned in Spain for a decade.

In 1947 Kate was made a member of the Irish Academy of Letters. She moved back to Ireland and spent the 1950s living and writing in Roundstone, Connemara. She returned to England in 1961, settling near Faversham in Kent. Her popular travel book, *My Ireland* (1962), clearly showed her appreciation of her native home. Despite this she lived in England until her death in 1974.

WIVES AND LOVERS

*'What will not a woman do who is firmly
and sincerely attached?'*
Dora Jordan

Eleanor FitzGerald, Countess of Desmond

1545–1638

Rebel and wife of Garrett FitzGerald, fifteenth earl of Desmond

The story of Eleanor FitzGerald is the story of an ancient Irish clan and its lonely and desperate stand against its mighty Tudor neighbour. Eleanor was born into conflict: conflict within her own family; conflict between the two greatest families in Munster, the FitzGeralds of Desmond and the Butlers of Ormond; and conflict between Ireland and England.

Eleanor was originally a Kilkenny Butler, a member of the Norman-Irish nobility. She was born into a life of ease and plenty in the family pile at Kiltinan, County Kilkenny. In 1558, when she was thirteen, two things happened that were to have a profound effect on her life: Queen Elizabeth I ascended the throne of England, and Garrett FitzGerald, her future husband, became the fifteenth earl of Desmond.

In the mid-sixteenth century, Gaelic Ireland was about to enter its death throes under a superior and ruthless force. The Tudors had impelled nearly all the leading families to submit to their cultural and economic domination. The name of the game was loyalty and assimilation: loyalty to the Crown, assimilation into the Anglo-Saxon way. This meant the Irish language would have to go, Catholicism was on its way to becoming illegal, ancient Brehon laws were replaced by the Latin law system, inheritance rules changed, autonomy was lost and old allegiances were split. For Eleanor and her family it also meant an unceasing, never-ending battle to try and hold it all together – all to no avail, for by the end of Eleanor's long life, her world, already fractured at her birth, would be smashed to pieces.

In 1565 Eleanor Butler, a tall and beautiful nineteen-year-old, married thirty-two-year-old Garrett FitzGerald, the fifteenth earl of Desmond. The bride was regarded as a great asset: she was intelligent, diplomatic, calm, resourceful and courageous. Their marriage was definitely a love match: Garrett would never have married a Butler otherwise for he passionately hated all Butlers, and one in particular, Eleanor's kinsman and his own contemporary, Thomas 'Black Tom' Butler, the tenth earl of Ormond.

Garrett FitzGerald was one of a dying breed of poet-warriors who had been brought up in the traditional Gaelic manner. He was single-minded about holding onto his land and his heritage, no matter what the cost. His estate, the biggest estate in the whole of Ireland or England, comprised most of the province of Munster and, within it, he ruled as a king. Garrett was undeniably brave, but also proud, highly strung and foolishly impulsive. He resented Tudor efforts to get involved in his estate and this was to lead him – and his family – disastrously to outright rebellion.

The first test of Eleanor's mettle came two years into her marriage. Just after the birth of her daughter, their first child, Garrett was arrested and taken to England where he was imprisoned in the Tower of London. He spent the next six years away from Ireland, imprisoned without trial, first in the Tower, and then under house arrest. The effect on him was traumatic: his pride took on an element of hysteria and his nerves were shattered. He was to spend the rest of his life obsessed with avoiding re-imprisonment.

In Garrett's absence, Eleanor ran the estate, obtained massive funding for his upkeep and cannily remanded into custody his closest rivals to guard against attempts to seize his property. Eventually she went to England to personally petition the Queen for her husband to be allowed home. Staying by her husband's side during his house arrest, she gave birth to his son and heir, James, in 1571. Heartbroken, she was then forced to hand the child into custody as a condition of Garrett's release.

Eleanor and Garrett finally got back to Ireland in 1575. Garrett spent the next eight years availing of his ancient lordly rights, but also making treasonable statements, skirmishing on the estate borders with Black Tom and failing to placate the Queen with her favourite present – money. Eleanor spent her time getting him out of trouble. She wrote conciliatory letters to the Queen, she negotiated with the Dublin authorities on his behalf, she guarded him from his enemies and she gave him sound advice, most of which he ignored.

By 1579 Garrett, who had never recovered from prison, was becoming physically frail, but his ambitious brothers, his 'unnatural brethren' as Eleanor called them, instigated what became known as the Second Desmond Rebellion (1579–1583). In the autumn of that year, to Eleanor's horror, the brothers propped the feeble earl onto a horse and informed him that he was to lead a rebellion against the English.

For the Lord Justice of Ireland, William Pelham, and the 'loyal' earl, Black Tom, it was good news: this was what they had been waiting for. As soon as they heard the word 'rebellion' they attacked Garrett's estate, ravaging his territories and laying waste to some of Ireland's finest farmland. Eleanor rushed to Garrett's side as the Crown drove the Desmond forces ahead of them, trying to starve them into surrender and killing indiscriminately. Despite the threat of punishment, no one betrayed the whereabouts of the earl and his countess.

Eleanor stayed with her sick husband, sleeping and eating under hedges and in caves. By day the FitzGeralds and their men regrouped and attempted to attack the Crown forces; at night, Eleanor rode out alone to distribute plans and communications for the following day. One night their party was attacked and she alone dragged the limping earl into a freezing river. They spent most of the night submerged as the soldiers hacked at the undergrowth around them. The soldiers stopped just before dawn, inches away from where Eleanor and Garrett were hiding. Eventually, Eleanor began to achieve mythical status among the English soldiers. They sometimes chased fleeting glimpses of the elusive Countess of Desmond on horseback, as she led them away from where her husband slept.

But it had to end. In 1583 Garrett made one final furious assault on Black Tom and the Crown forces, a supreme effort that immortalised him in legend and song. He was defeated and took to his heels for the last time as the freshly equipped Black Tom harried him across Kerry. Facing the cold and hunger of a fourth winter on the run, Garrett ordered Eleanor to leave him and save herself – better she should be in Crown custody than caught by soldiers, he reasoned. Plus there was their son to think of, who was still in custody in England. Sadly, Eleanor agreed to leave Garrett and give herself up to the Crown. She never saw her husband again.

Garrett's death came in November 1583 when he was run to ground by bounty hunters, who would be handsomely rewarded whether he was captured dead or alive. They decapitated him and sent his head to Black Tom, who sent it to the Queen, who had it spiked on London Bridge. Garrett FitzGerald, earl of Desmond, was fifty-one years old.

Eleanor spent the next four years as a pauper, mainly in Dublin, and another year in England attempting to see the Queen. In October 1588 she finally managed it and the Queen granted her a pension. She found it difficult to access the money in Ireland – the authorities there had no time for the 'wicked woman' who had been a 'chief instrument' of Garrett's rebellion – so she and her daughters moved to England full-time, trailing around after Her Majesty and managing as best they could. Eleanor's son, James, now aged seventeen, remained imprisoned in the Tower.

In 1597 Eleanor remarried. Her husband was Donogh O'Connor from Sligo, another hereditary landowner who was embroiled in legal battles in an effort to retain his birthright. It was a political alliance – the Lady of Desmond was still something of a catch – but the marriage was also a happy one, and Eleanor moved to Sligo full of optimism for the future.

She found she was still surrounded by politics. In the last years of the sixteenth century, the northern earls O'Neill and O'Donnell made nationhood seem tantalisingly possible. Buoyed by the mood of progress, Eleanor quietly tried to get back the FitzGerald earldom for her son. She even managed to get young James out of the Tower and over to Munster. But it was no use. James's spirit had been broken in captivity, just as his father's had been, and he had become institutionalised. He stayed a few months in Munster and then voluntarily went back into prison where he died in 1601, aged only thirty. A month later the O'Neill and O'Donnell forces were defeated at the Battle of Kinsale, and the Tudor re-conquest of Ireland was complete.

Eleanor lived out the rest of her life in Sligo Castle. Her husband died in 1609 and his indomitable widow inherited what was left of his land. After her years of glory as the Countess of Desmond, her years on the run as a rebel and her years of desperate poverty as a traitor's wife, she managed the Sligo estate and lived her final years in relative security and wealth until her death at the ripe old age of ninety-three.

Marie Louise (Louison) O'Morphi
1736–1815

Royal mistress

In the seventeenth century the Jacobite wars and the Cromwellian invasion meant that many Irish people, poor and rich, found it necessary to emigrate to Europe, and France was a favourite destination. The parents of Marie Louise O'Morphi, better known as Louison, were two such immigrants. Daniel Murphy, or O'Murphy, may have originally gone to France as a soldier in the army of James II. By the 1720s he was a shoemaker in Rouen and his Irish wife, Margaret Hickey, was a second-hand clothes merchant.

The Murphys had five good-looking daughters, and when

Daniel died, leaving the family predictably penniless, their mother moved them all to Paris and turned them towards the only lucrative professions within their reach – none of which were on the right side of respectability. The O'Murphy girls started to bring in money variously as actresses, dancers, artists' models, jewellers of fake jewels and live-in mistresses. The exception was Louison, the youngest. She was made use of by her older sisters as a servant girl – at least, they reasoned, she was out of harm's way. And so she was, until one day in 1751 a visitor came to see one of her sisters. He spotted the beautiful Louison scrubbing away in the kitchen and followed her to her room. The visitor's name was Casanova.

Casanova took Louison to see his friend, the artist François Boucher. Boucher was entranced. He had already painted at least one of Louison's sisters, but he was overwhelmed by Louison's beauty: she was tall, with curly brown hair, clear skin and a turned-up nose. She was also trim and round and he knew at once that she would be a great model. Before long, Boucher and Louison were lovers and he was painting her obsessively. As his work was commissioned by the French royalty, it was only a matter of time before risqué paintings of her adorned the palace of King Louis XV – even the chapel.

In the royal court, King Louis XV presided over the *ancien régime* with all the splendour and self-importance of an Egyptian pharaoh. He was in the prime of life and sex-mad, and he inflicted his insatiable appetites on every woman within his greedy reach. His favourite mistress, Madame de Pompadour, admitted frankly that she couldn't keep up with him – but she also knew that failing to pander to the king's every whim was risky. Should one of the many cultured ladies of the court succeed her as *maitresse en titre*, she would lose her powerful and influential position. So the clever courtesan hit on a plan. She drew the king's attention to the paintings of Louison adorning the walls of the palace, then, one day in 1753, she invited Casanova to introduce Louison to the king in person. Louison was just seventeen years old.

Louis XV was instantly captivated by Louison's looks, good humour and apparent *naïveté*. At one point she laughed in his face, something no one ever did. In short order, he found he had paid over a large amount of money to Louison's delighted mother and set Louison up in the palace. Initially, at least, Mme de Pompadour was happy with the arrangement – the ploy of using an uneducated, unambitious young girl who could satisfy the king's appetites and yet not pose a threat to her seemed to be working.

In 1754 Louison got pregnant. Mme de Pompadour and the king immediately took over the pregnancy and hustled her away to a secret location. The king really didn't need another royal bastard hanging around, so when the baby boy was born he instructed the nurse to tell Louison it was stillborn, and then have the baby taken away secretly and adopted. The following summer the same thing happened again. This time the baby was a girl, and she was whisked away to be reared in a convent, never to meet or know her mother and father. Louison accepted the loss of her babies: such was the lot of a royal mistress.

In 1755 Mme de Pompadour and the king married Louison off to an army officer in order to keep up appearances. She was now a lady of rank and lived in a château in Auvergne, in south-central

France. She still bedded the king, but her role was changing subtly. As well as being a bedmate herself, she started 'pandering' for him, in other words, procuring young virgins for his royal pleasure. This 'ideal' situation continued for some time. But it all went wrong when Louison, who had neither the brains nor the inclination to play at politics, became unwittingly involved in an anti-Pompadour court intrigue in 1757.

A courtier persuaded Louison to use her influence with the king at Mme Pompadour's expense, but she muffed her lines, the plot was uncovered and she was banished from Versailles. Cast out of court life and pregnant with another of the king's children, she suffered a second blow when her husband was killed in battle. She gave birth to a baby boy, and this time, as a punishment, the child was not acknowledged by the king. The king's action was to prove a blessing in disguise, for little Louis Charles was allowed to stay with his mother and would be her staunchest friend in the frightening days ahead.

After a few years in the wilderness, Mme de Pompadour and the king relented slightly towards Louison, and by 1759 they were seeking another husband for her. They found someone they deemed suitable and Louison, amenable as always, married without a murmur. Her new husband was given an important job as a steward to the king's brother. For Louison, this meant a move away from the wilds of Auvergne and back to her beloved Paris. Her continuing discretion and loyalty, and that of her husband, meant she was partially rehabilitated. Eventually, King Louis even summoned little Louis Charles to court as a page, thereby tacitly acknowledging the child's royal paternity.

The next twenty-five years were lived in comfortable prosperity by the one-time Cinderella. Her rival, Mme de Pompadour, died and was replaced by Mme du Barry; Louis XV died and was replaced by Louis XVI. Now a woman in her fifties, Louison was well-preserved and wealthy and secure in her position as a woman of fashion. But all this was set to change.

In 1789 widespread poverty and the deep unpopularity of Louis XVI led to the outbreak of the French Revolution. Louison's second husband died the following year, and in 1792 her son, Louis Charles, went to fight in the Franco-Prussian war. Left alone in Paris amid rioting and looting, Louison barricaded herself in her house. Finally, the unthinkable happened: King Louis XVI and Queen Marie Antoinette were arrested and the mob gained control of the palace.

Louison was one of the lucky ones. When the mob broke into her house they merely looted it, arrested her and packed her off to a convent. From her cell, she watched as the guillotine was set up outside her window and one by one all the members of the court she had known met a gruesome death, to rapturous public applause. In mid-October, Queen Marie Antoinette was guillo-tined, after which the mob turned on the royal mistresses. Mme du Barry was to be executed first and Louison was to be second. However, she was saved at the eleventh hour by her devoted son, who was going from strength to strength in the new republic and was as trusted and respected as anyone could be in those times. He arranged with the authorities for his mother to be transferred to a different convent prison and granted a reprieve. She kept her head down – and still on her shoulders – by changing her name back to

Louise Murphy, talking up her humble Irish roots and dissociating herself from her royalist past.

Between 1793 and 1794 the Terror reached its peak. Even Louis Charles found himself briefly but seriously on the wrong side due to the increasing radicalism of the revolution. But by December 1794 it was all over; Robespierre went to the guillotine and Louison was released from the convent. She returned to Paris and then, with her son, back to the old château in Auvergne. Louison, no longer as naïve as she had been in former days, liberated some jewellery she had hidden in case of emergencies and soon she and her son were able to afford a life of relative affluence. When Napoleon came to power in 1799, Louis Charles received a promotion; he retired as a general in 1803.

Louison lived under Napoleon's rule much as she had done under the two kings: she enjoyed a comfortable, privileged existence. Apart from an embarrassingly short-lived marriage to a man more than twenty years her junior, she grew old gracefully and discreetly. In 1812 her son died at the age of fifty-one. He had never married and remained devoted to his mother to the last. In spring 1814 the Bourbon monarchy was reinstated with the accession of Louis XVIII. Louison was there to witness the royal procession of the grandson of the man who had given her everything. She died less than a year later, and was buried in Pére Lachaise, Paris.

Eibhlín Dubh ní Chonaill

c.1743–c.1800

Originator of one of the most famous death laments in Irish,
'Caoineadh Airt Uí Laoghaire' ('Lament for Art O'Leary')

Eibhlín was born in Derrynane, County Kerry, one of the twenty-two children of Dómhnall Mór Ó Conaill, grandfather of Daniel O'Connell. When Eibhlín was fifteen years old she was unwillingly married off to an elderly man named O'Connor, from Iveragh, who obligingly died six months later. She then met and fell in love with the rumbustious, charming and handsome Art O'Leary of Rathleigh, near Macroom, County Cork. Art was a captain in the Hungarian Hussars, but he had little to his name except a bad reputation. He and Eibhlín were married against the wishes of her family.

The couple lived in Rathleigh and all went well until the high sheriff of Cork, Abraham Morris, laid criminal charges against Art O'Leary. Art defeated the charges in court in 1771, but the incident left bad blood between them and they were at feud with each other. Two years later matters came to a head when Art's horse, a superb bay mare, beat Morris's horse in a race. Under the terms of the Penal Laws, Catholics were not allowed to keep horses valued at more than £5 and, invoking the law, Morris insisted that Art sell him the mare for this insultingly low price. Art refused and then went into hiding to avoid the inevitable backlash.

Not long afterwards, Art became sick of life on the run and

decided to settle the matter between himself and Morris once and for all. On a spring day in 1773, Art lay in wait for Morris near the village of Millstreet, County Cork. The attempted ambush did not go according to plan, however, and Morris gave chase and shot and killed Art at nearby Carraig an Ime.

Art's blood-drenched mare galloped back to Rathleigh to a horrified Eibhlín. Pregnant with her third child, Eibhlín leapt on the horse and galloped back to her husband. She then knelt, keening over the body, and composed a traditional lament of the bereaved – the most famous of its kind to have survived to the present time. The most striking visual image contained in the lament is of Eibhlín bending over her husband's body and, in her grief, drinking his warm, spilling blood.

Five months later, Abraham Morris was acquitted of the murder of Art O'Leary. The story of Art's death was kept alive in the oral tradition until it was eventually written down in the nineteenth century. It has been translated many times and by many different writers. The following excerpt is from the translation by Eilís Dillon.

> Mó ghrá thu agus mo rún!
> Tá do stácaí ar a mbonn,
> Tá do bha buí á gcrú;
> Is ar mo chroí atá do chumha
> Ná leigheasfadh Cuige Mumhan
> Ná Gaibhne Oileáin na bhFionn.
> Go Dtiocfaidh Art Ó Laoghaire chugham
> Ní scaipfidh ar mo chumha
> Atá i lár mo chroí á bhrú,

Dúnta suas go dlúth
Mar a bheadh glas a bheadh ar thrúnc
'S go raghadh an eochair amú.

My love and my dear!
Your stooks are standing,
Your yellow cows milking;
On my heart is such sorrow
That all Munster could not cure it,
Nor the wisdom of the sages.
Till Art O'Leary returns
There will be no end to the grief
That presses down on my heart,
Closed up tight and firm
Like a trunk that is locked
And the key is mislaid.

from 'The Lament for Arthur O'Leary', Eilís Dillon

Dora Jordan
1762–1816

Popular comic actress and royal mistress

Dorothea Jordan's mother was an actress from Wales who married a young Irish army captain by the name of Bland. The young couple were married in Ireland by a Catholic priest but, because they were both minors, Bland's father objected to the match and was able to have the marriage annulled. Despite this, the couple continued to live together and produced a large family, including Dorothea (always known as Dora), who was born near Waterford.

When Dora was still a young child her father walked out and the family was plunged into poverty. For Dora's mother, survival became her daily grind and she was forced to call upon her children's help in order to put bread on the table. As there was an acting tradition in the family – as well as her mother, two of her aunts had also trodden the boards – Dora was introduced to the stage very early. In 1777, at the age of fifteen, she was already employed full-time playing tomboyish comic parts at Dublin's Crow Street Theatre. She was billed as Miss Francis – her mother's maiden name.

Portraits of Dora show a kind, pretty and expressive face. Her speaking voice was mellow and her singing voice extremely beautiful. She was good-natured rather than acerbically witty, and possessed easy charm in abundance. She was always popular with male theatregoers and was a big hit when she went on tour with the Crow Street Theatre Company. Dora's mother – an early example of a pushy stage mother – rejected several offers of marriage on her daughter's behalf because it was obvious to her that Dora would go far in her chosen career.

After this promising start, Dora ran straight into trouble. The manager of Crow Street was a particularly unsavoury character named Daly who liked using intimidation, and occasionally force, to gain sexual favours from his actresses. The newly married Daly set his sights on young Dora, and soon she was pregnant. As a result, she had to get away from Ireland. Dora, her mother and several siblings fled Dublin and the attentions of Daly in 1782, and Dora went to work for the great English actor-manager Tate Wilkinson in Yorkshire.

She lived the hard life of the travelling player. Heavily pregnant, she walked the hills and dales in all weathers as the company moved from one town to the next; the horses were used only to move the equipment. However, Wilkinson was good to her; he was the father figure Dora had been missing, especially as he singled her out for praise both for her acting talent and for her post-performance singing. Eventually, she threw off the name Francis so as not to upset her mother's family and took on the name Jordan; she threw off the title Miss when her baby was born and thereafter was known as Mrs Jordan.

Dora stayed with Wilkinson until 1785, then she moved to Drury Lane Theatre, Covent Garden, London. She did so against the advice of the great tragedienne Mrs Siddons who thought she simply wasn't good enough and told her so. But Dora proved Mrs Siddons wrong. She was an immediate success in London and played all the leading comedy roles of the day. A coterie of fans gathered around her, including Lord Byron, Charles Lamb, Sir Joshua Reynolds and William Hazlitt. In London, Dora was 'all gaiety, openness and good nature', according to Hazlitt; she was an actress who 'gave more pleasure than any other actress, because she had the greatest spirit of enjoyment in herself.' The loyal Dora was to stay at Drury Lane for the rest of her career.

During this time, in the late 1780s, Dora continued to be unlucky with men. She fell for a man named Ford and stayed with him five years. She had two daughters by him before he, like her father, absconded to marry an heiress. But her luck changed in

1790 when she met William, Duke of Clarence, son of King George III.

The lonely duke fell passionately in love with Dora at first sight, attracted by her straightforwardness, her generosity and her warmth. For her part, she was fond of him and was dazzled by his royal connections, although not so dazzled that she could resist an opportunity to make fun of him. When, early in their relationship, the duke reduced her promised annual allowance of £1,000 to £500, Dora sent him the bottom of a playbill bearing the words: 'No money returned after the rising of the curtain'. Dora continued to produce children at a phenomenal rate throughout this liaison. She suffered at least five miscarriages, but reared ten of the duke's children over twenty years. The duke installed Dora, her three daughters and their own ever-increasing brood at a beautiful estate in Bushy, Hertfordshire.

Dora had the classic working-mother problem: her family missed her if she were not at home; fans and managers were resentful if she were not at work. She did the best she could by continuous letter-writing to her family while on tour in the autumn/winter theatre season, and when something serious cropped up, like an illness, she cancelled performances and came hurtling home. Once, when the duke was ill, she performed a marathon mercy dash from Scotland to Bushy, which took several days by coach, with no time to stop even for a hot meal.

Throughout her relationship with the duke, Dora was earning vast amounts of money and giving it away almost as quickly as she got it. The duke was a particular drain on her: although he was a prince of the royal blood, he was penniless and was dependent on the charity of his father, George III, and his brother, the Prince Regent. The rest of the royals were quite happy to let Dora bail William out, but she was never acknowledged or accepted in royal circles, except by the Prince Regent.

Eventually the duke's money troubles got so bad that he was obliged to look for a rich wife and this, together with the fact that after two decades together he was probably tired of the now middle-aged Dora, meant the end of their relationship. Dora got the bad news in a letter from the chivalrous duke saying that he wanted to meet her to organise a separation. She was on tour in Cheltenham at the time and had promised to play for another actor's benefit. As she knew she was a major draw and that her absence would adversely affect the takings, she hid her broken heart and went on – though at one point she did burst into tears on-stage instead of the scripted laughter.

After the loss of her protector, the press wolves closed in on Dora and a storm of criticism broke over her. She stoutly defended herself and – generously – her duke. She persisted in seeing the best in him until her dying day, attributing his shoddy treatment of her to his parents' parsimony. But then, as she herself wrote in a letter, 'what will not a woman do who is firmly and sincerely attached?'

William had made Dora promise she would not go back on the stage; the maintenance money she received and the custody of her five daughters were contingent on that promise. But for once Dora disregarded the duke's wishes and, at the age of fifty, returned to the stage with gusto, thereby forfeiting the maintenance and her daughters. She thought it best for the girls to be with their royal father, and, in any case, she couldn't afford not to work. Back at Drury

Lane, Dora was as popular as ever and could command large fees.

All would have been well for Dora Jordan's old age were it not for two factors: a conspiracy against her on the part of the royal accountants who failed to sort out her tax and thereby allowed her to get into financial trouble; and her boundless generosity to her sons-in-law who ran up enormous debts in her name. When they finally came to light, the debts in Dora's name were so huge that she had no hope of paying them off.

In 1815 she was forced to leave the country to avoid arrest and imprisonment. Poor Dora lived in France in complete seclusion, under the assumed name of Johnson, first in Boulogne, then in Versailles and finally in St Cloud in a dilapidated old house. Deprived of the audiences which had been her oxygen for nearly four decades, her only comfort was receiving word from home. But despite all she had done for family and friends, the letters came infrequently and finally stopped altogether. Pathetically, Dora was reduced to sending a messenger to the post office specifically to look for any communication from home. When none was found, she would throw herself down and weep pitifully.

She pined away less than a year after arriving in France, not from actual want but from loneliness and homesickness. After her death her public couldn't quite believe she was gone and – not unlike certain other superstars since – reports that she had been spotted continued for years. Her children by the duke all did very well for themselves, and their eldest son eventually became the earl of Munster.

Sarah Curran

1782–1808

The beloved of Robert Emmet

The short and unhappy life of Sarah Curran began in Rathfarnham, south Dublin. Sarah was born into a home dominated by her
father, the most famous barrister in the country, John Philpot
Curran. Since Curran was a man known for his domestic aggres-
sion, Mrs Curran, not surprisingly, was something of a doormat.
Sarah, the youngest of nine and always delicate, was virtually
ignored by both her parents. When she was twelve years old, her
downtrodden mother summoned enough spirit to elope with a
local vicar.

Sarah's brothers all went to Trinity College. While there,
young Richard Curran met a shy patriot named Robert Emmet.
Robert came from a family of staunch Republicans and he joined
the secret Society of United Irishmen while still in his teens.
Rather than admit his membership, he dropped out of the university in 1797. Three years later, Robert first saw seventeen-year-old
Sarah Curran at a ball in Rath Castle, County Wicklow, where she
was making her début into Dublin society. She was slim, black-
haired and pale-skinned, with enormous dark eyes and a most
beautiful singing voice. Besotted at first sight, the twenty-two-
year-old Robert was too shy to approach her. Shortly afterwards,
he left Ireland to travel in Europe.

Back in Dublin again in 1802, Robert's college friend, Richard, invited the young idealist home to dine and to talk with his
family. After a number of such visits, Robert was deeply in love

with Sarah. For her part, she felt little more than friendship for him, but friendship in her loveless young life was important and she was happy to keep the relationship going. One day, Sarah's father, realising what Robert was up to and not approving of him as a potential son-in-law, banned him from the house. Sarah, showing some of her mother's spirit, continued to meet Robert, in secret. Letters flew between the two – usually carried by Robert's friend and colleague, Anne Devlin.

Months passed and Robert, confiding all his hopes and dreams to Sarah, even discussed the insurrection he was planning. The young idealist hoped to stage a rising that would forcibly take control of Dublin from the occupying English. On 23 July 1803, Robert led about eighty rebels in an attempt to storm Dublin Castle. Unfortunately, miscommunication, poor organisation and lack of popular support meant that the attempt was doomed to fail before it had even begun. The rebels broke up in disarray and the 1803 Rising was quashed in just one night. Hopelessly in love, Robert refused to save his life by absconding to the USA. He preferred instead to hang around south Dublin in the hopes of seeing Sarah. His cat-and-mouse game with the authorities came to an end on 25 August when he was betrayed and arrested by Major Henry Sirr, Dublin's chief of police.

Two of Sarah's (unsigned) letters were found on Robert's person during his arrest, and while he waited for his death he tortured himself with the thought that she would somehow be dragged into the mess. He even offered to plead guilty if the court would suppress the letters. Eventually, in his fear, he did a foolish but typically chivalrous thing: he bribed a warder and gave him a letter to take to Sarah, warning her of the danger she was in. The warder duly handed this letter straight into the hands of Major Sirr, who arrived on the Currans's doorstep in Rathfarnham shortly afterwards.

After watching while his house was ransacked for evidence of complicity, and furious at Sarah's defiance in continuing to communicate with Robert, Sarah's father informed her that she was 'blotted [from his] society, or the place she once held in [his] affections'. In effect, he made it impossible for her to remain at home. As Robert was living out his final days in Kilmainham Jail, contemplating the scaffold, Sarah was on her way to Cork. She saw neither home nor Robert again.

Robert Emmet was given a traitor's death. On the morning of 20 September 1803, he was taken to a spot outside St Catherine's Church on Thomas Street, Dublin, where he was publicly hanged, drawn and quartered. He was twenty-five years old.

In Cork, Sarah found a refuge with her friends, the Penrose family, with whom she stayed for more than two years. She felt partly responsible for Robert's death, and was described at this time as morose and guilt-ridden. It seems likely she suffered a nervous breakdown.

Despite the generosity of the Penroses, Sarah knew she couldn't live on charity forever and that the only practical course open to her was marriage. Strangely enough, the man prepared to take her on was a British Army officer, Captain Henry Sturgeon. Like Robert Emmet, Sturgeon was an honourable and good man. They were married in the winter of 1805 in what must have been a love match – there could have been no career advantage in marrying a penniless outcast with connections to a dead Irish rebel. As for Sarah, she was adamant that she could not forget Robert, but she admired and respected her new husband.

Ten months after the wedding the couple sailed to Sicily and, though homesick, Sarah seemed to enjoy the only peaceful period in her life. She was treated well by 'dear Henry', and when, in the summer of 1807, she discovered she was pregnant, she was delighted. But Fate had not finished with Sarah Curran.

Heading back to England a month before her baby was due, the ship on which they were travelling was struck by a storm outside Gibraltar. The crew and passengers were stranded as no other vessel could attempt a rescue due to the dangerous sea and weather conditions. Sarah went into premature labour on 26 December 1807. She gave birth the following day on the rocking, freezing floor of an empty cabin with no one to help her. She then sank into a fever. On the thirteenth day she was finally able to breastfeed her weakening baby son, and the ship finally docked at Portsmouth. But by the fifteenth day her baby was dead. 'My heart is bleeding and broken,' Sarah wrote to Anne Penrose, 'and I can't pray to God, for he has forgotten me.'

Sarah lingered a few months after her baby's death, but was unable to rally and died of consumption on 3 May 1808. She was only twenty-six. Her last request was to be buried next to her sister in the family grave at Rathfarnham, a request her father refused. She is buried instead at the family seat in Newmarket, County Cork. She has been immortalised in song as 'the beloved of Robert Emmet'.

'She is far from the land
Where her young hero sleeps
And lovers around her are sighing,
But coldly she turns
From their gaze, and weeps
For her heart in his grave is lying.'

from 'She is far from the Land', Thomas Moore

Katharine O'Shea
1845–1921

Mistress and wife of Charles Stewart Parnell

Katharine Wood was born into a titled family in Essex, England, and married Captain William O'Shea in 1867. After leaving the army, Willie O'Shea displayed a complete ineptitude with money and was unable to make any success of the several businesses he started. From 1874 onwards, it fell to Katharine to support them and their three children by taking a job as a paid companion to her rich Aunt Ben. Although the O'Sheas grew apart over the years and Willie kept his own private apartment in London, they shared an official family residence with Aunt Ben at Eltham, Surrey.

Katharine was very pretty, bright and headstrong. She had an interest in politics stemming from her husband's attempts to forge a career in that direction. In 1880, the year Willie O'Shea first entered Parliament as MP for Clare (where he owned land), Katharine sought out Charles Stewart Parnell, the leader of the

Irish Parliamentary Party, with a view to advancing her husband's career. At that first meeting, the attraction was immediate and she developed a fascination with the charismatic Charles. Within a few months, the two had embarked on a passionate love affair.

Instead of meeting clandestinely in hotels, Katharine and Charles arranged matters between them less conventionally, but more conveniently, by having Charles to stay – as a guest of both Mr and Mrs O'Shea – at Eltham. Their cover was that Willie had a political relationship with Charles and acted as a mediator between him and prime minister, William Gladstone, on the thorny Home Rule issue. In return for Willie's compliance, Charles helped him to a position as the MP for Galway in 1886 – an act that would come back to haunt him.

In 1881, while Charles was in prison for 'conspiring to defraud landlords of rents' – a charge arising from his work as president of the Land League – Katharine gave birth to his daughter, but the baby died soon afterwards. She was to have two more children by Charles, in 1883 and 1884, but all were registered under the name of O'Shea. Willie, apparently hoping for political advancement from Charles, seemed to turn a blind eye to what was going on, even through Katharine's pregnancies.

This civilised arrangement fell apart on Christmas Eve 1889 when, at the height of Charles Stewart Parnell's career and just when it seemed he had brought Home Rule within Ireland's grasp, O'Shea petitioned for divorce. He was backed by Katharine's family, all of whom were furious at not receiving anything in Aunt Ben's will. (Ben had died in 1887.) Willie made the unlikely claim that he had known nothing of his wife's nine-year affair, and he named Charles as co-respondent in the action; because he wanted to marry Katharine, Charles refused to defend himself. Despite attempts by Katharine to buy off her husband by promising him most of Aunt Ben's money, the divorce was finalised in autumn 1890 and the ensuing scandal destroyed Charles's parliamentary career.

The Irish Parliamentary Party split into pro- and anti-Parnellites, and their leader was accused of living under the thumb of a scheming, immoral Englishwoman. He was also accused of bribing O'Shea with the Galway parliamentary seat in 1886. In by-election after by-election, Charles fought the gossip and innuendo to retain pro-Parnellite candidates and keep the leadership of the party.

In June 1891, Charles and Katharine were married in an English registry office. This only made matters worse in the Irish press, which unanimously refused to refer to 'Kitty', as they called Katharine, by her new married name of Mrs Parnell. After the wedding, Charles went straight back to work, but it was clear to everyone that he was a broken man. Crippled with rheumatism and suffering from stress and exhaustion, Charles Stewart Parnell died in Brighton in October 1891. After his death his widow suffered the first of several nervous breakdowns, but she outlived him by another thirty years. Katharine never visited nor showed any further interest in Ireland.

Bridget Cleary
c. 1869–1895

Burned as a changeling

Bridget Cleary was reared near Fethard, south Tipperary. She married when she was eighteen and by the spring of 1895 she was living in a new house in the townland of Ballyvadlea with her husband, Michael Cleary, and her father, Patrick Boland. Michael Cleary was a cooper by trade and Bridget herself often worked as a milliner. This meant that, by the standards of the time, the Clearys were a relatively well-to-do, modern young couple.

In the spring of 1895 a gruesome crime was committed in this apparently happy home that changed everything. Michael Cleary burned his wife to death in her own kitchen and then buried her in a shallow grave. Shockingly, when Michael stood trial, in the dock with him were Bridget's own father, her aunt and four of her cousins, all of whom were implicated in her murder. It transpired that the whole family had believed that the real Bridget – their Bridget – had been stolen away by fairies, and that the woman killed in the kitchen was what was commonly known as a fairy changeling, that is, a fairy inhabiting the body of a human.

Connections with the unseen world were still strong in Irish rural communities in the nineteenth and twentieth centuries. Bad luck was often ascribed to the mischievous and sometimes downright malevolent 'little people', variously known as the gentlefolk, the Sídhe and, of course, the fairies. In a world where oral traditions were important, stories were handed down about supernatural interventions. They were a way of making sense of the apparent randomness of unexpected deaths, strange behaviours, ailing animals or bad harvests.

Belief in fairies coexisted quite happily with a sincere belief in Christianity, and people would think nothing of attending Mass and then going straight to a local wise woman, such as the famous Biddy Early, for advice on how to deal with a fairy problem. However, as with the notion of witches in previous centuries, there was a darker side to this belief in fairies. It was usually the difficult or unorthodox people in the community who were accused of involvement with the fairies – especially strong or domineering women.

Bridget Cleary fit into this category. She was not popular in the community. She was said to be outspoken, moody and somewhat high-handed. She was a good-looking woman and there was salacious gossip concerning herself and a male neighbour. Most importantly, she was suffering from the stigma of childlessness after seven years of marriage. In short, Bridget didn't fit into her community and was fitting in less and less as time went on.

Then Bridget became ill. She developed bronchitis and took to her bed for a few days. She was feverish and refused to eat. Not surprisingly, her manner was snappish and, to her husband, she literally seemed like a different woman.

As her condition worsened, Michael called the priest and had a Mass said over her. Then he called the local fairy doctor, under whose instruction Bridget's nearest and dearest menfolk forcibly enacted a series of fairy remedies to drive out the changeling they believed was inhabiting her body. These remedies included forcing her to ingest herbs steeped in new milk, slapping her, questioning her, holding her over the fire in the range and pouring urine on her.

Eventually, after nights of little or no sleep and consumed by the belief that a fairy was infesting the person of his wife, Michael Cleary leapt on Bridget in the kitchen, threw paraffin oil over her and burnt her alive. Her father, aunt and cousins were all witnesses, but not one attempted to save Bridget. Michael and one of the cousins then took the body and buried it.

Apparently Michael believed that once he had burnt the changeling, his true wife would emerge from a local fairy fort and he would be able to retrieve her as she rode past on a grey horse. He took a group of men and they went to wait their chance by the fairy fort. They waited and watched for three nights, but to no avail. Bridget did not appear. Shortly afterwards, Michael was arrested and tried for the murder of his wife.

The court accepted that the belief in changelings was genuine and that the crime had not been premeditated, accordingly the charge was reduced to manslaughter. Bridget's aunt received a suspended sentence, and the other accessories got between two and five years' imprisonment. Michael Cleary got twenty years' hard labour. He was released after fifteen years and emigrated to Canada, where he died.

Nora Barnacle
1884–1951

Wife and inspiration to James Joyce

Nora Barnacle was one of seven children born in Galway City to Thomas Barnacle and his wife, Anne Healy. The Barnacles were comfortably well-off townies: Nora's father had gainful employment as a baker, and she had an uncle, Michael Healy, in the civil service. But Nora's father, though a gentle man, was a drinker. When this habit began to get out of hand, Nora's mother, in an unusual move for the times, threw him out of the house for good. From then on, Nora had little to do with her father.

In a practice common until recently in large families in Ireland, Nora was fostered out to her maternal grandmother when she was about five years old. She was a confident, good-humoured little girl, though rather more independent and spirited than was appreciated by the elders of the Healy family. Nora was quick-witted and daring, and by the time she reached her teens she was already flouting convention. Shockingly, she enjoyed sneaking out at night dressed as a boy, purely for the freedom of movement it gave her. When she was discovered, her family considered her behaviour immoral.

Tall, clear-skinned and red-haired, young Nora was a looker and she knew it. It was this arrogance, coupled with the fact that she was 'walking out' with a young Protestant, that eventually got her the thrashing of her life from another of her uncles, Tommy Healy. But Nora's first beating was to be her last. Like her mother before her, she knew exactly where to draw the line with male family members. Immediately after the beating, she packed her bags and headed for Dublin without so much as a goodbye to anyone. She was twenty years old.

Several months later, in June 1904, Nora was walking down Nassau Street when she met twenty-two-year-old James Joyce, a dissipated graduate of University College, Dublin, and a struggling writer. They may have already been slightly acquainted since Nora was working as a waitress and chambermaid at the nearby Finn's Hotel on Leinster Street, but on this occasion Joyce asked Nora out on a date. Nora's acceptance of his invitation was to change both her life and literary history.

When Nora met Joyce he didn't look like such a great catch. He had received the best Catholic education, but his unhappy home life was dominated by his violent, extravagant father, John Stanislaus Joyce, as was his downtrodden, passive mother. He exhibited a deep hatred of the Church, a dislike of conventions (such as marriage), an incipient drink problem, a chronic shortage of money, an unhealthy predilection for prostitutes and a certainty of his own genius that no one else seemed to share.

But when Joyce met Nora, he saw that there was something about her. She was strong and realistic, a calm presence in a hectic world. She was bright yet earthy, honest but loyal. Later he would find that she was passionate and sexually uninhibited, yet she was genuinely guilt-free. She was funny and she teased him in an outrageous manner: he was an avant-garde genius, but to Nora he was 'simple-minded Jim'. Most of all she understood him, and in time she came to understand him better than anyone else. To James, Nora was indispensable.

Their first date was on or around 16 June 1904, a date that has since become world-famous as Bloomsday. After this, Nora and Joyce spent the summer falling deeply in love, and then in the autumn eloped to Europe. Three weeks after their elopement Nora became pregnant, and Joyce found work as an English teacher. In the summer of 1905, Nora gave birth to a son, Giorgio, followed in the autumn of 1907 by a daughter, Lucia. After the children were born, Nora wanted marriage and a home of her own, but Joyce found the idea impossibly bourgeois and refused to comply on both counts.

So began the long years of moving from one European city to another, pretending to be married, living in rented rooms and eating in restaurants. Over the next three decades the Joyces lived in Trieste, Rome, Trieste again, Dublin, Zurich, Trieste again, Paris, London, Paris again, Zurich again, and many places in between.

The Joyces's relationship with their native land was not that of most Irish exiles. Joyce's most famous works – *Dubliners* (1914), *Portrait of the Artist as a Young Man* (1916), *Ulysses* (1922) and *Finnegans Wake* (1939) – are all based around or in Ireland, and Nora was frequently described as 'very Irish'. It was said, rather sentimentally, that she represented Joyce's own 'little piece of Ireland'. But the Joyces themselves were out of love with the country. Hailing from a pro-Union background, Nora had never been a nationalist, and as for Joyce, he took a dim view of the lack of respect he received at home. His masterpiece, *Ulysses* (which had been banned in most countries on the grounds of obscenity), didn't need to be banned in Ireland because it wasn't even allowed into the country due to a customs dispute.

Joyce's stubbornness on the question of marriage aside, Nora was the boss of the family and Joyce generally deferred to her. In return, she nurtured him, supported him, cared for him and was his constant companion in everything he did. As the years went on and Joyce's sight began to fail, he became more and more dependent on Nora, physically as well as emotionally. For example, when Nora had to have a hysterectomy in later life, Joyce, unable to sleep without her, moved into her hospital room. This intense intimacy is reflected in the fact that most of Joyce's books feature Nora. He questioned her closely about her past and found her continually fascinating. Her loves and hates, her turns of phrase, the way she wrote, the clothes she wore, her personality and experiences, all seeped into his fiction. Joyce didn't just need Nora, the strong woman who took care of him, he needed Nora as a muse.

Nora and James's relationship was exclusive. They needed each other far more than they needed anyone else, including their children. Though undoubtedly they loved Giorgio and Lucia, their parenting skills were not all they might have been. Their peripatetic lifestyle made it impossible for the children to have a stable life. Giorgio and Lucia hardly knew what nationality they were, they were unable to make and keep close friends, their parents lied to them for years about their illegitimacy (which, quaintly, was still a huge stigma in the early 1930s) and as their education was never a priority they were never fit for careers. Sadly, the identity crises that ensued eventually led to Giorgio becoming an alcoholic and Lucia going spectacularly and permanently insane when she was only in her twenties.

So although the pram in the hall never killed creativity for James Joyce, his genius pretty nearly destroyed his own family – except for Nora. Nora was made of more resilient stuff than either of her children. She enjoyed her unconventional life, she revelled in the influence she wielded and she liked moving around and meeting famous people, such as HG Wells, Ezra Pound, Samuel Beckett, WB Yeats and Carl Jung.

Although his peers were in awe of his literary genius, Nora was not overly impressed with Joyce's work. In fact, she claimed she 'always told him he should give up writing and take up singing.' She never read *Ulysses*, even though she is the clear inspiration for one of the most realistic and memorable women in literature: Molly Bloom. Displaying characteristic honesty she said she simply found the book too difficult and rather dirty. Strangely enough, she loved the later, more difficult, *Finnegans Wake*.

In London, in 1931, when Nora was forty-seven, she and Joyce finally married in a registry office service. The couple continued moving around Europe, worrying continually about Lucia's future but finding solace in Joyce's increasing fame. When World War II broke out in 1939 they settled, with Lucia, in neutral Switzerland. In 1941, Joyce died there of a perforated ulcer.

Crippled with arthritis and largely forgotten by all the people who had flocked around the genius she had lived with, Nora quietly outlived her husband by ten years. She died in Zurich in 1951, aged sixty-seven, attended only by her son, Giorgio.

Kitty Kiernan
1892–1945

Fiancée of Michael Collins

Catherine Brigid Kiernan grew up on the main street of Granard, County Longford, and was educated first at the Loreto Convent in Wicklow and then in St Ita's, in Rathfarnham, Dublin. Her parents died within months of each other in 1908, leaving sixteen-year-old Kitty and her four siblings, Chrys, Larry, Helen and Maud, to run the family business, the Greville Arms Hotel in Granard. They were a respectable and prosperous little family, and all four Kiernan girls were acknowledged beauties.

As well as being very attractive, Kitty had a lively personality. She was bright and affectionate and something of a party animal. She liked fine clothes and sleeping late and romantic novels. She was fond of singing and dancing, but she was also deeply religious. She was unpredictably moody, and could be rather vain and self-centred. Surprisingly for the woman who was loved by Michael Collins, she seemed completely apolitical.

Michael Collins, then a member of the Irish Republican Brotherhood (IRB), first visited Granard in 1918. It was said that he was attracted initially to Kitty's sister, Helen, but Helen was already spoken for so he switched his attentions to the lovely Kitty and a flirtation ensued. He was not long making his presence felt in the town in other ways too: in April 1918 he made a seditious speech, was arrested and charged, but then broke bail and went on the run, cheered on by the inhabitants of the town, including Kitty Kiernan.

At the same time there was also another senior IRB man interested in Kitty – Harry Boland. Harry and Michael were friends and colleagues and were quite open in their rivalry for Kitty's affections; Harry referred to Michael as his 'formidable opponent'. But in the early days, Michael had a reputation as a womaniser, and Harry was much more serious about Kitty. The only thing stopping Harry Boland from proposing marriage was 'the Chief' – Eamon de Valera – who sent him to the USA in 1919, 1920 and 1921 to campaign for Sinn Féin. However, their relationship was considered serious enough for Harry's mother to write affectionately to her 'future daughter-in-law'.

By the time of the Truce between the rebel forces and the Crown in the summer of 1921, the situation was a triangle: Kitty was regularly seeing both Harry and Michael. But when Harry returned to the States in early autumn 1921, Michael took the opportunity to redouble his attentions towards Kitty. In winter 1921, Michael went to London to negotiate the Anglo-Irish Treaty. From London he wrote daily love letters to Kitty. Harry wrote frequent love letters from the US, pleading with her to come out and marry him there. Instead, Kitty visited Michael in London – she seemed to have made up her mind. Relations between Harry and Michael soured as Harry realised Michael was going to win the woman that, after all, he had seen first.

In spring 1922, after the Dáil had passed the Treaty by seven votes thereby creating a 'Free State' of only twenty-six counties, all hell broke loose in Ireland and the Civil War erupted. Michael, who had been chairman and finance minister for the pro-Treaty provisional government that set up the Irish Free State, became commander-in-chief of the Free State Army. Harry, who had opposed the Treaty, joined the Irregulars and worked 'like the devil', as Michael said, against his rival. However strenuous his efforts to defeat his rival politically, he was apparently gracious in his personal defeat. After Michael announced his betrothal in the Dáil, Harry sent a letter to Kitty congratulating her on her engagement.

As the summer approached, the war was fraying Michael's nerves, and he was suffering from extreme stress and exhaustion. Kitty desperately wanted to name the wedding day so she could take on the responsibility of caring for him full-time as his wife. But it was not to be. On 22 August 1922, just over a fortnight after Harry was killed in Skerries by the Free State Army, Michael Collins was ambushed and assassinated by the Irregulars at Béal na mBláth, in his own home county of Cork.

After Michael's funeral, Kitty's own health declined. She had invested everything in becoming Mrs Michael Collins, but as a mere fiancée she had no status, no money and no future. For more than a year she wandered from relative to relative, carrying the precious souvenirs of her dead lover wherever she went. Eventually, in 1925, she married Felix Cronin, an ex-Free State soldier who had known Michael. She had two sons by him: Felix Cronin Junior and Michael Collins Cronin. The marriage was unhappy and money was scarce. In 1945, after years suffering from an inherited kidney disease (nephritis), Kitty Kiernan Cronin died in a Dublin nursing home. She is buried in Glasnevin, not far from her true love, Michael Collins.

THE GREAT PRETENDERS

> '... I had a strong inclination
> for the army ...'
>
> *Kit Cavanagh*

Kit Cavanagh

1667–1739

Soldier

Kit Cavanagh was born into a family of maltsters in Dublin. Soldiering was in Kit's blood: her father was a Protestant, but he fought and was wounded on the Catholic King James II's side in the Jacobite wars of 1689.

Kit was a capable girl who enjoyed spending her time on the family farm in Leixlip, County Kildare. But when she was a teenager a relative of her mother's seduced her at the farm, and Kit subsequently fled to her aunt's pub in Dublin. She lived with her aunt for four years, helping out and learning the pub business, which she inherited when her aunt died. Shortly afterwards, Kit fell in love with and married one of the servants, Richard Walsh. They lived happily together for four years until one day, in 1692, Richard disappeared without warning or explanation.

Kit was pregnant with their third child and was distraught by her husband's disappearance. She searched for him everywhere, but for a whole year she heard nothing. Then she received a letter from the Netherlands. It was from Richard, describing how he'd got blind drunk on that last day in Dublin City and had woken up in Holland – he had been forcibly conscripted to fight for King William III against the French. Kit immediately put her children in her mother's care, cut her hair, dressed in one of Richard's suits and enlisted in the Duke of Marlborough's infantry under the name of Christian Walsh. She was twenty-six years old.

Immediately nicknamed the 'pretty dragoon' by her comrades,

Kit heard what she called the 'rough music' of cannon fire almost immediately and she was wounded in her first action, at the disastrous Battle of Landen (1693). She recovered and the following year was back in action, but was quickly taken prisoner by the French. She was exchanged after nine days, and returned to the front. All the time she continued to enquire after her 'brother', Richard Walsh, but no information was forthcoming.

This disappointment did not impede what Kit calls in her autobiography her 'natural gaiety of temper', and she admits she 'lived very merrily' with her comrades in their winter quarters. Amazingly, she managed to do this without being discovered: she ate with them, drank with them, slept with them, played cards with them, even urinated alongside them by using what she describes as a 'silver tube with leather straps'. No one was ever the wiser.

So convincing was Kit as a dragoon that when a young girl was attacked by a sergeant in the regiment, Kit fought for the girl's honour and wounded the sergeant in a duel, whereupon the grateful girl fell in love with Kit. She 'got off from this *amour* without loss of credit' when she cited her inferior rank as an impediment to marriage. On another occasion, a prostitute claimed that Kit was the father of her baby. Rather than prove the mother a liar and give away her own secret, Kit admitted paternity and paid for the child's maintenance.

Things continued in this manner until the end of the war in 1697. Kit returned to Dublin, still having had no news of Richard. By now she had grown resigned to the loss of her dear husband, but upon the renewal of hostilities in 1702, she discovered that her 'martial inclinations' had been awakened and she promptly re-enlisted. She spent the next two years fighting under the Duke of Marlborough's command, enjoying the marauding and looting that followed every battle, and intermittently enquiring after Richard. She was wounded in the hip at Schellenberg, but managed to get through Blenheim unscathed – and with her secret still safe.

In the autumn of 1704, as she was guarding prisoners after the Battle of Hochstat, Kit was idly gazing at a soldier from another regiment being embraced by a Dutch woman. The soldier turned – and Kit recognised her husband, Richard. Perhaps a touch unreasonably – it had been twelve years after all – she immediately felt herself 'divided between rage and love, resentment and compassion'. She secretly made herself known to him, but as a punishment for his infidelity and because she still had a 'strong inclination for the army', she demanded they live apart so she could continue her military career. Richard kept her secret and they carried on with the war in separate regiments.

In 1706 Kit was wounded again, and this time, to the general amazement of all, it was finally discovered that she was a woman. On regaining consciousness and realising her secret was out, her main worry seems to have been financial: she feared she might be 'prevented in [her] marauding, which was very beneficial'. However, instead of being drummed out of the army, Kit became a celebrity across the ranks for her quick-wittedness and 'indomitable courage'. She remarried her husband, on the battlefield this time, and was allowed to continue in his regiment as a 'sutler' – a kind of black marketeer, thief and cook combined.

But Kit's 'martial inclinations' were not entirely laid to rest. When she discovered her husband's Dutch ex-mistress had followed his regiment, she attacked the poor woman and cut off her nose. She then had her placed on a 'turning stool' – a charming local punishment for minor misdemeanours, whereby the victim was spun around at high speed until he or she vomited. 'The violence of my temper, which was a very jealous one,' an abashed Kit afterwards admitted, 'pushed me on too far in this business.' The Dutch woman had her nose stitched back on and retired, defeated. Sadly, Kit was destined to lose Richard one way or another. Six months after their remarriage, Richard was killed at the Battle of Malplaquet. A heartbroken Kit trawled the battlefield and turned over more than 200 dead bodies before she found her husband's corpse.

Within three months of Richard's death, Kit had married again, to a soldier by the name of Hugh Jones. It is possible this was a hasty match that she repented soon afterwards because when Jones was killed in action only one year later, she admitted she felt nothing like the grief which had seized her when she found her 'dear Richard Welsh [sic] among the dead'.

Two years later the war was over and Kit went to London, where she found her fame had preceded her. Living on pensions from Queen Anne and the Duke of Marlborough, she travelled back to Dublin. Two of the children she had left ten years earlier were dead, and the third was in the workhouse. She started another pub, but then her 'evil genius' for penniless soldiers entangled her in a third marriage with one named Davies, who, she said bitterly, always 'spent more than he got', mostly on drink.

The years that Kit had spent on the move with her regiment left her unsuited for settled living, and she spent the next twenty-seven years moving between Ireland and England. She lived on charity from her admirers among the top army brass and other members of 'the quality' who knew her story. She started and lost several pub businesses, and eventually managed to get her husband a job in the Chelsea Hospital, where she herself became an out-pensioner. She ended her days there and was buried with full military honours at St Margaret's Church, Westminster.

Anne Bonny
c. 1698–c. 1720s
Pirate

In the early eighteenth century, just over 100 years after the Elizabethan heyday of English and Spanish piracy, there were still motley crews of French, British and American colonials on the high seas. Women are rarely heard of in these situations, and those that do get a passing mention in history were probably 'companions' to the real pirates. But one Irishwoman stands out from this unappetising crowd and is able to claim the dubious honour of being a pirate in her own right.

Anne Bonny was born in County Cork *c.*1698, the daughter of a servant, Mary Brennan, and her married employer, local lawyer William Cormac. Due to the scandal caused by the illegitimate birth, Mary, William and baby Anne left Ireland forever and fled to the New World. They settled in Charleston, South Carolina, where William bought and ran a successful plantation. Anne's mother died and Anne grew up the spoilt mistress of a large house who was used to having her own way.

Anne was strong and sturdy and had a ferocious temper. In one account of her early life (*A General History of the Robberies and Murders of the Most Notorious Pirates* by Captain Charles Johnson *alias* Daniel Defoe), she is said to have knifed her maid for some minor misdemeanour. When she was the victim of a rape attempt, she beat up the would-be rapist so badly he took to his bed to recuperate. She is also said to have become an expert fencer and markswoman – skills that were to stand her in good stead later on.

The undisciplined Carolinas were full of people running away from past sins, and there was plenty of opportunity for a young woman with a wayward streak and an inheritance to get into trouble. As soon as she was old enough, Anne fulfilled the worst expectations of all who knew her by marrying one of the less savoury characters of the area – a pirate named James Bonny. Her long-suffering father appears to have disowned her at this point.

The couple gravitated to New Providence, in what is now Nassau, in the Bahamas, probably at James's suggestion because of its reputation as a gathering place for renegade seamen. Surrounded by a wide choice of men of a certain type, it wasn't long before Anne tired of her charmless partner and attached herself to a succession of lovers, eventually hooking up with someone quite exalted in pirate circles: Captain John Rackham, also known as Calico Jack.

When he found out, James Bonny charged his young wife with

desertion and took her to court where, according to one of the more overheated stories, Anne was forced to appear naked. Bonny succeeded in getting a court order to prevent Anne and Jack from meeting. Legend has it that, to remedy the situation, Calico Jack suggested James Bonny put his wife up for auction and pocket the proceeds. This was not as bizarre a suggestion as it sounds, since divorce law in the early eighteenth century was largely focussed on compensating the divorced husband for the loss of his 'property'. In any case, Anne's response to this was to ignore the court order, pull on a pair of men's breeches and elope with Calico Jack to his ship, *The Revenge*.

Once on board, Anne developed her reputation for a wild temper, but she was apparently competent and well able to use both sword and pistol in the performance of her duties, which mainly involved commandeering the goods of other ships. On one trip she met Mary Read from England – also dressed as a man and living the life of a pirate. Mary had actually been brought up as a boy in a vain attempt by her mother to secure an inheritance. When this ruse failed, Mary had continued in her male persona and run away, first to the army and then to sea. By the time she met Anne she was a pirate of some experience and was one of Calico Jack's lieutenants.

Inevitably the women's relationship has been the subject of much erotic speculation by earlier historians, many of whom pre-ferred to believe that they had a lesbian relationship or – even better – enjoyed a *menage à trois* with Calico Jack. Anne was 'not reserved in point of chastity,' as one biographer waspishly points out, and she 'took [Mary] for a handsome lad'. The story goes on to relate how Anne, intent on having her wicked way with the 'handsome lad', followed Mary into a cabin, threw her on the bed and ripped open her blouse to reveal not only her intentions but also her not inconsiderable bosom. The startled Mary startled Anne in turn when she responded by ripping open her own blouse. However, setting aside speculations, it is just about possible to believe, 200 years later, that Anne and Mary had a platonic relationship and worked, lived and fought side-by-side.

Around this time the British government issued a King's Proclamation pardoning all pirates who gave themselves up. Calico Jack immediately availed himself of this opportunity to lengthen his life expectancy, but as soon as money ran short and he didn't know how to get any more, he reneged on the deal and went back to sea. Soon Jack, Anne, Mary and the crew of *The Revenge* were up to their old tricks in the waters around Jamaica.

In November 1720 a pirate-hunter named Captain Barnet attacked *The Revenge*. Legend has it that Anne and Mary were the only two that stayed to fight on the deck, and became so enraged as the rest of the pirates, including Calico Jack, cowered below that, in between fending off Barnet's men, they fired their pistols into the hold, killing one of their own comrades and wounding others. Despite the women's valiant efforts, the ship was overcome and the whole crew was taken to Jamaica and charged with piracy. All were found guilty and hanged.

All, that is, except for Anne Bonny and Mary Read. The two notorious women were tried separately and each claimed that she was pregnant, which they knew automatically postponed their date of execution. Pregnant or not, Mary Read died shortly afterwards of what was called prison fever – probably dysentery or something similar. As for Anne, she had one more meeting with Calico Jack on the day he was being taken to the gallows. Instead of comforting her hapless ex-lover, she roundly berated him, telling him that had he 'fought like a man [on *The Revenge*], he need not have been hanged like a dog'.

Nothing more is known of Anne Bonny. It is possible that her rich and influential father took pity on her and got her off as she seems to have had at least one reprieve. One thing is certain: there is no record of her having been hanged.

Dr James Barry
c. 1799–1865

Army surgeon and Inspector-General of British Hospitals

The facts of the life of James Barry are more difficult to swallow than fiction. There are several mysteries surrounding her story, including her parentage and her correct age, but most puzzling of all is the question of her gender.

In the first years of the nineteenth century, a woman named Mary Ann Bulkeley came to London from Cork with her two daughters. Telling a sad story of having been forcibly ejected from the family home by her husband and son, she came to her brother looking for charity. Her brother was the talented but undisciplined artist James Barry RA (*d.*1806); their parents were well-known shipbuilders in Cork City.

In London, James Barry's main patrons were two powerful and influential men: a Venezuelan war hero named General Francisco Miranda (*d.*1812) and David Erskine Stuart, the earl of Buchan (*d.*1829). All three men were radicals in their own way – influenced, for example, by the feminism of Mary Wollstonecraft – and all three spotted early on that the younger of Mary Ann's two children was an extremely intelligent and precocious little girl. Such was her brilliance and promise, especially in her favourite science subjects, that it wasn't long before they decided she should live a life that fulfilled her potential. Instead of the female lottery of spinsterhood and poverty or marriage and an early death in childbirth, they believed Mary Ann's daughter should do the unthinkable: she should have a career in medicine.

The problem, of course, was that she was a girl. Girls, brilliant or otherwise, simply did not go to university and qualify as doctors (it would be another seventy years before the pioneers of the women's movement in Britain would make this possible). There was only one solution: Mary Ann's daughter had to be a boy. In 1809, swamped in a high-collared shirt and greatcoat, Mary Ann's small, slight, red-haired daughter enrolled at Edinburgh University as a boy and signed her name for the first time as James Miranda Stuart Barry, after her benefactors. Thus began a deception that was to last for the rest of her life.

Barry claimed to be ten years old at enrolment, but she may have been up to four years older than that. She was small and she had no Adam's apple, so she needed to pretend to be a prepubescent boy to deflect attention from her appearance. Nobody passed any remarks about the shy but clever student, and Dr Barry passed out of Edinburgh University with flying colours in 1812. A year later, having gained some work experience in St Thomas's Hospital, London, Barry enlisted in the British Army medical corps. She spent three years in Plymouth as a hospital assistant, and in 1816 was posted to the Cape colony as an army staff-surgeon – the start of a lifetime's service to the British Empire.

In Cape Town there was gossip about Barry's effeminate appearance and high, squeaky voice. A writer named the 'Count de Las Cases', who published a *Journal of the Private Life and Conversations of the Emperor Napoleon at St Helena* during Barry's lifetime, speculated in print after meeting Barry, who had come to examine his sick son. 'The grave Doctor,' wrote the Count, '… was a boy of eighteen, with the form, the manners and the voice of a woman, [but] was described to be an absolute phenomenon. I was informed that he had obtained his diploma at the age of thirteen, after the most rigid examination, and that he had performed extraordinary cures at the Cape.'

Phenomenally skilled she may have been, but Barry was also known for her phenomenally hot temper. On one occasion, a fellow officer protested against some of her more acidic remarks about one of the high-born ladies of the garrison, and Barry challenged him to a duel. They fought with pistols but, fortunately, neither was hurt, and both were able to retire with honour.

In Cape Town the dapper doctor was generally a favourite with the ladies because she was intelligent, fastidious, an excellent dancer – and, of course, she knew just how to talk to women. Privately, Barry spent a lot of time with the governor of the Cape colony, Sir Charles Somerset. Their relationship, obviously intimate though punctuated by ferocious rows, was almost lover-like in its intensity. Did she, a woman in her early twenties, trapped behind the myth of manhood, nurture an unrequited love for the governor? The biographer June Rose speculates that, not only was there a love affair, but that James Barry actually bore the governor's child.

Professionally, Barry was a stickler. Although skilled, she made herself unpopular by expecting the same high standards of everyone around her that she demanded of herself. She insisted on the modern fad of strict hygiene in hospitals – and added the outlandish idea of treating all patients equally, even the non-whites, lepers and lunatics. This policy extended to the prison hospitals, including that of the notorious Robben Island where serious offenders were housed. Barry also forced through smallpox inoculations some twenty years before these vaccinations became compulsory back in England. She also improved the standard of nursing care thirty years before Florence Nightingale by employing only respectable women as nurses instead of the usual drunks and thieves who regarded it as a cushy job.

In 1822, after six years' sterling service, Barry's superiors recognised her efficiency and she was promoted to Colonial Medical Inspector. Now she was in charge, the rather autocratic Barry continued to make herself unpopular with her colleagues in the Cape. This culminated in 1825 in a clash with the Colonial Medical Board over who had the final say on prisoners' welfare. The Board had decided one particular prisoner, Aaron Smith, was insane; Barry examined him and declared him sane. She took on all the powers at the Cape – including the governor – but eventually lost the case. For her pains, she received a suspended prison sentence for contempt of court and was demoted to Assistant Staff-Surgeon.

Despite her colleagues' impatience with her outspokenness and fastidiousness, Barry was a brilliant and respected doctor. In 1826 she was called out to an emergency childbirth. The mother was dying before her eyes, so Barry made the decision to perform a dangerous operation that she had only ever heard about and that in almost all other cases had resulted in the mother's death – a Caesarean section. It was only the second time on record this operation had been performed successfully, but thanks to the doctor's speed and dexterity both mother and child survived. The baby boy was named after Barry, and that baby's godson, named after him in turn, would be a future president of South Africa: James Barry Munnik. This exploit guaranteed Barry 'a celebrity for skill as a surgical operator' (*Manchester Guardian*, 21 August 1865).

In 1828, Barry was posted to Mauritius, but she did not like it and left soon after. After home-leave in 1831 she was posted to Jamaica, where she worked herself into poor health looking after the interests of the garrison's soldiers. By 1836 she was on the island of St Helena and was promoted to Principal Medical Officer. Here the marginal groups she chose for special protection were the thousands of female paupers and people of colour on the islands. On St Helena she disobeyed her superior on a matter of principle – this time because he was blocking supplies for her hospital – and eventually went over his head to the War Office. The result of this rash action was that she was arrested and court-martialled for 'conduct unbecoming to an officer and a gentleman'.

This was the lowest point in Barry's career. The old boys' network ganged up against her and, despite her brilliance, the doctor who had devoted twenty years of her life to healing the sick in the outposts of the Empire was once again demoted from Principal Medical Officer to Staff-Surgeon and sent home on extended leave.

Her next posting, in 1838, to the Windward and Leeward Islands in the West Indies, nearly killed her. She contracted yellow fever, and it was during her illness that she was seen naked in bed by two young doctors, one of whom was able to confirm, more than forty years later, that Dr James Barry had indeed been a woman.

When she recovered, Barry fought back to regain her exalted position — and her efforts paid off. In 1846 she was posted to Malta where she was specially commended by the Duke of Wellington for her work in improving public sanitation systems and for her role in quashing the 1848 typhus epidemic. This commendation from such a luminary eventually led to James Barry being made Inspector-General of British Hospitals — the highest rank a doctor could attain. This new position gave her immense status as an officer and as a doctor.

After Malta she was transferred to Corfu, where, by 1852, she was dealing with the wounded from the Crimean War. Always interested in the welfare of the common soldier, Barry spent her leave in the Crimea in 1855. Inevitably, she fell out with the famous and rather officious Florence Nightingale, whom she scolded and who later referred to Barry as a 'brute'.

In 1857 Barry received her last and most dismal posting. In its wisdom, the army transported the doctor who had served in tropical climes for forty years to the freezing wastes of Canada. Not surprisingly, Barry's health took a turn for the worse and despite being as enthusiastic in her work as ever, she retired in 1859 with a small pension and chronic bronchitis.

She returned to England and took rooms in Marylebone, London, where she lived out the remaining six years of her life in increasing eccentricity. The only creatures allowed near her were John, her West Indian servant, and her pets – a succession of dogs named Psyche, a cat and a parrot. She lived simply and kept to a strict vegetarian and teetotal diet. Despite these precautions, in the hot summer months of 1865 when dysentery was rife in filthy London, James Barry succumbed to the sickness she had managed to avoid her whole life in the tropics.

After her death, Barry's female gender was confirmed by a woman employed to lay her out. The woman even claimed that there was evidence that Barry had had a child. The story was widely circulated and, in a final injustice, Barry's military funeral was abandoned. The Establishment ignored the claim – it would never do that the Inspector-General had been a mere woman – and gagged the press. But the story of a woman who sacrificed her womanhood so she could do the job she loved has refused to go away.

WOMEN ON THE FRONT LINE

'I have raised hell all over
this country!'
Mother Jones

Anne Devlin

1780–1851

Patriot

On 18 September 1851, in a slum area of Dublin, a blind and broken old woman named Mrs Campbell died of starvation. She had recently told the sad story of her life to her only remaining friend, Reverend Brother Luke Cullen.

Anne Campbell had been born Anne Devlin seventy years earlier on a farm near Rathdrum, County Wicklow. She was born into an old rebel family, which had a revolutionary pedigree on both sides going back to the time of Red Hugh O'Donnell in the sixteenth century – one of her ancestors had been a messenger for Red Hugh. Anne's father, Brian Devlin, was a United Irishman, and from an early age, Anne, her three brothers and three sisters were reared with rebel politics. Of all the young Devlins, Anne was the most passionate in her desire to free Ireland from English rule.

Anne was just eighteen years old at the time of the 1798 Rising, but she was well aware of what was afoot. Four of her cousins were active rebels: Hugh O'Byrne, brothers Art and Pat Devlin, and Michael Dwyer. The Devlin household often offered shelter to these and other rebels.

After the Rising was crushed and its main leaders executed, Michael Dwyer and the others went into hiding in a cave in the Wicklow Mountains, where the brave and trusted Anne visited them, bringing news and provisions. From his hiding place, Michael carried out daring and provocative raids against those members of the loyalist militia, known as yeomen, who were burning Catholic homes and looting property. He became a folk hero in the process.

Soon after the Rising, Anne's father was arrested on suspicion of involvement with the rebels. The only breadwinner in the family, he was taken to Wicklow jail and imprisoned, without trial, for two and a half years. After his release in 1801, Mr Devlin moved Anne and the rest of the family from Wicklow to Rathfarnham, on the outskirts of south Dublin, and rented a farm.

One day, Anne's cousin, Art Devlin, a committed young revolutionary, came to call on them. He had a friend who was looking for a base from which to plan another rising. Art rented a house in Butterfield Lane, near the Devlin home, for his friend and introduced him to Anne. His friend's name was Robert Emmet.

Robert Emmet was born in Molesworth Street, Dublin, on 4 March 1778, the son of a prosperous doctor. He and his brother, Thomas, were members of the United Irishmen and friends and admirers of Theobald Wolfe Tone, one of the main leaders of the 1798 Rising. After Wolfe Tone's death, Robert moved to France and perfected his rebel education. He returned to Dublin in March 1803, under the assumed name of Ellis, and moved into the house at Butterfield Lane with fellow revolutionaries Thomas Russell and WH Hamilton. All three were strongly of the opinion that there should be another rebellion – and soon. They planned a rising for the night of 23 July 1803.

Anne, a passionate believer in the rebel cause, is usually described as Robert's servant or housekeeper, but in her memoirs she rejects this description. She wanted to play an active part in the coming revolution and did so without payment of any sort from

Robert – her expenses, she said, were always paid by her father. Intelligent and efficient, her main job was to organise the delivery of Robert's messages by hand, as a result of which she knew the names of more than fifty insurgents spread across the city. She was loyal to Robert, but she was not in love with him; she arranged for messages to get to his fiancée, Sarah Curran. Along with passing intelligence for Robert and running the household for her father, Anne was also receiving and packing consignments of ammunition and arms in preparation for the rebellion.

On 16 July, a few days before the date set for the rising, a rebel powder factory in Patrick Street was accidentally blown up, unsettling the rebels. On the night itself, Robert and his men were supposed to be storming Dublin Castle, but a tragic miscommunication resulted in a premature strike by some rebels stationed in the Coombe area. There was a serious problem with informers, resulting in low morale and poor communications; Michael Dwyer didn't even make it into town from his mountain hideaway. There was hand-to-hand fighting in the Coombe area, but as soon as the first yeomen fell in Bridgefoot Street reinforcements were brought in. Robert and the others were forced to retreat in disarray. The rising had failed, disastrously.

Robert went into hiding, his hopes for Ireland dashed. Within the week, a unit of yeomen paid a call to Rathfarnham and found twenty-three-year-old Anne and her eight-year-old sister at home. The yeomen questioned both girls as to the whereabouts of Robert and the other rebels, using bayonets to slash them both in an effort to procure information. When no information was forthcoming, one of the yeomen tipped up a cart, tied a noose around Anne's neck and hung her over the back of the cart until she lost consciousness. Still, she refused to speak.

The entire Devlin family was arrested on the night of 29 August, including Anne's youngest brother, James (nine), who was forced up from his sickbed. They were marched ten miles to Dublin Castle and separated. Spread throughout the Castle dungeons were no less than twenty-one members of the extended Devlin/O'Byrne family.

Anne was questioned by Major Henry Charles Sirr, Dublin's chief of police. Sirr harangued her for the names of those involved in the rising; Anne refused to answer. Sirr then claimed that her parents had confessed and had been allowed to return home, but Anne refused to believe him. Eventually he offered her £500 (about £35,000 today) and government protection to give the names of the people with whom Robert had been in collaboration. Anne simply replied: '[I will never] let the name of any man pass [my] lips.'

In early September 1803, Anne was transferred to Old Kilmainham Jail, while the rest of her family went to New Kilmainham. The old jail was nothing more than dungeons and was so dilapidated it was usually reserved for the most serious offenders. Anne's obstinacy and spirit had obviously not endeared her to the authorities. The governor of the prison, the notoriously cruel Dr Edward Trevor, took over as Anne's tormentor, keeping her in the male part of the prison, spitting abuse at her, accusing her of risking her family's lives and threatening her with public execution. Anne's proud, defiant response was invariably the same: 'Go to the devil and get someone else; I'll tell you nothing.'

Conditions in Old Kilmainham in the early part of the nineteenth century were unspeakable. Food – one quart of milk, a half-pound of bread and five pounds of potatoes daily – was usually contaminated. Sewers were open and sanitation was nonexistent. Anne's tiny cell had two unglazed windows and a bed of straw on a cobbled floor. There was no protection from cold or damp. There was no light except what came through the window of the cell. There were no reading materials, no visitors, no health care – except from Dr Trevor.

One day Anne was forcibly pushed into the prison yard, no doubt expecting some new punishment, only to come face to face with the man she had prayed was still free: Robert Emmet. He had just been arrested by Major Sirr. Robert, reasoning that he was a dead man anyway, pleaded with Anne to identify him as an insurgent and save herself. A distraught Anne refused and was taken back to her cell. On 20 September, Robert was taken from New Kilmainham Jail and publicly executed outside St Catherine's Church on Thomas Street. Dr Trevor ordered Anne to be taken to the spot in a carriage and shown Robert's blood staining the cobbles.

Anne was never formally convicted of any crime, but was incarcerated for three years nonetheless. She was in solitary confinement for most of that time and endured beatings, starvation and psychological torture. After the first winter her health started to decline and she developed a disease called erysipelas, a streptococcal infection that causes pain, inflammation and a reddening of the skin, particularly on the face and scalp.

In 1804 her sick young brother, James, still confined in

another part of the prison, was brought to her, only to die in her arms. According to Dr Trevor, he had died of 'prison fever' – another term for malnutrition and dysentery. A book published by the doctor in 1808 as a riposte to slanderous rumours, *Dr Trevor's Statement to Charges Brought Against Him*, tells how his tactless suggestion of a post-mortem on the boy was met by Anne in characteristically fiery style:

'... The said Ann Develin [sic], in the presence of the Deponent [witness], used very abusive language against said Trevor, and cursed him for having proposed to have the head of said boy, her brother, opened, to ascertain more fully the cause of his death, which operation would have been unnecessary had he died of a fever.' (Statement taken 23 July 1808.)

Compare Anne's attitude with that of her father, who sent what amounts to a begging letter pleading for the release of his family:

'... I hope, Sir, you will be pleased to consider the very great length of mine and my children's confinement ... I know, Sir, that a word's speaking in our favour, would have us all set at liberty ...' (Letter dated 4 August 1805.)

By the summer of 1806 all the Devlins had been released, except for Anne, who still refused to tell what she knew. She could not move without excruciating pain from her swollen joints and was maddened by pain in her head. Just when it looked as if she too were going to die, the much longed-for 'word' from Dr Trevor came. She was released with 'a soul unstained', as she herself said, but with her youth and health gone and her spirit shattered. She was twenty-six years old.

Not much is known of Anne's life after this date, except that she worked as a housemaid in Dublin from 1806 to 1810, and sat for her portrait by Lydon (which is now in the National Gallery of Ireland). When the playwright Richard Brinsley Sheridan asked her to let him write the story of her imprisonment, she was still so traumatised by her experiences that she turned him down. Whenever she met men in the street whose lives she had saved by her silence, she looked away. She was never involved in revolutionary politics again.

In time she married a man named Campbell and had two children. But after Campbell's death in 1845, Anne's situation went from bad to worse. Her family's deaths were hastened by what they'd been through, the country was gripped by famine and her children died before her. This is how desperate she was when Brother Luke Cullen found her and recorded her story. As she ruefully told him: 'the security I gave [the rebels] is the only thing on Earth that I have now to be proud of.'

Blind and starving though she was, her loyalty to the rebels and the rebel cause remained unchanged to the end. She died in 1851, sure in her conviction that Robert Emmet had been one of Ireland's greatest heroes. Anne was buried in a charity coffin in Glasnevin cemetery, but shortly afterwards her body was disinterred by an admirer – Dr RR Madden, the acclaimed United Irishmen historian – and replaced in 'the Circle' of the cemetery, where all the other great patriots lie. Her headstone features an Irish wolfhound – an ancient symbol of loyalty.

Mother Jones
1830–1930

Labour activist

Cork-born Mary Harris, better known as Mother Jones, was one of America's most outspoken socialists and labour rights campaigners. The woman who once said her home address was 'wherever there is a fight against oppression' was passionate in her hatred of unfettered capitalism and all its attendant ills.

Mother Jones's early life was not an easy one. Her family hailed from Cork City and were proud of their long Republican tradition. Poverty drove them to emigrate to the USA when Mary was a young child. Mary's father worked the railroads, but he managed to put Mary through school and she became a teacher in Memphis, Tennessee. In 1861 she met and married George Jones, an ironworker and committed member of the Iron Moulders' Union.

Tragically, in 1867, Mary's husband and all four of their children died in a yellow fever epidemic. In her autobiography, *The Autobiography of Mother Jones*, she relates how she laid out the little ones herself since no one would come near them for fear of contagion. After this she went to Chicago to start again as a seamstress, only to lose her business and her home in the great fire of 1871. She camped by the lake in the city with all the other homeless citizens, and faced the prospect of starting all over yet again at the age of forty-one.

At this point, Mother Jones experienced an epiphany. She looked at the people living in shacks around her and compared the insecure fortunes of the average worker with what she called the 'tropical comfort' and security of their fat-cat employers. She joined a society known as the Knights of Labor [sic], a secret assembly open to all skilled and non-skilled workers, which had been founded by Philadelphia garment workers in 1869. Within a short time Mother Jones was engrossed in the labour movement. Now, with no family, no home and no business to distract her, her life course was set.

For fifty years Mother Jones travelled, lectured and agitated for labour rights. She wrote for the socialist press and, as she put it, 'raised hell' all over the country. She co-founded left-wing workers' organisations, such as the Industrial Workers of the World (1905). She was jeered at, jailed, assaulted and, in 1912, damned as 'the most dangerous woman in America'.

Mother Jones was always most interested in the welfare of coal miners, who endured possibly the worst working conditions in the country. In the 1880s and 1890s she travelled to coalfields far and wide and witnessed first-hand the misery of fourteen-hour underground shifts, the company-owned shacks that miners' families lived in, the dead children buried by mothers who already had another on the way, the lack of medical and educational facilities and the exploitation of cheap immigrant labour. Eventually she became an organiser for United Mine Workers (UMW), which worked to protect and extend the rights of miners.

Mother Jones was campaigning at a time when brutal suppression of unions was the norm. Employers were often backed by the force of state troops and hired gunmen. In 1914, in Ludlow, Colorado, while visiting the coalfields, she witnessed a particularly nasty incident that was to become known as the Ludlow Massacre.

Coal miners at one of John D Rockefeller's Colorado mines had downed tools over a dispute about membership of UMW. As the strike wore on, families lost their homes and took to living in tents. Rockefeller sent for the state troops as a precautionary measure. One day some of the soldiers opened fire on the strikers, who returned fire. One soldier and five strikers died in this exchange. In retaliation, the infuriated soldiers attacked the tented city, razing it to the ground. At least two women and eleven children died. This incident led to statewide warfare for ten days until neutral federal troops were called in to quell the violence. Several months later a truce was called and the strikers were forced to return to work.

Mother Jones was also especially aggravated by child labour in textile mills. In order to report on the situation first-hand, she went to work in a succession of mills herself. She described how 'undersized, round-shouldered, hollow-eyed, listless sleepy' little children of six and seven years old routinely lost limbs while cleaning between spindles during twelve-hour night shifts. One female mill worker claimed she had a 'good boss': she had been let off early the night she gave birth, and allowed back with the baby two days later. The baby slept under the machinery its mother operated. The percentage of children working in such factories was high, for example, in 1903 a factory of 75,000 textile workers in Kensington, Pennsylvania, included 10,000 children, most under ten years old.

Mother Jones felt her mission was to combat all this and her tactics were nothing if not direct. During a coal miners' strike in Pennsylvania in 1899, she heard that the hated scabs, as strikebreakers were called, were undermining the action. She armed miners' wives with their own brooms and mops, and mobilised them into a physical charge against the scabs. This proved a psychological turning point in the dispute and the strike was a success. During another campaign, she organised a march of mill children from Philadelphia – a city, she claimed, that was 'built on the broken bones of children' – through New Jersey to New York City. The march helped change legislation, raising the minimum age of workers from twelve to fourteen.

Mother Jones was famous for her confrontational style. She admitted she had a tendency to 'put it strong' when speaking. 'I am not choice when the constitution of my country is violated,' she declared, 'I do not go into the classics. I am not *praying*.' She was also renowned for her sharp wit. On being refused entry to Canada by a border official, she threatened to take the matter up with her uncle. 'Who's your uncle?' asked the official. 'Uncle Sam,' replied Mother Jones.

Mother Jones always regarded herself as a 'patriotic American', but claimed that her hatred of oppression sprang from her Irish roots. 'I believe that this country is the cradle of liberty,' she said, citing the Irish Fenians as just one group that was afforded the liberty, in America, to continue their fight for freedom at home.

But Mother Jones's politics, though sincere, were in no way consistent. For all her talk of equality and liberty, she was bitingly critical of those fighting for women's rights. 'You don't need a vote to raise hell,' she declared to a group of suffragists in 1915. 'I have never had a vote and I have raised hell all over this country!' She maintained that politics was the 'servant of industry', and that plutocrats kept women oppressed by keeping them 'busy with suffrage and prohibition and charity'. She was characteristically blunt on this matter: 'I do not believe in "careers" for women, especially a "career" in factory and mill where most women have their "careers" … The training of the children – this is her most beautiful task.' Needless to say, with this attitude, Mother Jones was not popular with the women's franchise movements.

In her long career, the controversial Mother Jones agitated in almost every state in North America, including Illinois, Tennessee, Michigan, Kansas, New Jersey, Maryland, Pennsylvania, West Virginia, Arizona, Colorado, California, Alabama, Washington, and also in Canada, in British Columbia. At the age of ninety-one she travelled to Mexico to address the Pan-American Federation of Labour. Her last labour dispute was in 1924 (she was ninety-four), when she addressed a textile union strike in Chicago.

Although organised religion came in for much of Mother Jones's scorn – 'Don't listen to ministers,' she is reported as saying, 'we know the Lord as well as they do' – she died a devout Christian at 100 years of age. She is buried near strike victims in the Union Miners' cemetery in Mount Oliver, Illinois.

Madame Eliza Lynch
1835–1886

Regent of Paraguay

Eliza Lynch was born near Blackrock, County Cork. Although her own family was poor, she claimed an exalted Anglo-Irish family tree that included bishops, vice-admirals and magistrates. When Eliza was still a child, her life took a turn for the exotic when the Lynches emigrated to Paris in search of better living conditions.

At just fourteen years of age, Eliza married a vet from the French Army and moved to Algiers. The ill-advised match lasted only two years, after which time Eliza returned to Paris and, as a no-longer-respectable, separated woman, slowly entered the murky world of the courtesan. After several minor liaisons, she started an affair with Don Francisco Solano Lopez, eldest son of the president of Paraguay. When Lopez returned to Paraguay in 1855, Eliza went with him.

In due course, Lopez's father died and he became the marshall-president of Paraguay (population: one million). Madame Lynch, as she was now known, became his consort and main advisor. Everything was relatively tranquil for nine years until, in 1864, war broke out between Paraguay and the massed forces of Brazil, Argentina and Uruguay.

While Lopez took charge of the army, Eliza formed and commanded a female regiment made up of the women of Paraguay's native Guarani people, who fought alongside the men. As the situation became more serious, Lopez made Eliza the Regent of Paraguay so he could concentrate on fighting. The popular Eliza was now in charge of State affairs.

The war continued for four years, during which time Eliza had to leave statecraft and again take up arms alongside Lopez. In a desperate stand at Cerro in northwest Paraguay, she is said to have distinguished herself as a soldier. Two years later, in 1870, Lopez was killed by the enemy forces. Eliza tried to escape with her four sons, but this caused mutiny in the ranks and her eldest son was murdered. It is said she buried both her lover and her son in the same grave with her bare hands.

After capture by the Brazilians and eventual release, Madame Eliza Lynch returned to Europe and lived the rest of her life in poverty. When she died she was buried at Père Lachaise cemetery, Paris, but, in the 1930s, her body was re-interred in the Panthene do Los Heroes in Paraguay's capital, Ascuncion. Paraguay has since declared her a national hero.

Dr Kathleen Lynn
1874–1955

One of the first female doctors in Ireland and founder of the first hospital for children

Kathleen Lynn was born near Cong, County Mayo, the daughter and grand-daughter of Church of Ireland clergymen. Kathleen's locality was often worst hit during the recurrent famines of the nineteenth century, and she witnessed to how poverty and malnutrition caused the most disease and death in her father's parish. Realising that the local doctor was the most useful member of the community, she formed the outrageous notion of becoming one herself. She was educated abroad, and on her return to Ireland she attended the Royal University, Dublin (as the National University of Ireland was known until the early years of the twentieth century). The university had been conferring degrees on women since

1884, but upon graduating in 1899, Kathleen became one of the first women in Ireland to gain a degree in medicine.

Her gender proved an impediment from the outset as Kathleen could not find a hospital to accept her residency; the doctors at the Adelaide Hospital in Dublin all voted for postponing her appointment 'indefinitely', citing a lack of 'female accommodation'. Kathleen refused to take the hint. She got as much experience as she could working in the Rotunda Lying-In Hospital, the Coombe Lying-In Hospital and Sir Patrick Dun's hospitals, and then set up her own general practice in her home at 9 Belgrave Road, Rathmines, south Dublin (her next-door neighbour was Hanna Sheehy Skeffington). She did her postgraduate degree in the USA and, in 1909, became a Fellow of the Royal College of Surgeons in Ireland. Her style was brisk: she was a no-nonsense doctor who believed in fresh air, cold drinks and long cycle rides.

Through her struggle to establish her medical career, Kathleen became first a suffragist, then a labour rights activist and finally a nationalist. The fact that she was interested in women's rights was in no way surprising considering the treatment she had received professionally. Although she was not an 'extreme militant', according to Andrée Sheehy Skeffington, daughter-in-law of Hanna Sheehy Skeffington, her feminism 'inspired her political activities'. She tended hunger-striking suffragists in 1912 at the beginning of a combative phase of their fight for the vote.

Similarly, she treated starving workers in 1913 during Dublin's Great Lock-Out, and once she saw that the malnutrition and disease suffered by the majority of Dublin's workers and their children were even worse than at home in Mayo, she became a staunch supporter of Jim Larkin's and James Connolly's Irish Trades and General Workers' Union (ITGWU). These interests dovetailed naturally into nationalism: to Kathleen, Irish independence was a necessity if there were ever going to be equal opportunities for women and workers. A good friend of Connolly's, she joined his Irish Citizen Army (ICA) in 1913.

By the early months of 1916, Kathleen had been made a captain and chief medical officer of the ICA. She gave first-aid lectures and workshops to ICA and Cumann na mBan members, and she also collected and transported weapons in her car. During the Easter Rising of 1916 she was initially in charge of delivering medical supplies to the various stations. She was then ordered to go to City Hall, on Dame Street, with a regiment of about twenty-five men and women who were meant to be attacking Dublin Castle. Kathleen had found several insurgents at Christ Church Place and they all had to climb over the locked iron gates to get into City Hall. Heavy casualties were expected, so Kathleen set up a casualty station inside. After Seán Connolly, the officer in charge, was shot and killed on the roof of City Hall, she and Seán's fiancée, the labour rights activist Helena Moloney, took over as senior officers.

Kathleen, Helena and their comrades held City Hall throughout the night under a heavy bombardment, until eventually the British managed to break through a wall with grenades and machine guns and overpower them. As the senior officer present, Kathleen surrendered at bayonet-point and handed over the revolver she kept in her medical bag. She and the survivors were marched to Ship Street Barracks, and then she and Helena went on to Dublin Castle. From there she was sent on to Kilmainham, where she was jailed along with Countess Constance Markievicz.

Released in 1917 under the General Amnesty, the government continued to regard Kathleen as a subversive and she was 'on the run' for some of 1918 because she was on Sinn Féin's executive. Government forces raided her clinic and house continually. At the height of the worldwide 'flu epidemic of 1918 she was arrested and detained. A public outcry orchestrated by the lord mayor of Dublin ensured her release, so that she could go about her medical business. But she was watched.

As a result of the epidemic and soldiers returning from the war in Europe, Dublin's hospitals were severely overcrowded. Kathleen and her friend and ICA comrade, Madeleine ffrench-Mullen, developed a plan to open a new hospital. Originally intended for adults, Kathleen and Madeleine changed the idea to a children's hospital because of the horrifically high infant mortality rate in Dublin's slums; about 165 per 1,000 children died of preventable diseases. They borrowed money, bought 37 Charlemont Street and officially opened with just two cots in May 1919. The hospital was named St Ultan's (or *Teach Ultan* – the house of Ultan) after an early bishop of Meath who was also a famous healer.

St Ultan's grew and prospered under the women's guidance and it had sixty cots by 1937. One of its aims was to provide classes for mothers to combat the ignorance that was the cause of so many infant deaths. In 1934 they incorporated a Montessori school for the little patients. St Ultan's employed an all-female staff, partly to provide employment opportunities for women graduates. One staff member there was Dr Dorothy Stopford Price, a pioneer of the BCG vaccine, which eventually wiped out the common and deadly infectious disease, tuberculosis (TB).

Kathleen was on the board of the Irish White Cross (founded in 1920 for the relief of those affected by the War of Independence), which changed into the Children's Relief Association in 1922; she stayed on the board until it was disbanded in 1936.

In 1923 Kathleen was elected to the Dáil as TD for north Dublin. As an opposer of the Anglo-Irish Treaty, she refused to take her seat in Leinster House in support of Eamon de Valera and the republicans. Then, in the late 1920s, when de Valera's Fianna Fáil failed to embrace the social reform Kathleen had been looking for, she dropped politics altogether. Instead, she devoted the next thirty years of her life to the running of St Ultan's, which, at the end of her life, Kathleen was to regard as her greatest achievement. She gave up holding clinics just six months before her death in 1955, at the age of eighty-one.

At Dr Kathleen Lynn's funeral, three volleys were fired over her grave as a military honour in recognition of the part she played in the Easter Rising.

Delia Larkin
1878–1949

Trade unionist

Delia Larkin was born into an Irish working-class community in Liverpool. After her father's death from TB when she was nine years old, her older brothers helped support the family; James, the most famous Larkin, was then only eleven years old.

Delia supported her brother politically when he set out to organise a trade union in the Liverpool dockyards. When he moved on to Belfast and then Dublin, she left her job as a nurse to follow him. In 1909 James founded the Irish Transport and General Workers' Union (ITGWU), and two years later, with Delia's assistance, the Irish Women Workers' Union (IWWU). Delia became the IWWU's first general secretary.

The IWWU widened opportunities for women, maintained a strike fund and provided a forum for discussion. Delia helped funding by organising a choir and a drama group, which went on a very successful tour, and she managed most of the social life of both the ITGWU and the IWWU. On a more serious note, she represented the IWWU at the Irish Trades Union Conference three years in a row, and wrote a column in the *Irish Worker*, the organ of the ITGWU.

In 1913 the Great Lock-Out crippled Dublin City. Workers were locked out by their employers, who wanted them to relinquish union membership. Conditions were atrocious for the striking workers – many were starving and unable to provide for their families.

When James Larkin went to raise support in England, Delia was effectively in charge at Liberty Hall. When he returned, she switched her attention to managing the Liberty Hall soup kitchen, which tried to provide meals for some 3,000 starving children. She liaised with comrades in Britain to remove Dublin children there until the strike was over, but her efforts were quashed by massive

Church opposition. Many of Delia's IWWU members were not reinstated when the Lock-Out ended in failure in February 1914, so she took the drama group on tour again in order to raise money for those left without employment.

When James Larkin left for the USA in 1914, Delia quickly found that she did not get on with his successor as secretary of the ITGWU, James Connolly. She began to come into conflict with different factions in the labour movement. She dropped out of sight altogether during the preparations for the Easter Rising in 1916 – apparently she went home to war-torn Liverpool to work as a nurse – and did not appear in Dublin again until 1918, when she came out in support of the anti-conscription lobby.

By 1918 Delia and James were leaning towards Communism, and were seen as more militant than most members of the ITGWU and the IWWU; Delia's own union even refused to renew her membership. Delia started to write for *The Red Hand,* an opposition newspaper to the ITGWU, but stopped at the request of her brother who feared such overt disunity. In 1920, James was jailed as an anarchist for three years. While he was in prison, Delia married an ex-Irish Citizen Army (ICA) man, Patrick Colgan. She was forty-three years of age.

James Larkin came into conflict with the leadership of the ITGWU – whose membership now numbered some 100,000 – and he was eventually expelled from the union. Delia supported him and another brother, Peter, when they founded the left-wing Workers' Union of Ireland (WUI). She again founded a drama group for the union, but during the 1930s confined her labour activities to writing occasional articles for the *Irish Worker.*

Delia and her husband provided a home for James for the last ten years of his life in Ballsbridge, Dublin. He died in 1947 and Delia, who had long suffered from ill health, died two years later. She is buried in Glasnevin cemetery, Dublin.

Mairéad Farrell

1953–1988

IRA member

Mairéad Farrell was born in Belfast into a republican family. Her grandfather had been active in the 1919–1921 War of Independence, and had been imprisoned by the British. Mairéad joined the IRA at eighteen years of age, straight after leaving school. Soon after that, in 1976, she was convicted of involvement in bomb-making and imprisoned for fourteen years.

In prison in Armagh, Mairéad studied political science and economics and refined her political beliefs – later she was to refer to herself as a socialist as well as a republican. She became the officer-in-command of the women, a position she described as 'lonely'. On 1 December 1980, in a gesture of solidarity, Mairéad and two other women joined a hunger strike started six weeks earlier by seven male IRA prisoners in the Maze prison. The men, apparently believing their demands for political-prisoner status would be met, called off their strike on 18 December, followed by the women the day after. However, the demands were not met and Bobby Sands resumed his hunger strike on 1 March 1981. The

 Maria Edgeworth, 1767–1849

Lady Sydney Morgan,
c.1776–1859

Marguerite,
Countess of
Blessington,
1789–1849

 Lady Jane Wilde, c.1821–1896

Lady Augusta Gregory, 1852–1932

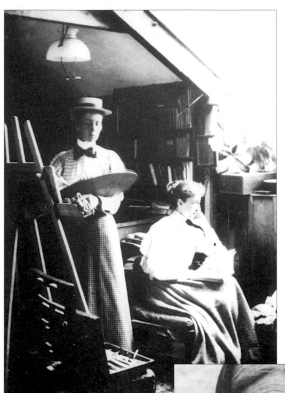

Somerville (left),
1858–1949,
and Ross,
1862–1915

Peig Sayers, 1873–1958

Dora Jordan, 1762–1816

Sarah Curran, 1782–1808

Kitty Kiernan, 1892–1945

Anne Bonny, c.1698–c.1720s

Mother Jones, 1830–1930

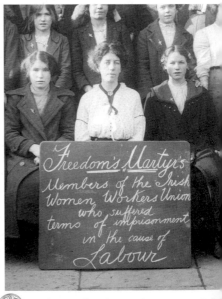

Delia Larkin (centre), *1878–1949*

Nano Nagle, 1728–1784

Mary Ann McCracken,
1770–1866

Ladies of Llangollen: Lady Eleanor Butler, 1739–1829,
and Sarah Ponsonby, 1755–1831

hunger strike resulted in the deaths of ten IRA men before the IRA finally called it off in October of that year.

Mairéad was freed in 1986. She immediately became politically active, touring Northern Ireland, lecturing and campaigning with other women against the practice of strip-searching in prisons. She also resumed her involvement as an active member of the IRA.

In March 1988 an SAS surveillance operation focussed on the island of Gibraltar, which Mairéad and two IRA men, Sean Savage and Danny McCann, had been recorded visiting on several occasions. The British Army suspected that they were planning to car-bomb a British military ceremony on 9 March. In the middle of the day on Sunday, 6 March an SAS team followed Mairéad, Sean and Danny as they walked down a Gibraltar street. The soldiers approached the three and shot them dead at point-blank range. This bloody and controversial event was to have tragic repercussions.

The three IRA members were flown home to Belfast to be buried in the same grave in Milltown cemetery. Some 10,000 mourners attended the funeral procession on 16 March, but during the graveside service the cemetery became the scene of new horror when a convicted criminal, Michael Stone from east Belfast, threw four hand grenades at the mourners and then opened fire. He killed three people and wounded about sixty before running away.

This particular trail of death was not yet over. Three days later two British soldiers mistakenly turned onto the street where the funeral of one Stone's victims was being held. Enraged mourners, believing their appearance was deliberate and aggressive, dragged them from their car, beat them up and handed them over to the IRA, who shot them.

Meanwhile, controversy about the manner of Mairéad's, Sean's and Danny's deaths continued to rage. The IRA admitted that all three had indeed been on 'active service' in Gibraltar, so the suspicions of the British authorities were confirmed. However, they had all been unarmed at the time of the shooting and, according to some eyewitness reports, had not been given a chance to surrender had they had arms. It was felt in some quarters that the authorities could and should have arrested the suspects, which could have been done at any time in the preceding month since they had been under continual surveillance.

The SAS gave a confusing and inconsistent version of the events of 6 March, which some commentators felt lent credibility to the accusation that they were trying to cover up a 'shoot-to-kill' policy. The British press made matters worse by victimising some witnesses who had contradicted the SAS version of events. This eventually resulted in large libel payouts by the papers. Margaret Thatcher's government then imposed a broadcasting ban on all paramilitary organisations, denying them what she called 'the oxygen of publicity'.

The issues arising from this case resulted in a judgement some seven years after the event by the European Court of Human Rights, which stated that the SAS, with their alleged 'shoot-to-kill' policy, had violated the right to life of Mairéad, Sean and Danny. It was judged that they had been 'unlawfully killed'. In Belfast, it is felt in some quarters that, had she lived, Mairéad Farrell would have moved away from guerrilla warfare and become prominent in the constitutional nationalism of the current peace process in Northern Ireland.

Veronica Guerin
1959–1996

Investigative reporter

At lunchtime on Wednesday, 26 June 1996, a thirty-seven-year-old working mother stopped her car at a set of traffic lights in Dublin. Two men on a motorbike pulled up alongside her car and one of them produced a revolver from his jacket. He pointed the gun at the woman and shot her five times at point-blank range, killing her instantly. The woman was Veronica Guerin; the men were emissaries from Dublin's drug underworld.

Veronica was born in Artane, north Dublin, the daughter of an accountant. She was a lively, sporty little girl with bags of confidence, renowned in her family for her combination of charm and tenacity. When she left convent school at eighteen years of age, Veronica went to work for her father in his accountancy firm. In her spare time she volunteered her services to Fianna Fáil, eventually mixing socially with the then-Taoiseach, Charles J Haughey.

Veronica's father died unexpectedly in 1981. She couldn't bear to work for another accountant and so took a job with Fianna Fáil. When her contract there came to an end she tried to start a public relations firm, but this foundered. Meanwhile, her personal life was more successful. Through her political contacts she enjoyed a lively social life and eventually met and fell in love with another Fianna Fáil party member, Graham Turley. She married him in 1985 and in 1990 gave birth to a son, Cathal.

By the time Veronica was in her early thirties she was desperate to use the surplus energy for which she was known. She had worked with journalists over the years and now became strongly attracted to the idea of writing for newspapers herself. What drew her was the idea of hunting down secrets, getting thoroughly involved in the research and then making known her findings. In 1990, with no journalistic experience at all, she managed to talk her way into a job on a national weekly, the *Sunday Business Post*, where she worked for three years. After this she worked for two more nationals, the *Sunday Tribune* and the *Sunday Independent*. It was at the latter that she really made her name.

Initially, Veronica did not work on crime stories, but with her accountancy background she felt comfortable with stories that involved complicated financial matters. This led naturally to an interest in financial stories of the illegal variety, and this in turn led to the juiciest stories of all – exposés of Dublin's drug underworld. Veronica always worked alone on these stories, using her car and mobile phone as her office. She worked on hunches, on intuition, but once she got a whiff of something she was like the proverbial hound with a bone – she simply would not let go. She relied on her contacts in law enforcement and in the criminal world, plus her legendary networking skills, to get all the information she needed. If these tactics failed, she pestered people, including drug barons, pimps and murderers, until they gave in to get rid of her. She thoroughly enjoyed her job and derived huge satisfaction from making life difficult for the bad boys of organised crime, and she revelled in the degree of fame that went with it.

At the *Sunday Independent* her stories just got better and better. She investigated gangland murders, armed robberies, underworld hierarchies, money-laundering enterprises and criminals' sex lives.

Public appetite for these salacious scandals grew and demand increased – as did the risk factor. In late 1994, less than a year after Veronica had started at the *Sunday Independent* as crime correspondent, warning shots were fired through the window of her house. Veronica ignored the warning. Three months later a gunman turned up at her house, rang the doorbell and, when she opened the door, shot her in the leg.

After this attack on her life and home, Veronica's bosses offered their highest-profile reporter safer work, but she refused to take it. She insisted that she would not be intimidated by gangsters. She stepped up what now amounted to her one-woman campaign against drug dealers, writing about them and disguising their identities only with transparent nicknames.

She continued her crime-busting work throughout the spring of 1996, interviewing known criminals in her own home and publishing the results. Up until now she had had a working arrangement with some of her shadier associates – a certain amount of back-scratching meant that in return for their information, they would get their own side of the story across in the papers. But it was only a matter of time before this dangerous arrangement would break down. It was inevitable that the conmen, armed robbers and killers would turn on Veronica – she knew too much. So on a busy weekday at lunchtime, on the outskirts of Dublin City, as Veronica was laughing and joking on her mobile phone, she was gunned down by a masked assassin and his accomplice. She had finally been silenced.

There was a national outpouring of grief and disgust at the journalist's death. Her funeral was attended by the president of

Ireland Mary Robinson, the taoiseach John Bruton and the archbishop of Dublin Dr Desmond Connell. Veronica was widely praised for her defiance and commitment, and held up as a martyr in the escalating war against drugs.

Two men were eventually brought to trial in connection with the murder of Veronica Guerin. In 1998 Paul Ward was convicted of murdering Veronica, and received a life sentence. The following year, Brian Meehan was also convicted of murdering Veronica and also sentenced to life imprisonment.

At the trial the judge said that Ms Guerin had contributed to the successful identification of Dublin's drug dealers and the destruction of their empire, adding that this would spare many young people from the scourge of drugs. Her death, he said, had not been in vain. The anti-crime offensive launched by the gardaí in the wake of Veronica's death has resulted in many convictions and has successfully tackled the once-spiralling problem of major crime. Their work has borne out the judge's words: Veronica Guerin's death has not been in vain.

AHEAD OF THEIR TIME

*'What is morally wrong can never
be politically right.'*
Mary Ann McCracken

Lady Arabella Denny

1707–1792

Philanthropist

The Honourable Arabella Denny was one of the great philanthropists of the eighteenth century, who devoted half her life to the welfare of foundling children and 'fallen' women. She founded the Magdalen Asylum, an early female philanthropic institution, which was the first charitable asylum of its kind in Ireland and became a model for institutions all over the country.

Lady Arabella was the second daughter of Thomas Fitzmaurice, the twenty-first lord (and later the first earl) of Kerry. Her mother was Anne Petty, the only daughter of Sir William Petty from England. There was considerable wealth on both sides of this landowning family, and Lady Arabella spent her youth in luxury at the family homes in County Kerry. As was usual for a woman of her class she was very charitable towards the tenants on her father's estates. As a teenager she started and ran an 'apothecary's shop', a basic medical dispensary for the poorer folk.

In August 1727, at the age of twenty, Arabella married Arthur Denny, a colonel in the British Army and MP for Kerry, and went to live at Lixnaw Castle, Tralee. Early in her marriage she was made miserable by the bullying behaviour of her husband's brother, who may have been put out by having to accept a new mistress at Lixnaw. As his behaviour continued, Arabella decided to tackle it in the head-on fashion that was to become her trademark. She secretly took shooting lessons and waited for an opportunity to show the brother what she was made of. One day, when he was being particularly obnoxious, she took him into the woods, demonstrated what she could do with a firearm and told him she'd kill him if he didn't stay out of her way. The direct approach worked and the unnerved brother caused no more trouble for Lady Arabella.

The colonel died of apoplexy in 1742, leaving Arabella a widow at the age of thirty-five. As she was childless, she was required by law to move out of the castle, which had been her home for fifteen years. The estate and its wealth passed to her husband's male relations, but she was left modestly well off by the standards of her class. By 1745 she was living in a house in Dublin's Stephen's Green, and by 1748 she had moved to the suburb of Blackrock, where she was to live for the rest of her life.

Georgian Dublin was a beautiful, modern city with many wealthy inhabitants and a rich cultural life. Regarded as the second city in the British Empire, it enjoyed the fruits of great prosperity. It was also a city where people starved to death every day. The Foundling Hospital had been established to shelter and feed the thousands of poor children who were abandoned by their desperate parents each year, either because of extreme poverty, illegitimacy or both. The hospital was a last resort: a mother would place her child in the purpose-built cradle at the gates of the hospital, ring the bell and leave quickly, usually never to see her child again.

Conditions inside the hospital were barely better than outside. The food was poor, clothing insufficient and disease was rampant. Severe crowding was the norm, with up to eight children sharing one bed – even the attached graveyard was overcrowded, with up to ten children to a grave. Staff were few and elderly, and the place was run by a treasurer who was able to act, in the name of the Board of Governors, with total autonomy and hardly any accountability. The death rate was phenomenally high, but those children who managed to survive to the age of twelve years were shunted out into the world to earn their living. Predominantly Catholics, these children were required to change their religion and were then apprenticed to Protestant tradesmen to ensure there was no backsliding.

Lady Arabella's involvement started in 1759 when she made a charity visit to the hospital with other well-to-do ladies. When the other ladies lost interest, she continued her visits alone and began to involve herself in a more immediate way. She engaged and paid for more qualified staff for the hospital and offered them cash incentives: instead of leaving sickly children to die, they received a bonus for every child they nursed back to health. She donated a clock that chimed every twenty minutes to call feeding-time for the young babies. She paid older children to produce their own lacework and knitted goods to inculcate the habit of working for a living. She spent more than £4,000 of her own money on extensions to the building.

A 'model of amiability and independence' was how Lady Arabella's nephew, William Petty-Fitzmaurice, first marquess of Landsdowne and later, briefly, prime minister of Britain, described his aunt. The diarist Mrs Delaney called her a 'very civil, sensible woman'. But Arabella brought more than these well-heeled qualities to her work at Dublin's Foundling Hospital. She brought a commitment unheard of in women of her social class, as well as generosity, originality and passion. As one biographer wrote: 'she brooked no delays, shortcomings or interference.' Lady Arabella's continuing work radically improved conditions inside the hospital and the death rate dropped dramatically. (Sadly when she retired, the death rate at the hospital immediately rose and kept rising until the 1840s when the hospital closed down.)

Her contribution was recognised in 1764 when the Irish House of Commons passed a resolution of thanks to Lady Arabella, and in 1765 she was presented with the Freedom of the City of Dublin. In 1766 she was the first woman elected a member of the Royal Dublin Society (RDS) – an honorary position, of course, as no women were allowed to be active in the hallowed group.

While Lady Arabella was reforming the Foundling Hospital, she came into contact with despairing and exploited young women who had been forced to give up their children, their homes and their families. Moved by the way a whole life could be blighted by one early mistake, she resolved on a rescue mission: to bring young women such as these back into a useful, self-supporting existence. The Magdalen Asylum, named for the reformed prostitute of the Gospels, Mary Magdalen, was established in Leeson Street in 1766, and its first inmate took up residence in August 1767. It was run by a committee headed by Lady Arabella.

As the asylum's governors later noted, the Magdalen was Arabella's 'own and favourite institution [and] she was constant and ardent in her attentions'. She raised funds tirelessly, shamelessly using as many of her high-ranking connections as she could. The *pièce de resistance* was when she managed to get Queen Charlotte, the wife of King George III, to act as patron. As a result, the charity became deeply fashionable and received substantial contributions from ladies who lunched.

When the Magdalen's adjoining chapel was opened in early 1768, Lady Arabella made sure the first service was attended by none other than George, viscount Townshend, lord lieutenant of Ireland. The chapel proved to be another source of funds for the institute: due to the high calibre of the preachers invited to speak, plus the fashion factor, it eventually became so popular that services turned into ticket-only affairs at one shilling each.

Inside the Magdalen Asylum, life was strict and well-ordered. Lady Arabella's deeply held religious beliefs ensured that women were more likely to be admitted if they were or were willing to become Protestant (Catholics tended to go to religious-run homes). They also had to be young enough to reject their 'former vileness'. The institute was 'not designed for the vicious, but for those resolved to be virtuous ...' In other words, battle-hardened prostitutes looking for a rest were not welcome.

While there, the penitents benefitted from anonymity and three square meals a day. They attended chapel, received religious instruction and were encouraged to 'private devotions and meditations' in their own rooms. When they were not doing this, they had to employ themselves doing something useful – generally reading or the never-ending needlework. Their health was attended to by the viceregal physician, Dr Robert Emmet (father of United Irishmen member, Robert Emmet), who acted as long-term medical supervisor to the institution. The penitents stayed for up to two years, ideally leaving only when they had decent employment to go to. On departure, they received a guinea to get them started, with a further small payment if they managed to stay out of trouble for a year.

Lady Arabella resigned from the committee in 1778, aged seventy-one, as she felt too old to cope with the rigorous day-to-day demands of running the institution. By the time she left, she had inspired the establishment of Magdalen Asylums all over Ireland.

She spent her declining years in her beautiful house in Blackrock with her cousin and 'adopted daughter' Katherine Fitzmaurice, in poor health but always cheerful. 'Thank God,' she wrote in spring 1779, 'tho' I am a cripple my mind is free and my spirit good.' Her only worry seems to have been a morbid fear of being buried alive. To prevent this she left clear instructions in the eventuality of her death. Burial should wait, she wrote, 'until I am certainly dead' and, to make absolutely sure, she desired to be left lying on her bed 'for at least 72 hours'.

After thirteen years of retirement, Lady Arabella died at the age of eighty-five; the burial was carried out according to her instructions. In her will she left money to the Foundling Hospital and to the Magdalen Asylum she had founded, regretting only that it could not be more.

Nano Nagle
1728–1784

Pioneering educator and founder of the Presentation order of nuns

Nano Nagle was born Honora Nagle in Ballygriffin, near Mallow, County Cork. She was the daughter of Garret Nagle, a landowner and one of the wealthiest Catholics in the country. Educated privately in the paternal mansion, she and her sister were sent to be 'finished' at a French convent, as was the custom for rich Catholic girls. France was a good choice for the Nagles: they had many important social connections in Paris, including Nano's father's cousin, Sir Richard Nagle, who had been the erstwhile speaker of the 'Patriot Parliament' held by James II in 1689, and who was then secretary of state for Ireland. After school, the well-dowered and attractive young Nano stayed on in Paris for several years, mixing with high society and having a lively time of it.

Nano realised she had a vocation at an unlikely moment. Returning home at dawn from an all-night ball, she was sleepily looking out of her carriage window when she saw a group of desperately poor Parisians waiting patiently outside a church to hear Mass. In order to worship God, these people had arisen even earlier than they had to and had fasted, even though they had a long day's backbreaking work ahead of them. Their faith was a revelation to Nano; she immediately swore to reject her wealthy society background and devote her life to the poor.

Returning to Ireland after her father's death in 1746, Nano determined that she would make a Catholic education available to the poor. But the eighteenth century was a time of virulent anti-

Catholicism and Nano came up against the Penal Laws. Born out of the ever-present Protestant fear of Catholic rebellion, these laws were designed to disempower the Catholic majority: they were not allowed to vote, hold public office, buy land or maintain long-term leases, marry Protestants, practise law, own weapons, join the services, or receive a Catholic education. The only legal education was that provided by the Church of Ireland, and even that was not generally available to the poor. Disheartened, Nano returned to France and entered a convent.

In the convent, Nano was haunted by voices calling her back to help her people. She sought the advice of her confessor and between them they resolved that God was indicating her life's purpose: to work among her own people in her own country. In 1749, with some trepidation, Nano sailed once again for Ireland.

When she reached Cork, Nano went to live with her brother and his family. Soon she had secretly started a small school of about thirty girls in a mud shack on Cobh Lane. Under the pretence of going to chapel to worship, Nano was actually going to the shack each day to teach. As she commented in a letter written nearly twenty years later, her 'design had to be kept a profound secret' – after all, what she was doing was totally illegal.

The cat got out of the bag one day when a poor man came to the Nagles's house and announced to Nano's brother that he wanted his daughter to go to 'Mrs Nagle's school'. Nano's brother was shocked at what Nano had been up to, but his initial opposition soon turned to strong support, and within a year the thirty students had become 200. By 1769 five schools had been set up for girls and two for boys. All the children were taught how to read and write and how to do basic maths, and they were all educated in their own religion.

Nano kept this up year after year, maintaining the schools from her own money and collecting door to door when the money ran out. As a helper she had Dr Francis Moylan, later bishop of Kerry and then of Cork, who had been ordained in Toulouse and was recently returned to Ireland. The two of them decided to expand the operation and, in 1767, they approached the Ursulines in Paris to start a foundation in Ireland – with French-trained Irishwomen. After a few false starts, and some understandable reluctance on the part of the Ursulines, they succeeded. In May 1771 four Irish novices and one fully professed nun landed at Cobh. Four months later they entered the convent that Nano had specially built for them.

But there was a hitch. Nano felt the Ursulines needed to modify their closed-order rule so they could visit the poor in their own homes, but the nuns themselves felt unable or unwilling to do this. In addition, they were more interested in educating middle-class children in the conventional way, as Nano herself had been educated, whereas for Nano the *raison d'être* of the schools was to educate the poor. This situation obviously wasn't working.

Nano's response to the problem was to start another, wholly original community, whose aims were related to hands-on care of the poor. In 1777, Nano and three other women took simple vows and started the Institute of Charitable Instruction, which later became the Order of the Presentation of the Blessed Virgin Mary. They were professed, adopted a uniform of black dresses and black-ribboned caps, and entered their new convent on Christmas

Eve of that year. Their aim was to become 'the servants of the poor'; their first act was to throw a banquet and personally serve fifty local paupers.

Nano was only in her forties when she confirmed her vows, but she did not have long to live. She had always suffered from poor eyesight and a chronically weak chest and both these conditions were worsening all the time. In spite of this, she and her companions ceaselessly travelled from school to school and visited the sick and the old in their own homes.

Nano became known as the Lady with the Lantern because she often worked long into the night, and it was said there wasn't a garret in Cork she did not know. Nano worked on like this for eight years. One of her last acts, in 1783, was to establish a home for the elderly poor.

Nano eventually died of an inflammation of the lungs at the age of fifty-six, and was buried in the Ursuline convent graveyard at Douglas Street, Cork. By 1900 her seven schools had grown to fifty in Ireland alone, and there were others in North America, Britain, Australasia and India. Her foundation spread to become one of the most respected in the teaching profession. The cause of Nano Nagle for beatification is now being pursued.

Ladies of Llangollen

Lady Eleanor Butler, 1739–1829
and Sarah Ponsonby, 1755–1831

Eccentrics

Lady Eleanor Butler was born into the Catholic branch of one of Munster's oldest and most prestigious families, whose lineage in Ireland stretched back to Norman times. She was the third girl to be born in her family, a worrying event for parents who were obsessed with succession. Eighteen months after Eleanor's birth, however, her mother gave birth to the long-awaited son, and Eleanor was quickly relegated to the sidelines. To make matters worse, she was not very pretty and, when she was old enough to converse, she proved somewhat sharp-tongued and 'satirical'.

In due course Eleanor was packed off to a convent education in Cambrai, France, after which she was expected to come home to the family seat at Kilkenny Castle and make a decent marriage. But Lady Eleanor had other ideas. She objected to the idea of giving herself a master, and instead gave her heart to the person she regarded as her soulmate: Sarah Ponsonby.

Sarah was a slight, fair, but rather morose and over-sensitive girl, some sixteen years younger than Eleanor. Orphaned early, she had been brought to the home of her grand, wealthy relations who lived at Woodstock, near Inistioge, twelve miles away from Kilkenny Castle. They sent her to a nearby boarding school and, because she had no money of her own, she was effectively forgotten. She first met the twenty-nine-year-old Eleanor when Eleanor paid a duty visit to her school. Sarah hated school, being quiet and naturally melancholic, so Eleanor took the miserable girl under her wing and a friendship developed. When Sarah was eighteen she left the boarding school and returned to her guardians at Woodstock. Sarah and Eleanor were now able to spend a lot of time together at Kilkenny Castle, and their relationship became more meaningful.

Nineteenth-century society did not decree that the idea of a 'romantic friendship' among females was as subversive and threatening as such a connection between males. Nonetheless, the two women encountered strong family opposition to their growing attachment – after all, there was no point to girls unless they married advantageously and swelled the family coffers.

It was at this point that Eleanor and Sarah decided to run away together. Various myths came to surround their elopement: it was said that Eleanor's family was forcing her into an engagement; that both sets of families were heartlessly cruel; that Sarah's guardian was showing an unhealthy interest in her, and so on. The truth was more prosaic. There was no place in grand houses for unmarried or unmarriageable women, and all Eleanor and Sarah wanted was to make a home with each other.

The first time they ran away it was a fiasco. They disguised themselves as men but, after spending the night in a barn, they were found and brought back. They were forbidden to communicate with each other, and Eleanor's family threatened to place her in a convent in France. But the audacious Sarah sent for Eleanor to come and visit her at Woodstock, and then hid her ladyship in a cupboard. When they were discovered, about a week later, they boldly faced down their families, booked a passage on a small boat leaving from Waterford, took their maid, Mary Carryl, and left for good.

Looking for somewhere where they could retire from the world and be themselves, the pair happened upon the small village of Llangollen on the beautiful River Dee in Denbighshire, North Wales. They built a cottage there named Plas Newydd, and lived there together in man-free bliss for the next fifty years.

Their way of life being rather insular and unusual, the ladies soon became known locally and were regarded as eccentric though kindly. For a start, there was their style of dress. A contemporary comedian, Charles Mathews, claimed that, when seated, 'there [was] not one point to distinguish them from men'. At a time when it was plainly indecent for women – and ladies, in particular – to wear anything even remotely resembling men's clothing, Lady Eleanor and Miss Ponsonby sported identical habits made exactly like men's coats and finished with 'well-starched neckcloths'. They also had cropped hair, powdered in the (men's) fashion of the day so that it was 'rough, bushy and white as snow'. Their outfits were topped with black fur hats.

The ladies lived in extreme simplicity and made their thirteen acres at Plas Newydd very productive. They were charitable and always employed local poor people in preference to outside help. Despite their seclusion, they were well-educated and cultured – they spoke several modern languages and kept up an excellent library. They collected old carved oak and covered Plas Newydd with it. Miss Ponsonby was an artist while Lady Eleanor was a musician, and they both produced exquisite embroidery. Their maid, Mary Carryl, was just as happy. She was treated more as a member of the family than as a servant, and she had immense status among the other working folk in the area. She was to stay with the ladies until her death.

The ladies travelled around Wales and to London occasionally, but preferred instead for friends to come and visit them. The famous French children's author Mme de Genlis, who visited them in 1788, was utterly charmed by the unconventional set-up and felt the ladies were not as well-known as they ought to be. She was won over by the 'grace, cordiality and kindness' she received, and by the 'mutual attachment' the ladies exhibited.

Since Llangollen was on the main Dublin–London route, many other famous visitors came to witness this charming arrangement, including Charles Darwin, William Wordsworth, Sir Walter Scott, Richard Brinsley Sheridan, Edmund Burke and the Duke of Wellington. Most visitors only got as far as the garden; the ladies were sticklers for good manners, and if they looked through the window and thought their approaching visitor might be uncouth or unrefined, they simply sent down a message to say they were not at home.

Lady Eleanor died, aged ninety, on 2 June 1829. Although so much younger, Sarah Ponsonby could not bear life without her companion and duly followed on 9 December 1831. They are both buried, along with faithful Mary Carryl, in Llangollen's churchyard.

Mary Ann McCracken
1770–1866

Mary Ann McCracken's diverse interests included political reform, workers' welfare, philanthropy, women's rights, education and Irish music

Born in Belfast of Scottish stock, Mary Ann's family was Presbyterian and, under the Penal Laws, suffered nearly as much discrimination as Catholics. In contrast to most Catholics, however, they were well-to-do: her father was a prosperous sea captain and her mother's family were textile merchants. Mary Ann was the second youngest of seven children born to the McCrackens. She was a sickly child but grew into a young woman with an iron constitution. She was a lifelong believer in hard work, but she also believed in the therapeutic qualities of recreation; she herself was renowned for her playfulness until the end of her days. She was also extremely musical.

All the children in the McCracken family were well-educated in a pioneering co-educational school. Her unusually modern education, plus her background of religious dissent, helped mould Mary Ann into an independent-minded non-conformist who believed passionately in human rights. Mary Ann felt that parliamentary representation for all Irishmen was a basic human right. She and at least three of her siblings – the most famous being her older brother, Henry Joy McCracken – supported universal male suffrage, and to this end young Harry, as Henry Joy was known, was a founding member of the Society of United Irishmen in 1791.

The United Irishmen started out as a constitutional group

looking for parliamentary reform in certain areas, such as the eligibility of *all* men (though not, of course, women) to vote, regardless of their religion. The society's small voice for reform increased in volume until eventually it was silenced by the government. Driven underground, the now secret society evolved into a truly republican group, espousing complete separation from England.

As the United Irish cause became more radical, Mary Ann became more radical along with it. She herself had broken out of the usual female mould by starting a successful muslin business with her sister, Margaret. She saw this as a way of combating Belfast's unemployment as well as a means to make a living. By the mid-1790s, she had developed a particular interest in social reform and was influencing her brother's opinions on the subject.

In 1796 the authorities rounded up many United Irishmen, including Henry Joy McCracken and his colleague, Thomas Russell, and threw them into Kilmainham Jail. Harry was released after a year. As was usually the case in these circumstances, women involved in the movement then had a chance to become active, and it was around this time that the Society of United Irishwomen was formed. Mary Ann may or may not have been a member, although we do know that she assisted the cause by concealing arms from the authorities on at least one occasion.

Nonetheless, Mary Ann was basically a pacifist. She was opposed to the violent insurrection of 1798 in which her brother played such a prominent role. 'What is morally wrong,' she wrote, 'can never be politically right.' In other words, the end did not justify the means. Mediation was more in her line, and she was close enough to the leadership of the United Irishmen to make her presence felt in disputes. However powerful and influential she was on a personal level, she criticised an all-male society's tendency to 'keep the women in the dark and … make tools of them without confiding in them' – something that would be echoed by Hanna Sheehy Skeffington some 140 years later. In 1798, the men forged ahead with their plans for a rising, and nothing Mary Ann could say would sway them from their course.

In June 1798 Harry found himself unexpectedly taking command of the Antrim brigade in the rising. The Battle of Antrim was a rout, the rising was a failure and Harry took to the hills. Afterwards, it was Mary Ann who went out, on foot, looking for her brother. She made arrangements for Harry to be hidden, got him a forged passport and organised an escape attempt to the USA. It was all in vain: Harry was captured trying to board the ship to America. He was imprisoned again in Kilmainham and quickly tried and found guilty of armed insurrection, the penalty for which was execution.

During Harry's trial and subsequent imprisonment, as she came to terms with the fact that she was going to lose her favourite brother, stoical Mary Ann wrote and visited often to keep his spirits up while continually lobbying the authorities on his behalf. Her pleas fell on deaf ears; Harry was sentenced to a traitor's death. He was to be taken to a public place of execution and there hanged by the neck until he was dead.

During the last day of Harry's life, Mary Ann personally begged the governor for mercy. When this failed she spent his final hours with him in his cell, and walked with him to the scaffold. After he was hanged, she held him in her arms and attempted to resuscitate him. When it was obvious that all hope was lost, she made the necessary arrangements for his burial, which took place later the same day.

After Harry's death, Mary Ann discovered he had fathered a four-year-old daughter, Maria. Despite massive familial and societal disapproval, Mary Ann took the illegitimate child in, reared her as her own, gave her a home and provided for her education. She treated Maria as her own daughter for the rest of her life.

Mary Ann remained involved in the United Irishmen's cause after the rising. She had been close to Thomas Russell, Harry's comrade. Jailed in 1796 but never charged, Thomas was only released from prison in 1802 and immediately started organising support for Robert Emmet's abortive rising of 1803. After that rising failed and Emmet was arrested, Thomas went to Dublin to try and arrange his rescue, but instead he himself was arrested, tried for treason and sentenced to death. In a sad echo of the events of five years previously, Mary Ann visited her friend in Kilmainham Jail, lobbied on his behalf and paid for his defence. Again, her campaign was in vain; in October 1803, Thomas Russell was taken to Downpatrick, County Down, and executed.

After Thomas's death, Mary Ann withdrew from radical politics. She became more involved in the cultural life of Belfast, particularly the musical side. (Mary Ann was a lifelong friend and foster-sister of the famous traditional-music collector, Edward Bunting, who, as a child, had been taken in and brought up by her parents.) She had always been involved in the Belfast Charitable Society in an unofficial capacity, but now, after her textile business collapsed in 1815, she became more active.

The Charitable Society was run by an all-male Board of Governors, but Mary Ann saw the need for a counterpart ladies' committee. The committee, with Mary Ann at its head, took special interest in the girls who were cared for by the Charitable Society, teaching them useful skills, such as needlework and housework. The committee also found employment for them and mediated in disputes between them and their employers.

Always interested in the education of children, Mary Ann then employed what she called 'active and enlightened' people to look after and teach the children and, very much against the wishes of the governors, incorporated time for play, reading and rewards into the new régime. From the 1820s till the 1850s she successfully took on the all-male board in matters of money, equipment, hygiene and food for the children, berating them for feasting themselves while the children in their care had scarcely enough food to survive.

In the meantime, Mary Ann added abolitionism, temperance, the plight of child chimney sweeps and the Ladies' Industrial School to her list of causes. The industrial school had been set up in 1847 in an attempt to help women stricken by the Great Famine. One of Mary Ann's duties, at the age of seventy-seven, was to go door-to-door asking for financial support for the industrial school, a job she hated but never shirked.

As for the abolition movement, Mary Ann had supported the great abolitionist William Wilberforce from the early days. Although slavery was abolished in Britain in 1833, she continued to campaign for its abolition in the USA. As late as 1859, when she was in her eighties, she was at Belfast's quayside, leafleting returning Americans and claiming that America was not so much 'the land of the brave' as 'the land of the slave'. The author and expert on the United Irishmen, Dr RR Madden, with whom Mary Ann enjoyed a twenty-year correspondence, shared her interest in abolitionism. He acknowledged her invaluable help in compiling his seminal work, *The Lives and Times of the United Irishmen* (1842–46; 1857–60).

Despite a deep and increasing attachment to her own Presbyterianism in old age, Mary Ann remained as free of bigotry as in the early days of the United Irish cause. She visited the first Catholic convent in Belfast as a very old lady and found the nuns delightful, though she privately thought they could be more useful if they had more 'liberty'.

Mary Ann died peacefully in the home of her adopted daughter, Maria, at ninety-six years of age. She was buried in Belfast.

Kate Tyrrell
1863–1921

Shipping company director and owner

Kate Tyrrell was the second of four daughters born to Edward and Elizabeth Tyrrell of Arklow, County Wicklow. Edward was the owner of a small shipping company and captain of his own schooners. The whole family was steeped in the backbreaking life that was nineteenth-century shipping, from the hard manual labour of dealing with the sails, repairs and so on to the uncertain fortunes and prolonged absences of deep-sea fishing. The bread-and-butter work was import-export coastal runs between Ireland and Wales.

Slim, waspish and energetic, Kate was just like her father and in many ways she took the place of the son he never had. From early childhood she hung around the shipyard, at first getting in her father's way but gradually becoming indispensable to him; from the time she was twelve he trusted her to fill in shipping journals. As time went on, Kate became the obvious choice to succeed her father, and he promised her that, one day, she would be the owner of her own ship.

In spring 1882, Kate lost one of her younger sisters to the White Plague, as tuberculosis (TB) was then known. Her mother subsequently sank into depression and illness. Her condition became so debilitating that, at the age of nineteen, Kate had to take control of the bookkeeping side of the business and run the household at the same time. Late in 1882, Mrs Tyrrell died of the same disease that had killed her daughter. Kate now had her hands full helping her surviving sisters, doing the books for the business and managing domestic affairs, but occasionally she still had time to go sailing with her dad.

In 1885, Mr Tyrrell bought a Welsh schooner named the *Denbighshire Lass*. Although all three sisters had equal shares in it, the ship was registered in Kate's name, and it was Kate who sailed the sixty-two-tonne vessel home from Wales. The *Denbighshire Lass* was the best ship the Tyrrells had in their small fleet. Its cargoes typically included coal, iron ore and textiles, and more fragile goods, such as bricks and tiles.

The *Denbighshire Lass* sailed the rest of 1885 and into 1886, but in the July of that year, while on a trip to Wales, Kate's beloved father died on board of a heart attack. Kate now took over the family business fully, sold the other ships and became the sole owner of the schooner.

Although Kate was the owner, she could not have her name on any of the ship's documentation, according to the dictates of the maritime authorities, because she was a woman. Instead, a trusted employee called Brennan was named as the 'master' on all documents pertaining to the ship. But it was Kate who ran the business as her father had done before her, sending the *Denbighshire Lass* to Liverpool, Swansea, Cardiff, Bristol, Cork, Dungarvan, New Ross, Wexford, Belfast and Dublin, and it was Kate who inspected it for repairs and retained total financial control over everything. As a manager, Kate was known as a disciplinarian, for example, she was totally intolerant of the grog traditionally so beloved of sailors, and anyone found drunk on board was immediately dismissed.

In 1888 Kate lost another younger sister, aged only twenty, to TB. Now it was just Kate and her older sister left in the family home. Her sister kept house while Kate supported them both. A workaholic and a hands-on boss, Kate didn't need to go on many trips with the schooner, but she went anyway: she loved life on the sea and enjoyed captaining the ship herself. She became adept at the more difficult aspects of sailing, such as familiarity with shipping regulations and navigation.

Inspired by the women's suffrage movement, which was gaining ground in the 1890s, she continued her battle to have her own name instead of Brennan's on all documents relating to the *Denbighshire Lass*. Her perseverance finally paid off in 1899, the year she was officially recognised as the owner – fourteen years after she became the skipper.

In 1896 Kate married John Fitzpatrick, a nephew of Brennan's and a friend since childhood. He had been working as mate and occasionally as master on the *Denbighshire Lass* since her father's death. John and Kate complemented each other perfectly: he was easygoing where she was fiery. In 1900 a son, James, was born to Kate and John, followed in 1905 by a daughter, Elizabeth. But this last pregnancy nearly killed the forty-two-year-old Kate, whose health was never the same afterwards. The once-agile sailor now experienced difficulty moving and started to stay at home more and more until eventually she was completely housebound.

Meanwhile, the *Denbighshire Lass* sailed on. It sailed the land-mined Irish Sea right through World War I (without insurance), and had the distinction of being the first ship to fly the Irish tricolour in a foreign port. Partly because of competition and partly because of age, the ship's sailing life came to an end just four years after Kate's own death in 1921.

Countess Constance Markievicz
1868–1927

Revolutionary, labour activist and the first female MP elected to Westminster

Born into the upper echelons of Anglo-Irish society, Constance Gore-Booth, better-known as Countess Markievicz, turned away from the luxuries offered by her position. She chose instead a life that involved confrontation, hardship, imprisonment and, finally, an early death in the public ward of a Dublin hospital.

Constance was one of the Gore-Booths of Buckingham Gate, London, and Lissadell, County Sligo. Hers was an incredibly privileged background: at the time of her birth the Ascendancy was still going strong, and there were servants to look after the family and work the estate and tenants to pay for the lifestyle that the Gore-Booths enjoyed. Constance loved Lissadell and the people there, and there are many stories of her spontaneous generosity towards the tenants, from whom, of course, she was supposed to keep her distance. According to WB Yeats, a lifelong friend to Constance and a regular visitor to Lissadell, she was universally 'respected and admired', though was often in trouble for 'some tomboyish feat or reckless riding'.

At the age of nineteen, in 1887, Constance was presented at Queen Victoria's court. Tall and attractive, multilingual, an excellent shot and, according to Kathleen Behan, 'the greatest horsewoman in Ireland', she was a shining example of the sort of energetic gal-about-town the Ascendancy produced. But there was much more to Constance Gore-Booth. She was no empty-headed society miss whose main goal in life was to land a rich Protestant husband. She was interested in *all* the people around her and, in stark contrast to the rest of her class, she was genuinely egalitarian. This quality would eventually lead her to break completely with her background and become actively involved in all aspects of the struggle for equality in Ireland: in nationalism, in labour relations and in women's rights.

Constance enrolled at London's Slade School of Fine Art in 1893, and in 1897, aged twenty-nine, she travelled to Paris to further her study. In Paris, the unconventional Constance came into her own. She smoked, rode a bicycle, had her own circle of non-Ascendancy friends and, just when her family had despaired of her ever finding a husband, fell in love. He was a fellow artist, Count Casimir Markievicz, and he was Polish, titled, handsome – and Catholic. In 1900 she married 'Casi' and became Countess Markievicz or Madame, as she was known to the end of her life. The Markieviczs's only child, Maeve Alys, was born in 1901 at Lissadell.

In 1903 the Markieviczs settled in Dublin and spent the next five years painting for a living, riding horses, attending functions at Dublin Castle, shooting in the country and generally enjoying themselves. But Constance grew more and more dissatisfied with her comfortable existence. She loved Ireland passionately, but she could see injustice all around her – the begging, the homelessness, the enormous disparity in wealth, health and dignity between the few and the many. There had to be *something* she could do.

Constance's closet nationalism grew more and more difficult to reconcile with her pampered lifestyle. In 1908, at the age of forty, she finally showed her true colours by joining the revolutionary nationalist women's group, Inghínidhe na hÉireann (Daughters of Ireland). This was a whole new start for her. She immediately began to contribute to the organisation's magazine, *Bean na hÉireann*, and became more and more radical as she came under the influence of devoted nationalists, such as Helena Moloney, also a labour rights activist, Patrick Pearse and James Larkin.

At the same time her domestic life receded. She and Casi pursued separate lives although they remained good friends, and Maeve Alys seemed happy enough at Lissadell. As a mother, Constance was not good at intimacy and always remained rather distant from her daughter. Instead she preferred to spread herself thinly, and had a gift, according to the journalist and artist Sydney Gifford, for 'impersonal friendship'. Eventually she would shrug off even the pretence of being a 'good' wife and mother, and put politics first.

Although Constance came late in life to the world of Irish nationalism, it did not take her long to forge ahead by using her initiative. In the summer of 1909 she founded Fianna Éireann (Soldiers of Ireland), an organisation for young, Catholic, nationalist boys. It was a new idea, loosely based on the boy scout organisation in England but wholly nationalistic in outlook. Instead of the knot-tying and fence-mending of Baden-Powell's scouts, the boys of Fianna Éireann learned how to route-march, send signals, apply first aid and use real firearms. It was not for nothing Constance had named them after Fionn Mac Cumhaill's legendary band of warriors – she intended the boys of Fianna Éireann would fight for Ireland's freedom one day.

For Constance, one potent symbol of everything that was wrong with Ireland in the hands of the British was the filthy slums of the north Dublin tenements. In 1910 Maud Gonne of Inghínidhe na hÉireann and Hanna Sheehy Skeffington of the Irish Women's Franchise League (IWFL) organised a committee to distribute food to the slums' malnourished children. Con was an enthusiastic member. Meanwhile, she also received something from the tenements in return – she used them as a recruiting ground for the Fianna. Constance gave over her own house and all her time to 'her boys' in the Fianna, who adored her unconditionally. An incurable tomboy herself, it appeared she much preferred the company of her boys to her own daughter and she drew no boundaries around what belonged to her, including her clothes, her money, her house and her time.

By 1913 Constance's political horizons were widening to include the labour struggle. In the summer of that year many of Dublin's workers were made to choose between membership of the Irish Transport and General Workers' Union (ITGWU) or dismissal. The ITGWU, led by James 'Big Jim' Larkin and James Connolly, called a strike over the injustice of this ultimatum, an action that led to what became known as the Great Lock-Out. It lasted for six months, during which time the women's organisations set up soup kitchens for the strikers' starving families. Constance worked in one such soup kitchen and also attended demonstrations in support of the workers. One Sunday in August, Constance was at a rally at which Jim Larkin was speaking when police baton-charged the crowd and beat to death two people. Constance herself got kicked and punched in the face during the mayhem. That infamous day became known as the first of Ireland's 'Bloody Sundays'.

After this violent incident, Constance's position hardened. She believed that recourse to arms was a necessity, and the sooner the better. Her thinking was shared by many of her compatriots. In 1914 Larkin and Connolly set up the Irish Citizen Army (ICA), a socialist militia formed to protect workers from police brutality. A second nationalist, military-style organisation sworn to fight for Irish independence, the Volunteers, was formed under the chairmanship of Eoin MacNeill a few weeks later. The Volunteers had no room in its ranks for women, preferring instead to offload its female supporters into a separate wing known as Cumann na mBan.

In contrast, the ICA under James Connolly's leadership (he took over from Big Jim Larkin as commandant in 1914) displayed no such bias. Connolly was a feminist and he not only welcomed Constance's application to enlist, he made her staff-lieutenant. Constance was the only woman to be a member of both Cumann na mBan and the ICA.

The ICA and the Irish Volunteers were the main protagonists in Ireland's most famous rebellion against English rule. On the sunny Easter Monday of 1916, the Rising took place in Dublin City. Constance was second-in-command to Michael Mallin (later executed) of the regiment of men positioned at St Stephen's Green. They were engaged in digging trenches and, as she said herself, 'tackling any sniper who was particularly objectionable'. In full officer's uniform, and surrounded by the Fianna Éireann boys, Constance Markievicz traded fire with British soldiers for the whole of Easter week before surrendering on Sunday, 30 April.

In the blood-soaked aftermath of the Rising, Constance was the only woman to be court-martialled. She was sentenced to be shot, which was commuted to life imprisonment 'solely on account of her sex'. As she waited in her cell in Kilmainham Jail, she could hear the British firing squad executing some of the fifteen rebels who were shot in the following days; two of those executed, Con Colbert and Seán Heuston, were ex-Fianna boys. The executions at Kilmainham were finally halted on 12 May, and Constance was transferred to an English prison.

Constance was released in 1917 under the General Amnesty and she returned to Dublin to a hero's welcome. She had watched the rebels praying over the dead and dying during the dark days of the Rising, and it had affected her so deeply that her first act on arriving in Ireland was to convert officially to Roman Catholicism. Later that year, she was imprisoned again, this time in Holloway Women's Prison, north London. Her crime was to stage a peaceful protest against the forcible conscription of Irishmen during World War I.

In December 1918 there was a general election in Ireland that Sinn Féin, led by Eamon de Valera, won by a landslide. From her jail cell in Holloway, Constance became the first woman in history to be elected to the House of Commons as a Member of Parliament. On her release in March 1919, she, along with the other members of Sinn Féin, refused to take her seat at Westminster in defiance of British policies on the Irish Question.

Instead, Eamon de Valera ignored the British government and set up the first Irish rebel parliament, Dáil Éireann, on 21 January 1919. He appointed Constance minister for Labour; she was the only woman serving in the cabinet. During Britain's attempts to suppress the Dáil and the ensuing War of Independence, Constance held her ministry while on the run from the Black and Tans. She came out of hiding again and again to speak at public meetings as a minister of Dáil Éireann, relying on the support of the crowd to get her away before the authorities arrived.

Sometimes she avoided capture only by the skin of her teeth, and sometimes she did not. In these troubled times, Constance served two more prison sentences, one in Cork and one in Dublin.

Constance had joined Cumann na mBan at its inception, but it was only in the period after the Rising that she became active in the organisation. As president of Cumann na mBan, she was ferociously anti-Treaty during the debates of early 1922, which followed the end of the War of Independence.

During the Civil War she again took up arms for the republicans and saw active service in Dublin's O'Connell Street. After the republican surrender in 1923 she was re-elected to the Dáil as a TD for St Patrick's Ward in Dublin. Also in 1923 she underwent her last period of imprisonment after she was found guilty of campaigning for the release of political prisoners. She was subsequently released after starting a mass hunger strike. In all she served five jail sentences between 1916 and 1924, amounting to more than three years in total, during which she experienced conditions that certainly shortened her life.

In her final years, Constance devoted herself to the poor of Dublin, among whom she became a legend. The little rich girl from Lissadell Estate lived in tenement rooms or slept on the floor in friends' houses. She wore rags and shoes with holes in them, and pawned her few remaining possessions to pay her neighbours' rents. In early 1927 there was a fuel shortage and Constance rushed around in her car organising wood-cutting parties and collecting turf from the bogs. According to Hanna Sheehy Skeffington, she worked 'like a navvy' carting heavy bags of fuel up countless tenement stairways.

In 1927, her last summer, Constance threw herself into electioneering for Eamon de Valera's new Fianna Fáil party. Her perseverance was legendary: on one occasion she broke her arm while cranking the car, but still insisted on speaking at two meetings as she had promised, while the arm hung uselessly at her side. She was re-elected to her previous Dublin seat of St Patrick's as a party member, but just one month later she died from cancer, aged only fifty-nine.

The Free State government refused to allow Constance's body to lie in state in City Hall, instead republican friends arranged for her open casket to lie at the Rotunda Hospital on Parnell Square. Thousands of working-class Dubliners filed past her and her Fianna Éireann guard of honour to pay their last respects, and thousands more lined the streets as the Countess's coffin was carried to the republican plot in Glasnevin cemetery and there laid to rest.

Hanna Sheehy Skeffington
1877–1946

Feminist, nationalist, labour activist, pacifist

Hanna Sheehy Skeffington was born Johanna Mary Sheehy on 24 May 1877 in County Dublin. Her family was Roman Catholic and nationalistic. Originally from County Limerick, Grandfather Sheehy was an Irish-speaking pacifist who was pro-Home Rule. Hanna's father, David – at one time MP for south Galway as well as being a member of the Irish Republican Brotherhood (IRB) – served time in a variety of prisons for his own nationalist beliefs. Her uncle, Fr Eugene Sheehy, was jailed for his support of the Land League and was also a member of the first committee of the Gaelic League.

Hanna's mother, Bessie McCoy, also a Limerick woman, was a strong-minded individual who insisted that the education of her four daughters was as important as that of her two sons. Hanna's schooling took place at the Dominican convent school in Eccles Street, Dublin, and later at the Royal University (later University College, Dublin).

Her mother's early and unusual advocacy of equal education rights inspired in Hanna a passionate desire to enfranchise the women of Ireland. Her serious interest in politics started when she was an undergraduate and realised that, because they had no vote, women had no voice and were legally in the same category as criminals and lunatics. This inequity prompted Hanna to become active in her lifelong ideals of suffrage, socialism and Irish independence.

Hanna's personality was warm, down-to-earth and fair-minded. She was a hard worker and an original thinker who preferred, as her daughter-in-law Andrée noted, to 'keep her emotions private'. Initially a devout Catholic, during her life she disagreed more and more with the teachings of the Church until eventually she was an avowed atheist.

When Hanna married the Cavan-born academic Francis Skeffington in 1903, it was a marriage of minds. Their decision to combine their surnames was symbolic of the spirit of equality that lay at the foundation of their relationship. As Frank once said when called upon to rein in his wife, he considered himself 'merely the male member of the Sheehy Skeffington household' – a far cry from the universally held notion of the husband as the head of the household and, in law, the *owner* of his wife.

Together, Hanna and Frank embarked on a journey directed towards realising their ideals. They settled in Rathmines, south Dublin, and Frank worked as the registrar of UCD, while Hanna taught at St Mary's University College, Donnybrook. When Frank resigned from UCD on a point of principle in 1904 – he wished openly to support the admission of women to the college, which was in defiance of the rules of employment – Hanna financially supported them both. Frank thereafter concentrated on his career as a journalist, while Hanna carried on teaching.

In her late twenties, Hanna became more and more active in the cause of women's suffrage. She began to write articles for the cause and, in what was described as her 'clear, unhesitating voice', she spoke at public meetings. She also started to host a weekly 'At Home' – a forum for political and intellectual debate that convened every Wednesday at her house. Looking towards England, she was impressed by the banner-waving, law-breaking, hunger-striking militancy of Emmeline Pankhurst and her daughters, Christabel and Sylvia.

In 1908 Hanna co-founded, with Margaret Cousins, the Irish Women's Franchise League (IWFL), an activist organisation formed to win the right to vote for women. Theoretically, the IWFL was open to all women of any social class, but in practice, as with the Women's Social and Political Union (WSPU) across the water in England, membership was largely middle class. Only the relatively affluent could afford to use precious reserves of time and energy for doing something other than earning a basic living, which was a lot of women in the so-called lower orders.

Around this time, a potential split among women in the nationalist movement became apparent. Hanna was a nationalist as well as a feminist, but many nationalist women felt they were nationalists first and feminists/suffragists second. As a result, they objected to the notion of Irishwomen attaching themselves to the coattails of Englishwomen in their fight for suffrage, when their problems at home in Ireland were of a totally different order. What was the point in calling for 'votes for Irishwomen', they reasoned, when, once won, such votes could be used only to elect an alien Westminster Parliament, whose authority was not recognised by radical republicans.

Unfazed by this disunity, Hanna doggedly continued lecturing and writing on the subject of votes for women, briefly interrupted in May 1909 by the birth of her only child, Owen. Faced with a wall of silence from the press, Hanna and other members of the IWFL started a publicity campaign. They heckled visiting ministers at public meetings; they boycotted the 1911 census; and they physically clashed with police at the United Irish League Convention in 1912.

That same year Hanna and Frank started their own pro-suffrage, pacifist and nationalist newspaper called the *Irish Citizen*, and Hanna was jailed for the first time. Her arrest followed an appeal by the IWFL to guarantee votes for women. The Home Rule leaders rejected their appeal, whereupon Hanna led a direct action, which involved breaking windows at government buildings, including the GPO and Custom House. She was arrested and briefly imprisoned in Mountjoy Jail, where she demanded and received political prisoner status.

The following summer saw Dublin's factory owners and managers move against trades unions. They locked out of their premises all those workers who refused to give up union membership, thereby setting in motion what became known as the Great Lock-Out of 1913. On the issue of a worker's right to belong to a union, Hanna and Frank strongly supported the socialist and labour activist James Connolly, who was the deputy chairman of the Irish Transport and General Workers' Union (ITGWU). Along with Countess Markievicz and others, Hanna served in the soup kitchens set up for the starving families of locked-out workers. During a demonstration, the 5ft 2in (1.58m) Hanna was jailed a second time for 'assaulting a policeman'.

Frank Sheehy Skeffington had communicated his pacifism to his wife, so when World War I broke out in the summer of 1914, they both wrote strongly against recruitment and conscription in the *Irish Citizen*. For this, Frank was jailed for six months in Mountjoy Jail, where he immediately went on hunger strike. He was released under the terms of the Cat and Mouse Act (passed in spring 1913, originally to deter suffragettes from hunger striking), and escaped to the USA. In his absence, Hanna took over sole editorship of the *Irish Citizen*.

Frank came home in time for Christmas 1915. Well aware of the stirrings of rebellion in the winter of 1915 and spring of 1916, he played no active role in the Easter Rising. He was a pacifist and, as he always said, he was prepared to die for Ireland but not prepared to kill for Ireland. Instead, on Tuesday, 25 April, the second day of the Rising, Frank went around the city assisting the injured and trying to prevent looting. He and two other unarmed newspaper editors encountered an army patrol and were arrested. They were taken to Portobello Barracks where, early the following morning, they were shot dead without trial. The officer who ordered and carried out the murders was Captain Riversdale Bowen-Colthurst.

Hanna and her seven-year-old son were told nothing of this atrocity. Their first inkling that something was wrong came on the Friday of Easter week when the army turned up at Hanna's home, without explanation, and shot out the windows. They then raided the house and went through everything – looking for evidence to justify the murder. They took papers and personal possessions away, much of which was never returned.

Knowing a mistake had been made, the army attempted a whitewash after Frank's murder and Hanna was pressured to accept compensation. This she quietly and persistently refused to do, insisting instead on a government inquiry into her husband's death. The ensuing inquiry resulted in the arrest of Bowen-Colthurst. He was court-martialled, declared insane, imprisoned – and released after eighteen months. Meanwhile, Hanna's house continued to be raided and her movements were constantly monitored.

Hanna did not fall apart after her soulmate's death. Instead her nationalism came to the fore and she worked towards the cause of Irish independence, touring and lecturing in the USA. She pulled off a publicity coup for republicans when she was invited to Capitol Hill to meet president Woodrow Wilson. She was, she later remembered, 'the first Irish exile and the first Sinn Féiner to enter the White House, and the first to wear there the badge of the Irish Republic.' During her visit, she presented the president with an uncensored petition for Irish freedom from Cumann na mBan – and also managed to slip him a copy of the Easter 1916 Proclamation.

On her return in June 1918, she was again arrested by the furious authorities and imprisoned in Holloway Women's Prison, north London, for going to the USA 'without permission'. She immediately went on hunger strike and was released after two days.

During the War of Independence (1919–1921), Hanna served as a judge in the republican law courts in Dublin, which had been set up by the rebel republican government to supplant the British courts. Like Countess Markievicz, Kathleen Clarke, Maud Gonne and the members of Cumann na mBan, Hanna was anti-Treaty in 1921, but, as a pacifist, she abhorred the Civil War (1922–1923) and formed a deputation along with Clarke, Gonne, Louie Bennett and others to persuade the pro- and anti-Treaty leaders to negotiate. This attempt failed.

During the Civil War, the Free State government imprisoned some 7,000 republicans, and, in reply, Hanna helped set up the Women's Prisoners' Defence League (WPDL) with Maud Gonne and Charlotte Despard. The WPDL campaigned for prisoners' rights and fund-raised to give relief to their families. The group would meet to 'take tea' at cafés such as Bewley's once a week, and the adjoining tables would be full of CID men, also taking tea and trying to overhear the women's conversation. It was not long before the government banned the WPDL.

When Eamon de Valera's new Fianna Fáil party was inaugurated in 1926, Hanna was elected to the executive – a post she immediately resigned when she realised de Valera himself was a conservative who was against equal political opportunities for women. She continued to be an active republican, however, and in the early 1930s she edited both the *Republican File* and *An Phoblacht*. She served her fourth and final jail sentence when she was in her fifties, for an anti-partition speech she made in Northern Ireland.

She continued to campaign for women's rights in the workplace. She came out strongly against the 1935 Conditions of Employment Bill, which bluntly prohibited women from working in industry. Two years later, Eamon de Valera's 1937 Irish Constitution contained the following articles:

> *41.2.1: The State recognises that by her life within the home, woman gives to the State a support without which the common good cannot be achieved.*
> *41.2.2: The State shall therefore endeavour to ensure that mothers shall not be obliged by economic necessity to engage in labour to the neglect of the duties in the home.*
> *45.4.2: The State shall endeavour to ensure that the inadequate strength of women and the tender age of children shall not be abused, and that women and children shall not be forced by economic necessity to enter avocations unsuited to their sex, age or strength.*

The inclusion of these articles predictably failed to rehabilitate de Valera in Hanna's eyes. Like Maud Gonne and Kathleen Clarke, she campaigned against the Constitution, which she viewed as a repudiation of the equal rights and opportunities that were the very spirit of the 1916 Rising. Their protests fell on deaf ears and the Constitution was passed.

'She liked people, and particularly women, to be independent,' wrote her daughter-in-law, Andrée Sheehy Skeffington, because 'she herself was fiercely independent.' It was appropriate, therefore, that in 1943 Hanna stood as an Independent in the general election. She was one of four Independent female candidates, the others were Margaret Ashe, Miss Corbett and Miss Phillips. They campaigned under slogans such as 'equal pay for equal work' and 'equal opportunities for women'. After a press boycott made sure none of the women got elected, Hanna pointed out that there were now fewer women TDs than there had been in 1918 – only three out of 138 TDs. The political dice were and would continue to be loaded in favour of the boys who were still, as she said, 'allergic to women'.

In her sixties, Hanna enjoyed a wide range of non-political interests – botany and theatre to name but two – and continued to write on the political subjects close to her heart until at last her health gave out. Her final public political act was support for a teachers' strike in 1946. When her health started to fail, she was nursed by her loving son, Owen, until the end. She died in April 1946, refusing deathbed absolution from the Church and calling herself an 'unrepentant pagan'. She was buried beside her beloved Frank in Glasnevin cemetery. After her death, her close friend Maud Gonne praised her as 'the ablest of all the fearless women who worked for Ireland's freedom.'

Dame Kathleen Lonsdale

1903–1971

Crystallographer

Kathleen Yardley was born the youngest of ten children to a post-master and his wife in Newbridge, County Kildare. When she was five years old her mother left her father and moved the family to Essex in England. At school, Kathleen quickly became interested in science, but in order to pursue her interest she had to attend the local boys' school as well as the girls' school – physics, chemistry and higher maths were not included in the girls' curriculum.

At sixteen years of age, Kathleen won a scholarship to Bedford College for Women in London, and graduated with honours in physics in 1923. A brilliant student, she was immediately offered a research position under Nobel Prize-winning physicist WH Bragg, first at University College, London, and then at the Royal Institution.

Her research was largely based on experimentation in the field of x-ray crystallography techniques, with a view to applying her findings to medical problems. X-ray crystallography involves the use of controlled x-ray beams to study the structure and composition of crystalline materials by examining the patterns that can be seen in the x-rays that have passed through the material. A loose analogy of this complicated technique can be given by comparing it to calculating the shape of a bridge by examining the interaction of the ripples caused by the bridge a few miles downstream.

In 1927 Kathleen married a fellow research student and moved to Leeds, where she worked part-time at the university. But Professor Bragg persuaded her to come back and work with him at the Royal Institution, where she remained until his death in 1942. Meanwhile she raised three children and supported the family through a series of fellowships.

Kathleen and her husband became Quakers in 1936. This had obvious ramifications in the uncertain political climate of 1930s Europe, and during the war Kathleen was interned briefly as a conscientious objector in Holloway Women's Prison. Her pacifism and interest in human advancement continued after the war, to be joined by an interest in penal reform. In the 1940s she opposed nuclear testing and became prominent in the Women's International League for Peace and Freedom (WILPF). She also became involved in an international Quaker movement to fund science education in developing countries. In 1957 she published a book outlining her pacifist philosophy, *Is Peace Possible?*

In 1945 Kathleen and Marjory Stephenson, a sixty-year-old Cambridge don in biochemistry, were the first women to be admitted as Fellows to the Royal Society of London. Kathleen subsequently went on to become vice-president and was awarded the prestigious Davy medal. She became a professor of crystallography at University College, London, and then, in 1949, head of department.

Kathleen published various well-received works on crystallography and in 1956 was made Dame Commander of the Order of the British Empire. She was much in demand by the scientific community for her leadership qualities. She performed as president of several organisations, including the Association of Atomic Scientists (AAS), the British Association for the Advancement of Science (BAAS) and the International Union of Crystallography (IUC), to name but three. She continued her lab work into her retirement years, but died of cancer at the age of sixty-eight.

POLITICAL ANIMALS

'I don't like this exclusion of women from the national fight, and the fact that they should have to work through back-door influence if they want to get things done.'
Maud Gonne

Gormlaith

c.955–1042

High-queen of all Ireland

Gormlaith was born at a time when the Norsemen who had been invading and settling Ireland since the eighth century were reaching their full strength against the native kingdoms. In Gaelic Ireland, many areas traditionally had their own separate chieftains, or kings, and Gormlaith's father, Murchadh, was the hereditary overlord of north Leinster. Marriage alliances between Norse and native were not unusual, and when Gormlaith was a teenager she was married off to the powerful but elderly Olaf Cuarán, king of the Viking town of Dublin. She had five children by Olaf, including her favourite and most ambitious son, Sitric Silkbeard.

Shortly after his marriage, Olaf became high-king of Ireland, or *ard rí*, by conquest, making Gormlaith his high-queen (*ard bean-rí*). However, in the year 980 his position was challenged by the young king of Meath, Malachy. The treacherous Gormlaith looked at the young challenger's chance of success against her old husband – and decided to opt for the winning side. She used her influence in her home province of north Leinster and in her adopted city of Dublin to help Malachy take the high-kingship by force. Malachy then drove Olaf into exile in Scotland and married Gormlaith, making her high-queen for a second time. He also made her half-Viking son, Sitric Silkbeard, king of Dublin in 994.

Meanwhile, in the west of Ireland, Brian Ború, the king of Munster, was becoming ever stronger. Eventually, Malachy was forced to cede territory to him. Gormlaith took this opportunity to change sides once again and persuaded her brother, Mael Mordha, who had by now inherited the kingship of north Leinster, and her son, Sitric, to attack Malachy and take his remaining lands.

This plan backfired when the powerful Brian Ború came to Malachy's defence, but the tide turned once more in Gormlaith's favour when Brian Ború realised that the high-kingship was his for the taking. He accepted Gormlaith's political and sexual advances, made her brother and son his allies, and achieved a position of supremacy over Malachy. After taking the high-kingship from him, Brian married Gormlaith, making her high-queen for the third time, with her third king. Brian Ború's kingship, which lasted until his death in 1014, is regarded as the first time in history that Ireland came close to being a country united under one native leader.

Twenty years and one child later, Gormlaith was up to her old tricks again. She was manipulating Brian to gain advantages for herself and her family. Tired of her endless wheedling demands, Brian repudiated her. Once again she incited Sitric and Mael Mordha to rise up against the high-king. This resulted in the astute Brian Ború again allying with Gormlaith's ex-husband, Malachy, and laying siege to Dublin City. He was unconcerned that Gormlaith was in the city at the time.

Sitric gathered together a mighty host, or army, from Norse allies, relations and connections in Britain and Ireland and made war on Brian Ború and Malachy. The decisive moment was the famous Battle of Clontarf, fought on Good Friday 1014, which resulted in a resounding victory for Brian's forces – and also saw

Brian's death on the battlefield. The Battle of Clontarf ended forever any hopes the Vikings might have had of domination in Ireland. Gormlaith lost her youngest son in the battle. Afterwards she retired to a quiet life and died in a convent in 1042. Her son by Olaf, Sitric Silkbeard, remained king of Dublin for many years.

Charlotte Despard
1844–1939

Philanthropist, suffragist and nationalist

Charlotte Despard was one of the Victorian era's great eccentrics. A vegetarian, a Marxist, a Theosophist and a pacifist, she worked all her life towards three main aims: to change the law to improve the lot of London's slum-dwellers, to achieve female suffrage in Britain and Ireland and to see Irish independence.

Charlotte was born on an estate in Kent, England, into a wealthy Norman-Irish dynasty. Her father, Captain William French, was an irascible naval officer; her mother, Margaret Eccles, a mentally unstable Scottish heiress. Charlotte had four sisters and a baby brother, John (later to become the lord lieutenant of Ireland). She suffered the sort of Victorian middle-class childhood in which she was expected to bring herself up. When she was ten years old, her father died; when she was fifteen her mother was committed to a lunatic asylum; when she was twenty-one, Charlotte found herself orphaned and wealthy.

The Frenches were a wayward, independent-minded family,

and Charlotte was the most strong-willed of them. From her very early years she had a determined, free-spirited nature, and she hated authority of any kind. At twenty-six she met and quickly married a man from an identical background, Maximillian Despard, and lived with him in India and London. Charlotte and Max were an odd couple: where he was calm, she was passionate; where he was cautious, she was spontaneous; where he was calculating, she was reckless. Despite their differences, it was a happy marriage, although Charlotte deeply regretted that they did not have any children.

In 1890, after twenty years as a wife, Charlotte became a widow. She grieved for several months and then threw herself into the cosmetic and largely useless charitable works expected of all rich widows, such as sending flowers to the poor and visiting the sick. From these beginnings, within a year of Max's death, she began a process that would transform her from a well-meaning pillar of genteel society into a radical force for reform.

Charlotte, who could afford to live anywhere she chose, chose to live in Wandsworth, one of the roughest parts of south London. She had conceived a desire to be *among* the poor and, as she watched the sickly, stunted children wandering the streets in winter, she felt a need to help them directly. She opened her own home to provide basic medical help for the children of the area, then a basic play area for them, which eventually developed into the Despard Club. A couple of years later she moved to an even rougher part of London, Nine Elms, and started a second Despard Club among the poverty-stricken London-Irish.

Through this hard work, Charlotte started to get interested in the English workhouse system. The Poor Laws Act (1834) regarded poverty as a moral failing and gave no relief to the able-bodied poor, except that which could be 'earned' by labouring in workhouses. These were institutions where everyone was thrown in together – if you wanted help, you had to live there, usually in atrocious and degrading conditions. When, in 1894, Charlotte was elected a workhouse supervisor in Vauxhall, south London, it launched her public life – and heralded nine years of much-needed reform in south London's worst institutions.

Through the horrors she witnessed in the workhouse and the slums, it was natural for the empathetic Charlotte to make the political journey towards red-blooded socialism, and through that towards female suffrage. Around 1901 she joined the International Labour Party (ILP), and in 1906 she joined the Women's Social and Political Union (WSPU), a militant suffrage organisation founded by the Pankhurst family. In 1907, Charlotte was jailed for the first time, for leading a noisy WSPU demonstration to Westminster.

The sixty-three-year-old Charlotte was only just getting started. She left the WSPU, citing despotic management as the cause, and became president of the Women's Freedom League (WFL), which had a broader, more democratic and less militaristic outlook. Her style as president was much criticised – she was chaotic, overly blunt, democratic to the point of anarchy and unpredictable, but she continued to be much-loved as leader for many years.

While all this had been going on in London, Charlotte's adored brother, John, had been going from strength to strength in his own career. He became, in quick succession, a cavalry officer, an author, a well-respected veteran of the Boer War, a field marshall in World War I, a viscount and, in 1918, lord lieutenant of Ireland. John clearly thought his sister was slightly mad, but Charlotte was proud of John's achievements in his own field and the two kept in touch until their passionately opposing views on Irish independence finally estranged them.

The first time Charlotte had actually seen Ireland had been on her honeymoon, but she was, as her close friend Maud Gonne said, 'intensely Irish in feeling'. After she became politically active, Charlotte had bought a house in Dublin and had travelled often to Ireland, speaking at suffrage meetings, supporting the workers in the 1913 Dublin Lock-Out, canvassing support for Sinn Féin at election time, and founding an organisation known as the Irish Workers' College, in her own home, to promote education for workers. However, as a courtesy to her brother and his political career, she stopped going to Ireland when he became lord lieutenant.

Then, in October 1920, Terence MacSwiney, the lord mayor of Cork was allowed to starve to death in a British prison after seventy-four days on hunger strike. The horror and anger among the Irish community in Britain was intense, and Charlotte's passions once again flared. She realised she could not stay away from Ireland any longer. In London, her stature was now considerable and her stand for pacifism and civil rights had started to pay dividends. When she spoke, people listened. In Ireland this could help the people in their fight against colonial rule, while her pronouncements would have the incalculable extra benefit of coming from the lord lieutenant's sister.

In 1921 Charlotte and Maud Gonne travelled through Cork and Kerry collecting evidence of war crimes committed by Crown forces during the War of Independence. Using her high-class connections, Charlotte shamelessly gained access to all areas under martial law: each time they encountered a roadblock, she simply mentioned her brother and was waved through. The two ageing revolutionaries came back armed with information that was damning to the British government. The killing of boys and old men, the razing of homes, the curfew – all were totally unacceptable to Charlotte Despard, even if the laws that made them possible had been passed by her own brother.

At the age of seventy-seven she took up permanent residence in Ireland. She threw herself into her work for prisoners' rights and for the White Cross, a fund set up with Irish-American money to offer relief to victims of the War of Independence. She formed the Women's Prisoners' Defence League (WPDL) in 1922 with Maud Gonne and Hanna Sheehy Skeffington and became its first president. She lived with Maud Gonne in Dublin, but was always considered an outsider by rank-and-file republicans – the very people she wanted to help.

By 1926 Charlotte had joined the Connolly Club, a short-lived, Communist organisation, run by James Connolly's son, Roddy. She was beginning to realise that the underlying problems of a republic were economic. She now considered Communism, which she regarded as 'the true unity of men and women', as the only hope for the future. Around her eightieth birthday she underwent a period of depression that stopped her being active, but, unbelievably, on the achievement of one of her life's great dreams in 1928 – equal suffrage for British women – she rallied and came back into public life at full strength. She was eighty-four.

In 1930, Charlotte travelled to Russia with Hanna Sheehy Skeffington in a group called Friends of Soviet Russia, and on her return lectured extensively on the superiority of the Russian penitentiary system. She was half in love with the Soviet Union and would have liked nothing better than to see Communism thrive in Ireland. This espousal of Communism affected Charlotte's credibility and most Irish people came to regard her as totally outlandish. A practising Catholic herself, she was also condemned by the clergy.

Undaunted by her unpopularity, Charlotte electioneered for de Valera in 1932, and spoke out against the rising tide of Fascism the following year. Now aged nearly ninety, she gave away her house and most of her possessions in Dublin and moved to Belfast to spread the Communist word. There, white-haired, arthritic and nearly blind, she wrote speeches calling for the workers to unite, rise up and destroy the Northern Ireland government. But the working man did not care to hear Charlotte speechifying and, in any case, they were too bitterly divided along sectarian lines to present a united front. Charlotte had become an irrelevance.

One day, a mob burned down her house and Charlotte moved out of the city into a small, coastal town called Whitehead, where she knew no one. Shortly afterwards, after decades of unstinting generosity towards her many causes and individuals, she was declared bankrupt.

She was now suffering from the isolation that too often afflicts the elderly, and her brain was no longer sharp. Horrified, she watched as Fascism took hold in Europe and war was declared.

Two months after the beginning of World War II, Charlotte was hospitalised after a fall down a flight of stairs. She died in her sleep three days later. She is buried in Glasnevin cemetery, Dublin.

Fanny Parnell, 1849–1882
and Anna Parnell, 1853–1911
Co-founders of the Ladies' Land League

Fanny and Anna were the younger sisters of Charles Stewart Parnell, the president of the Irish National Land League and Home Rule MP of the 1870s and 1880s. Born into a wealthy Protestant background, their County Wicklow father and Irish-American mother separated when they were young, and they spent their youth roving between Paris, London, Dublin and New Jersey. Fanny studied art in Paris and wrote poetry, while the independent and wayward Anna was a voracious reader of US journals and a feminist ahead of her time.

The girls' strong-willed mother, Delia, entertained the deepest animosity towards British rule in Ireland, which she passed on to her daughters. When they lived in Upper Temple Street, Dublin, Fanny would walk around to the offices of the Fenian newspaper, *The Irish News,* and hand in nationalist poems for publication. In 1877 when Charles was following a course of obstructionism and filibustering in the House of Commons, Fanny sat watching him from the Ladies' Gallery in a gesture of support that lasted twenty-six hours.

In 1879, Delia, Fanny and Anna moved to Bordenstown, New Jersey, where they fundraised against a famine that was threatening Connacht (the potato crops had failed four years in a row). When Charles became involved in the Land League movement in 1879, Anna and Fanny actively supported him and Anna wrote about the League in American journals. The Land League demanded the 'three Fs' for those who lived and worked on the land: fixity of tenure, fair rent and free sale. The non-violent campaign largely involved delayed or non-payment of unfair rents by tenant farmers, obstruction of evictions and mass protests. Much of the Land League's financial support came from the USA, buoyed by the campaigning of Anna and Fanny.

By 1880 it was becoming obvious to the Land League leadership that their organisation would eventually be banned and that they would be imprisoned. The founder of the Land League and secretary of the Irish Republican Brotherhood (IRB), Michael Davitt, had the idea of forming a caretaker organisation to continue the protest, and to lead it he chose Anna, whom he referred to as 'a lady of remarkable ability and energy of character'.

The inaugural meeting of the Ladies' Land League was held in New York and the following year, against the wishes of her brother who felt a woman's place was in the home and not in politics, Anna became president of the organisation in Ireland. It was the first time that women had formed an official body specifically to engage in Irish political reform.

In 1881, at the height of the land agitation movement known as the Land War, the government banned the Land League and imprisoned most of its leadership. It was time for Anna and the

Ladies' Land League to step in. While Charles, Michael Davitt *et al* were languishing in Kilmainham Jail, the ladies kept the movement going by financially supporting evictees and prisoners' dependants, preventing land-grabbing and liaising with local branches.

The ladies started by overhauling the administration system. The League's 'records' were chaotic, so the ladies compiled from scratch what became known as the 'Book of Kells' – a damning report into rents, evictions, numbers of tenants, land evaluations and even the characters of local agents and landlords. They continued distributing the League's newspaper, *United Ireland*, which Home Rule politician William O'Brien edited from his jail cell.

When the paper was banned and its staff imprisoned, the ladies actually manned the printing presses and distributed the paper themselves. They personally travelled vast distances across Ireland to attend evictions and to arrange for wooden huts to be built for evictees to live in. All this was disgraceful and unfeminine behaviour for the times, and brought down upon the ladies what Anna called the 'cold atmosphere of censure' from the press, the Church and the police.

To Charles's dismay, it was not long before the ladies' movement was more radical than its male counterpart. They advocated all-out and escalating resistance, and some admitted that they were not averse to violence. In America, Fanny toured, raised money and became a political celebrity in her own right, while at home Anna's enormous public meetings often turned into direct action to stop evictions. This was not what their brother had planned. He saw mass agitation as a means to constitutional power and Home

Rule, whereas his sisters viewed agrarian revolution, a change in land ownership and expulsion of the 'foreign enemy' as the desired end.

In December 1881 the government banned the Ladies' Land League and started imprisoning its members. The ladies responded to this persecution, as William O'Brien wrote, 'by extending their organisation and doubling their activity'. By the following year they had 500 branches all over Ireland – and even some in Britain. But by then Charles felt that the Land League had served its purpose. He negotiated the Kilmainham Treaty with the government, which agreed to a cessation of agitation in exchange for concessions for tenants. On his release in May 1882, Charles, as president of the organisation, dismantled both the Land League and the Ladies' Land League.

It would be an understatement to say that Anna's efforts and those of the other members of the Ladies' Land League were not fully appreciated by her brother and his male colleagues. At the same time as congratulating them, Charles publicly humiliated his sisters and the other ladies by cutting off their funds and accusing them of having spent too much money on aid while he had been in prison. The reality was that he considered Anna and the women too radical. For her part, Anna felt betrayed by him and what she saw as his abandonment of agrarian reform. But Charles saw his chance to forge ahead as the leader of the Irish Parliamentary Party and make Home Rule a central issue, and he was not going to be side-tracked.

In July 1882 Anna's much-loved sister and closest ally, Fanny, died suddenly of a heart attack at the age of thirty-three. Charles was distraught at the loss of his favourite sister – but this did not prevent him from refusing to allow Fanny to be buried in Ireland. He was aware of her popularity and was worried that her funeral would become a focus of political disunity. After this, Anna had a nervous breakdown. She had in abundance what Davitt referred to as the Parnell 'resoluteness of purpose', and she used it to excise her brother from her life. She never spoke to him again.

Anna Parnell retired from political life and pursued her childhood interest in painting. She changed her name to Cerisa Palmer and moved to an artists' colony in Cornwall, England, but continued to support nationalist organisations, such as Inghínidhe na hÉireann and Sinn Féin, from afar. She died in a freak swimming accident at Ilfracombe, Devon, at the age of fifty-nine. She outlived Charles, who had died in 1891.

Maud Gonne
1865–1953
Revolutionary

Of all the names associated with revolutionary Ireland, that of the 'beautiful wild creature', Maud Gonne, is one of the best-known. However, her links with the country she loved were tenuous, for her family, though of Irish descent on her father's side, was wholly English on her mother's, and she was born in Aldershot, Surrey, England.

Maud's mother, Edith Cook, died of tuberculosis when Maud

was four years old, and subsequently she and her younger sister, Kathleen, were reared by governesses in Kildare and France. When Maud was sixteen, her father, Tommy Gonne, an army colonel, moved to the Curragh, Kildare, taking his daughters with him.

Maud loved her carefree life with the Dublin Castle set – the horse-riding, the parties, her personal popularity – but her adored father died of typhoid at just fifty-one years of age and her life was changed forever. His dying wish (according to Maud) was that he could have done more to redress some of the injustices he could see all around him. Twenty-year-old Maud, devastated by her loss, vowed to take his place, and so began her lifelong love affair with Irish revolutionary politics.

The well-known, rather square-jawed photographs of Maud Gonne do not do her justice. Contemporary accounts never fail to mention that, standing nearly 6ft tall (1.8m) with masses of auburn hair and fiery golden eyes, she was majestically beautiful. WB Yeats, who fell deeply in love with her at first sight in 1889, wrote of a 'beauty like a tightened bow, a kind / that is not natural in an age like this'. People literally used to stop and stare at her in the street so much did she seem, said he, 'of a divine race'. Maud was well aware of this: 'I do not say that the crowds are in love with me,' she said, only half in jest, when rejecting the advances of the lovesick poet, 'but they would hate anyone who was!'

In 1902 Maud was to give an unforgettable performance as the personification of Ireland in Yeats' 'Cathleen ni Houlihan', and inspired by her, Yeats was to write some of the greatest poetry in the English language. In addition to her fantastic looks, Maud Gonne also exuded charisma from every pore. She had an abundance of what we would today call 'star quality', and she traded on this to help her in her life's work: to free Ireland from English rule.

Maud's passion for Ireland was always at least partly informed by her hatred of England. After her father's death she lived in London with an uncle, and she disliked both the country and her guardian in equal measure. Liberation came in the form of a kind aunt who took her and Kathleen back to France, where Maud immediately succumbed to the charms of a most unsuitable lover – Lucien Millevoye, a handsome but married French patriot and journalist. It was through Millevoye that Maud first became active in revolutionary politics. Indeed, her first revolutionary act was for France, not Ireland, when she played a minor role in her lover's ongoing plans to regain the territory of Alsace-Lorraine from Germany.

After her French adventures, Maud was back in Ireland by 1889, determined to throw herself into the Irish nationalist movement. But she was blocked by members of the old guard, such as Michael Davitt, founder of the Land League, who simply did not trust women in politics. Eventually, she managed to win the respect of the former Young Irelander and Fenian, John O'Leary, and also the future leader of Sinn Féin, Arthur Griffith, who vouched for her, thus giving her the entrée she needed. In less than a year she was living in rooms on the corner of Nassau Street, central Dublin, and presiding over a group of young nationalists. She was on the road to revolution.

Maud was brave, generous with her time and money, passionate and very sincere, but she had her limitations. She was melodramatic, narrow-minded and had a very unpleasant tendency towards anti-Semitism. She herself admitted she was not 'intellectual', but she would go to almost any lengths to achieve her ideals. 'More and more I realised,' she wrote, 'that Ireland could rely only on force, in some form or another, to free herself.' Her view of independence was over-simplistic: she wanted a reinstatement of the traditional values of an ancient Irish world, before urbanisation, before industrialisation, before, in short, British rule.

There was a niche for Maud in the nationalist movement. As well as her freakish good looks and mesmeric stage presence, she also had a thrilling voice, and she turned out to be a natural at public speaking. Thus her gift to the nationalist cause was to inspire others. The Princess Diana of her day, Maud became what Micheál mac Liammóir called 'the nation's last great romantic heroine'.

The 1890s were a particularly turbulent time for Maud, both politically and personally. She travelled around Donegal helping to mount resistance against the shameful evictions of 1889 and 1890, in some cases actually physically rebuilding the burnt-out houses of evictees. This made her very popular with the country poor, who named the fantastical presence in their midst the 'Woman in Green' or the 'Woman of the Sídhe' (fairies). Maud also conducted lecture tours in Europe and the USA. Her message was always the same: England has no right to Ireland and must be banished, with force if necessary. She also had a lifelong interest in penitentiary reform, and campaigned vigorously for the release of the Irish 'TreasonFelony' prisoners in Portland Jail, who were kept in conditions so inhumane – for example, solitary confinement in the dark – that some of them lost their minds.

In 1890 Yeats made a proposal of marriage, the first of many over the next twenty-five years. Maud turned him down – they were a perfect spiritual match, but she needed to be free. Unknown to Yeats, one of the things she needed to be free for was her continuing illicit relationship with Millevoye. Maud's affair with Millevoye produced two illegitimate children: a boy, Georges, in 1890, and a girl, Iseult, in 1895. Tragically, Georges died of meningitis when he was only eighteen months old.

Even though Maud hadn't been there for much of his baby-hood, the loss of her son devastated her; she carried Georges' little bootees with her for the rest of her life. But at a time when single motherhood would have made her a total social outcast, Maud was never able to publicly mourn her dead son or to acknowledge her living daughter; she always referred to Georges as her 'adopted' child and to Iseult as her niece or 'kinswoman'. Nonetheless rumours, both true and untrue, flew around Maud and what she got up to when she was not in Ireland, and she lived the rest of her life under a moral questionmark. Her relationship with Millevoye ended shortly after Iseult's birth.

In 1897 the British Empire celebrated the Golden Jubilee of Queen Victoria, or the 'Famine Queen' as Maud dubbed her. In Dublin, amid the ostentatious feasting and partying in the streets, Maud marked the occasion by draping a coffin with a black cloth and parading it through the city.

Meanwhile, far beyond the Pale, in Mayo, the potato crop had failed again and there was yet another famine threatening. As soon as she got word of this, Maud headed west. Once in Mayo she travelled around, whipping up support among local people and the clergy. She called a public meeting in Belmullet and personally addressed a crowd of 10,000, demanding food and money from the local Board of Governors on their behalf. Once she had the crowd on her side, she intimidated the local authorities into giving the people what she had promised. After this the legendary status of the Woman of the Sídhe increased still further.

In 1900 Maud founded Ireland's first women's nationalist organisation, Inghínidhe na hÉireann (Daughters of Ireland), and she met her future husband, Major John MacBride. John was a famous soldier and revolutionary hero just returned from South Africa, where his Irish Brigade had been fighting the British in the Boer War. He was good-looking, gallant, charming and had an obvious passion for Irish independence. Perhaps it was these qualities that attracted her to him, or perhaps his soldierly bearing reminded Maud of her father, or maybe Maud just felt that two icons belonged together for Ireland's sake, in any event, against all advice, Maud married John in 1903. The marriage, which produced a son, Seán, in 1904, was unhappy right from the start, and within two years Maud had obtained a civil dissolution.

Her women's organisation fared better than her marriage. Maud herself was never a woman's woman, but she was frustrated by the way that women's abilities were ignored or subsumed into the men-only business of politics. Like the Gaelic League, Inghínidhe na hÉireann ran Irish classes, promoted Irish goods and so on, but, unlike the League, it was also unashamedly political. For example, its stated aim was the re-establishment of Irish independence, and it was vehemently pro-suffrage and anti-conscription. One of its first actions was 'the Patriotic Treat'. This was a huge children's party, planned to coincide with Queen Victoria's visit to Ireland in the spring of 1900, which successfully upstaged the government-sponsored festivities.

In 1910 Inghínidhe na hÉireann battled malnutrition among Dublin's poorest children by setting up a School Dinner Committee, comprising their own members and members of IWFL. Due to high levels of unemployment, working-class mothers often acted as a family's sole breadwinner on a wage of just a few shillings a week and children's diets were pathetically inadequate as a result. For a nominal fee (or for free if necessary), the Committee organised a system whereby poor children got a plate of hot stew every day. This action finally led to a change in legislation in 1914, when the Provision of Meals Act was extended to include Ireland.

Another of the organisation's contributions to the nationalist movement was its journal, *Bean na hÉireann (Woman of Ireland)*, the first ever women's paper to be produced in Ireland, which ran from 1908 to 1911. *Bean na hÉireann* focussed on feminist and nationalist issues, and published articles by Hanna Sheehy Skeffington, James Connolly, Constance Markievicz, Mary MacSwiney and Arthur Griffith.

In 1914, Inghínidhe na hÉireann merged into the newly formed Cumann na mBan – the female wing of the militaristic Irish Volunteers. Meanwhile, now living in France, Maud devoted herself to ambulance work in that war-torn country. Ever since leaving John MacBride, she had lived mainly in France because she was afraid of losing custody of Seán; early twentieth-century family law courts often awarded custody of children to the father. For Maud this situation was resolved by fate when, in May 1916, Major John MacBride was one of fifteen men executed by the British Army in reprisals after the Easter Rising.

The following year Maud returned to live in Dublin. However, she was now less popular than before. It may have been felt that she basked a little too much in the reflected glory of her ex-husband's martyrdom: certainly she only started to use his name after his death and she insisted on wearing black for many years, although she claimed this gesture was for Ireland rather than for MacBride. She was also unconventional in conventional times, and her 'grand romantic dottiness', as Micheál mac Liammóir called it, was a quality much less forgivable in an ageing divorcée with a murky sexual past than in a young, pure and beautiful symbol of Ireland.

In 1918 some seventy nationalists, including Maud, were arrested by the authorities on the spurious excuse that they were in league with Germany against Britain. Maud was interned for six months in Holloway Women's Prison, north London, where she shared her imprisonment with Kathleen Clarke and Constance Markievicz. Conditions were comparatively good, but Mrs Clarke later said that Maud was like a 'caged wild animal ... like a tigress prowling endlessly up and down.' Not surprisingly, the woman whose horror of prisons had led her to campaign for prisoners' rights for more than twenty years found her own incarceration absolutely unbearable. She was the first of the three to be released, on the grounds of ill-health.

During the War of Independence, Maud worked for the White

Cross, which supplied financial relief to the families of victims of violence. In 1921 she was anti-Treaty, but as a long-time loyal supporter of Arthur Griffith, who supported the Treaty, she was uncharacteristically quiet on the matter. However, her position hardened after Griffith's death in August 1922, fuelled by the fact that she hated WT Cosgrave's Free State government. She became disillusioned with her great admirer, WB Yeats, due to his decision to serve in the Irish Free State Senate in 1922, and he in his turn wrote regret-filled poetry about how she had wasted her beauty and passion, most famously in his 1916 poem 'No Second Troy'.

Also in 1922, along with Hanna Sheehy Skeffington and Charlotte Despard, Maud founded the Women's Prisoners' Defence League (WPDL) for the 'help, comfort and release of' republican prisoners. A serious thorn in the side of the Free State government, the organisation of 'Mothers', as Maud called them, was banned in early 1923. Tall and gaunt in her everlasting widow's weeds as she continued to lead placard marches around the city, Maud's appearance was now so eccentric that Dublin wits took to calling her 'Gone Mad', while they referred to the hyperactive Charlotte Despard as 'Mrs Desperate'.

In 1923 the Free State government arrested Maud again for her activities with the banned WPDL. Her crime was to parade peacefully down a street carrying anti-Free State placards. Inside the dreaded Kilmainham Jail, she immediately joined a hunger strike with ninety-one other inmates. Meanwhile her close friend, the seventy-nine-year-old Charlotte Despard, was staging a solitary protest against her illegal imprisonment: she waited on a chair at the prison gates, day and night, for twenty days until Maud was stretchered out, suffering from malnutrition but still defiant.

Maud continued to lecture and tour for the still-banned WPDL throughout the 1920s and early 1930s. She did not stop agitating until 1932, when Eamon de Valera released the prisoners on his accession to power. To Maud's disgust, however, de Valera began his own campaign of jailing republicans. In protest she started a news-sheet and fired off many an angry letter to the press, but as a political force she was spent. Instead she watched as her son, Seán MacBride, took an active role in republican politics. He became the IRA's chief-of staff in 1936, founded a new political party, Clann na Poblachta, in 1946 and served as minister for External Affairs from 1948 to 1951.

Maud Gonne lived to be a legend in her own lifetime. One of the first modern female nationalists, she had the sad experience of outliving all her old friends and comrades: WB Yeats, Arthur Griffith, Hanna Sheehy Skeffington and Countess Markievicz. The free spirit who could not bear to be caged became, as she put it, 'a prisoner of old age, waiting for release.' Her release finally came in April 1953, at the age of eighty-seven. She was buried, holding her dead baby's bootees, in Dublin's Glasnevin cemetery. Her grave is in the 'republican plot', near the graves of Countess Constance Markievicz, Cathal Brugha and Jeremiah O'Donovan Rossa.

Louie Bennett
1870–1956

Suffragist, pacifist and labour leader

Louie Bennett was born in Dublin to a prosperous merchant family. In her early life she had literary aspirations and published two unremarkable novels, *The Proving of Priscilla* (1902) and *A Prisoner of his Word* (1908). In 1911, Louie changed direction dramatically when she co-founded the Irishwomen's Suffrage Federation (ISF) with her lifelong friend and ally, Helen Chenevix. As a feminist, Andrée Sheehy Skeffington remembers that she was 'not militant'. However, she was involved enough to act as the editor of Hanna's suffrage newspaper, the *Irish Citizen*, while Hanna was on a lecture tour in the USA.

Louie became deeply involved with labour rights during the 1913 Great Lock-Out in Dublin, and worked in the soup kitchens set up by various women's organisations. The same year she started the Suffrage Federation and Reform League in an effort to bring women's suffrage and women workers' rights together in one forum. This was typical of her thinking: Louie, a lifelong pacifist, looked to mediation and conciliation rather than outright conflict to advance the interests of different groups.

Louie and Helen's pacifism led them, in 1914, to join the Women's International League for Peace and Freedom (WILPF). During the war, Louie was the only Irish representative given leave by the government to attend the Women's International Conference for Peace in The Hague (in the event she did not go because the authorities prohibited her boat from sailing).

In 1917, after labour rights activist and nationalist Helena Moloney was imprisoned for her part in the 1916 Rising, Louie replaced her as secretary of the Irish Women's Workers' Union (IWWU). This organisation had been set up in 1911 as a sister organisation to James Larkin's Irish Transport and General Workers' Union (ITGWU). Louie was to act as the matriarch of this organisation for the next forty years, imposing her strong personality and individualistic views on it from the start – because of this, and because of her own massive authority, the organisation was not as democratic at that time as it later became.

During her leadership, membership of the IWWU increased and it won important concessions for printing, laundry and textile workers. By the 1930s it represented some 5,000 women trade unionists. It protested the Conditions of Employment Act 1935, which virtually banned women in industry. Strangely enough, Louie's own views on female employment were somewhat inconsistent. While arguing for equal pay for equal work, she also felt that the increasing numbers of women in industry was 'a menace to family life'. Louie was not convinced that married women had a right to work if their husbands were employed, because she viewed jobs as a resource to be shared around.

In 1955, a year before her death, Louie retired from active participation in labour affairs and handed over the leadership of the IWWU to her loyal friend, Helen Chenevix, who did the job until 1957. The IWWU lasted as a women-only trades union until 1984, when it amalgamated with the Federated Workers' Union of Ireland (FWUI).

Mary MacSwiney
1872–1942

Republican

Mary was the eldest of seven children born to a County Cork father and an English mother. When she was a child, the family moved from England to Cork, and her father attempted to set up a tobacco factory there. When this enterprise failed he emigrated to Australia, leaving his family to cope as best they could.

Mary was a bright but solemn little girl. At seven she developed an infection in her foot and had to have it amputated, which forced her to limp along in a surgical boot for the rest of her life. Since this incident precluded her from the usual rough and tumble of childhood, Mary became bookish and rather introverted. After her father's departure, she felt a huge sense of responsibility for all her siblings, especially her brother, Terence, who was five years her junior.

At twenty years of age, Mary secured a teaching post at a strict Benedictine-run convent school in Kent, England. Mary was a deeply devout Catholic and, while she never actually joined a religious order, she joined a lay Catholic organisation whose members pledged themselves to lives of chastity and study.

In 1904 Mary's mother died and she returned to Cork to help look after the family. The next ten years saw Terence become more and more committed to his political ideals, while Mary, a member of both the Gaelic League and Inghínidhe na hÉireann, became more politically aware through supporting him and discussing matters with him.

She joined the Munster Women's Franchise League (MWFL), but she was lukewarm about feminism, describing herself as a 'conservative suffragist'. Mary had little argument with women's and men's respective roles in society, but she wanted women to have more access to education and career opportunities. Eventually, Mary abandoned the cause of suffrage altogether to devote herself to the cause of Irish independence. Meanwhile, alongside her growing political career, she carried on teaching.

By 1914 Terence was deeply immersed in Sinn Féin and Mary was holding Cumann na mBan meetings in the MacSwiney living room. In those days she was not keen on the idea of armed conflict – though she later came to see republican fighting as 'a just war' against oppression – and she felt the Easter Rising of 1916 was premature.

Immediately after the Rising, Terence was arrested and sent to a prison in Frongoch, North Wales, while Mary's role in 'holding the fort' in Cork during Easter Week led to her arrest in her classroom at school. She was subsequently sacked, whereupon she borrowed money and moved to Dublin to open St Ita's in Belgrave Place, Rathmines, a school for girls that modelled itself on Patrick Pearse's boys' school in Rathfarnham.

As Terence continued to be arrested, released and re-arrested for his political activities, Mary also became more active in the Cork branch of Cumann na mBan, campaigning vigorously against British attempts to impose conscription during World War I. In the general election of 1918, Terence was one of the thirty-six candidates elected to the first Dáil Éireann from their jail cells and Cork became a republican stronghold.

In March 1920 the lord mayor of Cork, Tomás MacCurtain, was murdered in his own home by members of the Royal Irish Constabulary (RIC). Terence MacSwiney took his place as mayor and shortly afterwards was arrested by the authorities on a trumped-up charge of possession of 'sensitive' documents. He immediately went on a hunger strike in protest at the illegality of his arrest. He fasted all the way through his trial, conviction and journey to imprisonment in England. On 25 October 1920, seventy-four days after beginning his strike, he died at Brixton Prison, London.

Mary managed the publicity surrounding her brother's hunger strike and death. Always direct and confrontational, she made it plain that she believed the British government had let her brother die deliberately to provoke the sort of outrage that would require martial law to be deployed in Ireland. Her own response to his death was to become completely single-minded in her desire for an unequivocal Irish republic. After his funeral, she and Terence's widow, Muriel, embarked on a well-attended American lecture tour, publicising Terence's death and campaigning for his ideals. As she became more confident in the public eye, her style became more aggressive and she became known for her intractability.

Mary was still in the USA during Ireland's general election of 1921, but her name was put forward and she was easily voted in as TD for Cork City. She was horrified when Michael Collins and Arthur Griffith signed the Anglo-Irish Treaty in 1921, and was convinced most of her colleagues in the Dáil would reject it. But despite her three-hour speech in defence of 'the Irish Republic and the government of the Republic of Ireland, which is Dáil

Éireann, against all enemies, foreign and domestic' – the cause for which her brother had died – the Dáil voted narrowly in favour of the Treaty. Mary found herself going head-to-head with those who had a different approach to the issue of Irish independence.

Mary threw her support behind Eamon de Valera during the Civil War. She toured Ireland, arguing her brand of resolute republicanism and maintaining her opposition to the provisional government and her loyalty to the First Dáil of 1919. She was eventually arrested in Dublin and jailed in Mountjoy where she deployed her most effective weapon: hunger strike. It was obviously unthinkable that Terence MacSwiney's sister should starve to death in the same way he had. This fact, plus Cumann na mBan's huge publicity campaign, ensured Mary's release in late 1922, four days after she had received the Last Rites from a Catholic priest.

In 1923 Mary toured again, was arrested again, went on hunger strike again (this time in the company of Maud Gonne) and was again released. She joined the Women's Prisoners' Defence League (WPDL), a band of mothers, wives and sisters of imprisoned and executed republicans.

When Eamon de Valera started to engage in constitutional politics with the hated Free State government, Mary was appalled and became estranged from her leader; she refused even to recognise the legitimacy of the Free State government. In 1926 she refused to join de Valera's Fianna Fáil party and lost her Dáil seat the following year.

Thereafter, Mary became less and less relevant as her intransigence in the face of changing realities isolated her more and more from the main political action. Throughout the 1930s she continued to regard herself as the true voice of 'old-guard' republicanism, which still believed in the legitimacy of the First Dáil of 1919. She fell out with de Valera, Sinn Féin and even Cumann na mBan over the purity of their republican ideals. Believing that she, and she alone, occupied the moral high ground, Mary also fell out with the Roman Catholic Church. Eventually, the surviving members of the First Dáil signed over their authority to hard-core republicans: the newly resurgent Irish Republican Army (IRA).

Now in her sixties, Mary was beginning to suffer a variety of illnesses and was going blind due to cataracts. She had to reduce her political activity to writing furious letters to the newspapers. The mainstay in her frustrated life was Terence's now-teenaged daughter, Máire Óg, whom she lovingly reared after his death. Although she remained an unrepentant republican to the very end, her political activities continued to decrease until her death at her Dublin home in the spring of 1942. She is buried in Cork City, near her brother.

Kathleen Clarke
1878–1972

Revolutionary, senator and the first female lord mayor of Dublin

Kathleen Daly was born into a political family in Limerick in 1878. Her father, Edward, and his brother, John, were active Fenians and had both served time in prison. When Edward died, aged only forty-one, Uncle John cared for Kathleen and her nine siblings. With his history in the Irish Republican Brotherhood (IRB) and his experiences in the notorious Portland Jail, he was a major political influence on the family. When he was voted mayor of Limerick in 1899, one of his first acts was to remove the royal coat of arms from the wall of Limerick Town Hall.

Kathleen's biographer and grand-niece, Helen Litton, describes her relative as 'forthright, outspoken and passionate, with a single-minded commitment to one idea above all others'. Kathleen herself said her family occasionally described her as pig-headed. She certainly demonstrated an independent streak at the age of eighteen when she started and ran a successful dressmaking business by herself, refusing to go into the family bakery because she did not wish to be 'under' her older sisters. Later she would manage her courtship and marriage in a similarly stubborn manner.

At the age of twenty-one, Kathleen met and fell in love with the forty-year-old Thomas J Clarke, a Fenian who had just completed a fifteen-year stretch in Portland Jail for 'Treason-Felony'. He was a member of the old IRB and, having lived much of his life in the USA, had become a key member of Clan na Gael, an Irish-American pro-independence organisation.

Tom was a well-respected revolutionary, but, according to the Dalys, not much of a catch for Kathleen, being relatively old and completely penniless. Kathleen ignored all opposition. She went to New York in 1901 to be with Tom, and married him the day after she got there. Their first son was born in 1902, followed by two more boys in 1908 and 1910 respectively.

The Clarkes were passionately committed to the ideal of Irish independence. In New York they joined Clan na Gael, the Gaelic Society and the Irish Volunteers, and ran a newspaper, the *Gaelic American*. They raised funds and planned for the future. After six years of store-keeping and market-gardening punctuated by active politics, they returned to Dublin in 1907 to realise their dream.

The Clarkes considered their fellow countrymen and women in Edwardian Dublin to be apathetic about the struggle for self-determination, and they threw themselves into the task of shaking things up. They started a bookshop in Amiens Street and, later, one in Parnell Street, which became popular nationalist haunts. Tom started another newspaper, *Irish Freedom*, and set up the militaristic Irish Volunteers, which Kathleen's only brother, Ned, immediately joined. Kathleen was a founder member of Cumann na mBan in 1914.

The Volunteers courted controversy from the outset by refusing to kow-tow to the Irish Parliamentary Party (led by Charles Stewart Parnell's successor, John Redmond), on the grounds that they were too closely aligned with the Establishment at Westminster, whose authority the Volunteers refused to recognise. Kathleen courted controversy of her own when, under her presidency, Cumann na mBan ran first-aid classes and rifle practice – not activities in which the chauvinistic Volunteers wanted to see their women engaged. In this way the years went by in a whirr of subversive activity until that fateful day: Monday, 24 April 1916.

Some time before the Easter Rising in Dublin, the Supreme Council of the IRB had placed Kathleen in a position of special responsibility. In the event of the arrest and/or death of the leaders, it would be her job to pass on their plans and decisions to key men all over the country so that their network of intelligence would not collapse. Therefore, she had to be kept informed of all the decisions made by the Council, memorise all the relevant personnel and avoid imprisonment. She was also responsible for the welfare of the Volunteers' families should anything happen to their menfolk.

When Tom set out on the morning of Easter Monday, Kathleen knew that it was quite possible she would never see him again. By the end of Easter Week she knew that he and his comrades had surrendered and that, as the first signatory on the Proclamation of Independence, Tom would be among the first to be executed. She was right: Tom Clarke was shot dead by a firing squad on Wednesday, 3 May, and Kathleen's brother, Ned Daly, was shot on Thursday, 4 May. Shortly afterwards, Kathleen lost the baby she had been expecting.

Demonstrating what Constance Markievicz later called 'a hero's soul', Kathleen focussed determinedly on the work that had been assigned to her by her husband. By the end of the first week following the executions, she had established the Irish Volunteers' Dependants' Fund, which financially supported families of dead and imprisoned Volunteers.

In 1917 Kathleen was elected to the Sinn Féin executive under Eamon de Valera. In 1918, after two years of being continually watched and followed by 'G-men', she was arrested as part of a round-up of Sinn Féin activists and jailed in Holloway Women's Prison, north London. Sharing her imprisonment were Countess Constance Markievicz and Madame Maud Gonne MacBride.

Kathleen's attitude to the two aristocratic revolutionaries was mixed. Something of an inverted snob, she did not care for their backgrounds. They came from the 'English element', as she called it, while she felt herself to be 'purely Irish'. In addition, 'little Mrs Clarke' found herself being patronised relentlessly by the ladies who had a much higher profile than she. Maud Gonne was released early, but Kathleen and the Countess continued a combustible inmate relationship; the tactless Constance seemed to forget the role Kathleen had played and how heavy her losses had been. Despite their constant bickering, however, the two revolutionaries remained close, and after their release in early 1919, Kathleen provided the homeless Countess with somewhere to live.

The bloody years of 1919–1921 saw the War of Independence raging uncontrollably. Martial law was declared, there were curfews across the country, mercenaries known as Black and Tans were shipped in to intimidate the populace, and republicans were on the run. The Black and Tans (named for the colour of their uniform) were untrained, undisciplined and deeply unpopular, and did much to turn public opinion in favour of the rebels. Kathleen herself was kept under surveillance by detectives, and her house and her mother's house in Limerick were continually raided by the army.

Things took a turn for the worse in 1920 when the army demolished Kathleen's mother's house, burnt the contents and beat up her mother and sisters who were living there. Despite this continual harassment, Kathleen remained politically active, attending Sinn Féin meetings and sheltering rebels. During the War of Independence, the republicans set up judicial courts to supplant those run by the British administration. Kathleen became chairperson of the north Dublin judiciary, and then president of the Court of Conscience and the Children's Court.

In July 1921 a truce was called. Five months later, Michael Collins and his five colleagues signed the Anglo-Irish Treaty, which partitioned Ireland, and by early the following year civil war was raging between anti- and pro-Treaty factions. Kathleen was a hard-line republican and vociferously anti-Treaty; she believed that acceptance of it betrayed the ideals for which her husband, brother and others had died. She continued to be harassed by the military – but this time the military were her own countrymen in the Irish Free State Army.

In 1926 Kathleen joined Eamon de Valera when he broke away from Sinn Féin and formed the Fianna Fáil party. Ideologically she also moved from the military to the political, reasoning that the people had had enough of war and that changing policy was acceptable so long as the objective remained the same. But the election in September 1927 saw her defeated by a Cumann na nGaedheal candidate in north Dublin, thus ending her brief career as a TD.

Instead, Kathleen was nominated a member of the Senate, where she served until its abolition in 1936. It was her only paid job in politics. Throughout the 1930s she became less and less enamoured of Fianna Fáil, even though she remained a member of its executive. She was publicly critical of many of the party's policies – particularly of the 1937 Constitution and its treatment of women, which she and Hanna Sheehy Skeffington loudly condemned.

In 1939 Kathleen was still a member of the Fianna Fáil executive and a Fianna Fáil member of Dublin Corporation. In June of that year her name was put forward to stand as lord mayor of Dublin, and she was won the majority vote: she was the first woman to be elected to the office. Her first action was reminiscent of her Uncle John's priorities as mayor of Limerick forty years previously: out went the many portraits of British royalty, including an enormous one of Queen Victoria herself; out too went other 'colonial trappings', such as the previous lord mayor's English-made chain of office, which she replaced with an Irish-made chain; in came the Clarke family crest, which featured the first motto in Irish to be seen in the Mansion House.

Kathleen was the incumbent during the beginning of World War II and supported Irish neutrality. She did not support IRA bombing in England during wartime, but opposed the imprisonment of IRA members by de Valera's government. When her term as mayor was up in 1941, she resigned from public life. She resigned from Fianna Fáil in disaffection in 1943.

Kathleen spent the 1940s on the boards of various hospitals and maintaining the graves of the nationalist dead. She tried unsuccessfully to stand for election to the Dáil in 1948. In 1965 she moved to Liverpool to live with her youngest son, Emmet, and in 1966 she received an honorary doctorate from the National University of Ireland. Although she suffered ill health all her life, Kathleen Clarke lived to the age of ninety-four. She was given a State funeral in Dublin and is buried at Deansgrange cemetery, Dublin.

SAINTS AND SINNERS

*'My heart was naturally good ... but the
natural good was frequently perverted
by evil examples.'*
Margaret Leeson

St Brighid
c.453–524

Patron saint of Ireland and founder of the first monastery in Ireland

The earliest Christian priests were canny: they merged ancient pagan rituals with new Christian thinking in order to improve Christianity's chances of taking root in the general populace. The cult that grew up after St Brighid's death is a good example in that it is an amalgamation of a legendary woman with a real woman and her real achievements. The legendary woman was the daughter of a Celtic goddess; the historical woman was the daughter of a Christian slave.

The story goes that Brighid was born *c.*453 at Faughart, near Dundalk, County Louth. Her mother, Broicsech, was a bondswoman or indentured servant, and her father was Dubhtach, probably a member of the warrior class. Brighid's mother was a Christian and she reared her daughter in the faith; some stories say the child was baptised by St Patrick himself.

At an early age, Brighid became renowned for her acts of charity. In Lady Augusta Gregory's retelling of Brighid's life, she relates how 'every-thing she put her hand to used to increase … she bettered the sheep and she satisfied the birds and she fed the poor.' (*A Book of Saints and Wonders,* 1906.) According to *Ancient Legends of Ireland* (1888) by Lady Jane Wilde, Brighid also had the gift of healing and was able to cure lepers.

Of course, Brighid was also very beautiful and very marriageable. In due course her father did the obvious thing and selected a high-status husband for her, but Brighid prayed to God to make her ugly and preserve her chastity. Her prayers were answered: she developed a pox that disfigured one side of her face while leaving the other as beautiful as ever. Now unmarriageable, she was free to form the first community of nuns in Ireland, which she did with just seven other like-minded women.

Chaste she may have been, but Brighid, whose name means the 'fiery arrow', was no shrinking violet. She is reported to have been direct, confident and outgoing. She was a very skilled chariot driver and she travelled all over the country, making conversions, tending the sick and starting religious communities. Despite her vow of chastity, she was at ease in the company of men, all of whom she treated as equals – even the great chieftains she visited and attempted to convert.

Near the end of the fifth century, a local chieftain granted Brighid the area of land now known as the Curragh in Kildare (in Irish Kildare is *Cill Dara,* meaning Church of the Oaks), where she founded the first monastery in Ireland. Brighid gained the land by trickery: the chieftain said he would only give her as much land as her shawl would cover, to which terms Brighid agreed. Six months later she arrived back with the shawl and in front of the chieftain gave the four corners of it to four nuns, who ran north, south, east and west. The magical shawl unravelled until it covered the whole of the Curragh.

Once the new community had been established, Brighid turned it into a large double abbey, comprising celibate nuns and monks working side by side, healing the sick and helping the poor. Although there was a bishop responsible for the monks, Abbess Brighid outranked him, such was her undisputed standing in ecclesiastical circles. She had jurisdiction over all the churches in her area. Some sources report that she was actually made a bishop herself (she is seen holding a bishop's staff in some early monuments), but rather than this story being the literal truth, it may have been a way of emphasising just how powerful she was. Such was her influence that even after her death, her successor abbesses continued to benefit from her precedent, having more episcopal power than was usual.

In keeping with the druidical associations of the oak grove at Kildare, Brighid adapted a pagan symbol for her own use – the eternal fire – as reported by the twelfth-century Welsh historian Geraldus Cambrensis. The eternal fire, tended by nineteen nuns, one of whom was constantly on watch, had been burning for 600 years by his time, but, according to him, there were never any ashes. On the twentieth night the nuns left the fire in the care of the spirit of Brighid with the words: 'Brighid, take care of your own fire for this night belongs to you', and in the morning the fire would still be burning brightly.

The fire was extinguished in 1220 by Henri de Londres, archbishop of Dublin. The fire-house, said to be located at Kildare Cathedral, remained an important part of local folklore. In the eighteenth-century, Austin Cooper sketched the remains as they then stood, and recorded it as the 'fire-house of the Nuns of St Brigid at Kildare'. Today, there is very little left to see, just a low, square wall to the north of the cathedral.

Another of Brighid's miracles concerns the story of Dara. One night she was sitting with Dara, a sister nun who was blind, and they were discussing God. They talked all night and as the beautiful dawn broke, Brighid felt a great compassion and desire that Dara should see God's work with her own eyes. Brighid placed her hands over Dara's eyes and miraculously removed her blindness. Dara sighed with delight when she saw the beauty around her, but immediately asked to be returned to darkness. When the world was so visible, she said, God was seen less clearly in the soul.

Brighid died c.525 at Kildare. About fifty years after her death, her body was disinterred and subsequently re-interred at Downpatrick, County Down, in order to protect it from the marauding Vikings who had invaded the south and east. There, according to tradition, Brighid was laid to rest beside St Patrick and St Columba.

One of the ways in which she is remembered today is the St Brighid's Cross, a cruciform of equal lengths made out of rushes with which, it is said, she converted a pagan on his deathbed. Every St Brighid's Day (1 February), schoolchildren all over Ireland make these crosses and they are to be seen in most homes and businesses.

Often compared to one of the holiest women of all time, the Virgin Mary, and known as 'Mary of the Gael', St Brighid continues to hold a special place in the canon of saints in Ireland. As well as being a patron saint of the country, she is also particularly responsible for babies and illegitimate children, the sea and fishermen, dairy-workers, healing, learning and metalwork.

Dame Alice Kyteler
c.1280–c.1330

Ireland's first convicted witch

In medieval Europe, witch-hunting was a serious business. It is estimated that some 100,000 men and women were executed on suspicion of being witches at this time (*c.*1000–1500), and laws against witchcraft remained on English statute books as late as the mid-nineteenth century. Overall, Ireland had comparatively few witch-hunts, so the incredible events of 1324 caused shockwaves throughout the country.

Dame Alice Kyteler was a wealthy, landowning woman of Anglo-Norman descent whose family had settled in Kilkenny in the twelfth century. Her father was a banker, and Alice prospered in her own right in the generally male pursuit of money-lending. She married well but was widowed often – suspiciously often. Her first husband was William Outlawe of Kilkenny, a banker; her second, Adam le Blund of Callan; her third, Richard de Valle. By 1324, still only in her forties, she was married to her fourth husband, Sir John le Poer.

Dame Alice lived in a beautiful and prominent house in the middle of the town, and her increasing prosperity made her the subject of envious speculation by the citizens of Kilkenny. Scandal and gossip surrounded her ability to outlive her husbands. Her knack for financial gain made people wonder: how does she do it?

In 1324 the speculation turned to savage action. There were complaints made against Dame Alice by her adult stepchildren.

Privately, they felt she financially favoured her own eldest son, William Outlawe Junior, at their expense. Publicly, their accusations were much more serious: they claimed she had bewitched and poisoned her first three husbands. Furthermore, they said, her current husband, Sir John, was losing his hair and his nails – in other words, exhibiting signs of poisoning.

The rumour mill provided plenty of 'evidence' against Dame Alice. One night, while sweeping out her house, she was apparently heard to recite:

> *'To the house of William, my son,*
> *Hie all the wealth of Kilkennie towne!'*

Incriminating stuff – but it was to get much worse. It was said she was receiving nightly visitations from a large black dog who turned into a demon lover named Art Artisson; she was mixing strange potions in the dead of night; she sacrificed animals; and she spoke incantations.

Against this background of gossip and local hostility, Dame Alice, her faithful personal servant, Petronilla of Meath, plus several other women, were arrested and charged with heretical sorcery. The official charges included:

1. *Failing to go to Mass and receive Holy Communion.*
2. *Consorting with demons.*
3. *Sacrificing animals.*
4. *'Excommunicating' their own husbands.*
5. *Concocting devilish potions, including a stew made of dead men's nails, spiders, pubic hair and parts of*

dismembered cockerels.

6. Murder and attempted murder through sorcery.

Enter the English zealot Richard de Landrede. He was the Franciscan bishop of Ossory and the Church's representative in the matter. It may have been that he was convinced of Dame Alice's guilt, or it may have been that he was sick of the minor nobility, such as Dame Alice and her ilk, growing as wealthy as the Church and challenging its authority. Either way, he lost no time in wholeheartedly jumping on the bandwagon and accusing Dame Alice of heading a coven of witches.

If Dame Alice's wealth and position had caused dangerous levels of envy in the first place, they now protected her against bishop de Landrede's first efforts to have her imprisoned. A delegation of Kilkenny's most influential citizens, including the Seneschal (the administrative head of the area) Sir Arnold le Poer (no relation of the ailing Sir John), met the bishop to speak on Dame Alice's behalf. When the bishop refused to drop the charges, the citizens rather rashly had him imprisoned in Kilkenny jail for seventeen days to give him a chance to rethink his position.

When the furious bishop was released, it became a matter of personal pride to him to convict and condemn Dame Alice. So when the archbishop of Dublin summoned de Landrede and Sir Arnold to appear before him, the bishop responded enthusiastically.

In Dublin, Sir Arnold put forward his strongest case against the witchcraft charges: the bishop was only a dirty Englishman who excommunicated anybody who disagreed with him and who thought all Irish people were heretics anyway. Furthermore, he said, Ireland could not possibly harbour any witches since it was universally acknowledged to be 'the island of saints'. Despite these compelling arguments, he lost his case when the archbishop heard about the outrageous imprisonment of bishop de Landrede in Kilkenny. To the bishop's glee, it was decided that a faction from the Dublin court would go down to Kilkenny and try Dame Alice and her coven.

After a thorough interrogation, Dame Alice was found guilty as charged and handed over to the authorities. They sentenced her to be whipped through the streets of Kilkenny and then burned to death in full sight of all in the centre of town. But the wily Dame Alice was not beaten yet. The night before her scheduled execution, with the help of other members of the Anglo-Norman nobility, she escaped from the jail and fled Kilkenny into an exile that lasted the rest of her life. As it turned out, Dame Alice was the lucky one.

The enraged bishop excommunicated Dame Alice *in absentia*, confiscated her property and ritually burnt a cloth bag containing witches' paraphernalia that purportedly came from her house. He then turned his attentions to her remaining followers: Petronilla, Dame Alice's faithful servant, Petronilla's daughter, Sarah, and nine others. He accused them all of sorcery, but for the worst treatment he homed in on the most defenceless – Petronilla, a servant and a poor, vulnerable, middle-aged woman who, abandoned by her employer, now had no hope of protection of any kind.

Petronilla was arrested, imprisoned and flogged every day for a week – the only time that torture was employed in a witchcraft trial in Ireland. Not surprisingly, a confession to witchcraft, implicating Dame Alice and all the others, was soon forthcoming. The major advantage of her confession, according to the bishop, was that Petronilla could now go to her death with a clear conscience. Accordingly, Petronilla was burnt alive in front of bishop de Landrede and a large crowd at the market place on 3 November 1324. The Tholsel (built in 1761), now stands near the spot where the poor woman met her horrific end.

For Dame Alice's son, William Outlawe Junior, the outcome was rather different. As with his mother, power and position held sway. While his mother's servant was burnt to death for her 'crime', William's penance was to attend three Masses a day for a year, pay for a lead roof for St Mary's Church and feed a certain number of paupers. The other accused all seem to have been able to buy their way out of trouble, for there is no record of any other executions.

It is said that in England, Dame Alice became close to the family of King Edward III. She managed to persuade the king to confiscate bishop de Landrede's lands and possessions, but the tenacious bishop cleared his name, regained his property before his death in 1360, and is buried in style at St Canice's Cathedral in Kilkenny. The Kyteler house remains standing in a prominent position on High Street in Kilkenny; it is now a bar and restaurant called the Kyteler Inn.

Margaret Leeson

1727–1797

Brothel-keeper

Margaret Leeson was born Margaret Plunkett in Killough, County Westmeath. There were twenty-two children born to the family, although only three boys and five girls survived to adulthood. Their father was a Catholic man of property and, for the times, Margaret and her sisters received a good education.

When Margaret was still young, her mother contracted a fever and died. Her father was unable to cope and the children were scattered around to various relatives. When they returned to the family home some years later, they found that their eldest brother, Christopher, had taken over as master of the house. Unfortunately, Christopher was a tyrant who regularly beat and starved his siblings. He also prevented the young Margaret from getting married – not once but twice – whereupon Margaret ran away from home to the bright lights of Dublin.

In Dublin, Margaret was quickly seduced by a lawyer friend of her brother's and became pregnant. In her memoirs, written more than half a century later, she appears philosophical about this fall from grace. She rather delighted in the fact that, because of it, she acquired her own home, which her lover rented for her in Clarendon Street.

After the birth and death of the baby, this relationship ended, and there were many more lovers of ever-decreasing respectability. Margaret had children by nearly all of her 'protectors', but none of them survived infancy. In her memoirs, written when she was a

⅋ *Countess Constance*
Markievicz, 1868–1927

⅋ *Hanna Sheehy*
Skeffington,
1877–1946

Charlotte Despard,
1844–1939

Maud Gonne,
1865–1953

Mary MacSwiney,
1872–1942

Kathleen Clarke,
1878–1972

Venerable Catherine McAuley,
1787–1841

Grace O'Malley (left),
c.1530–1603

Máire Rua O'Brien,
1615–1686

Lola Montez,
c.1820–1861

ÉIRE 28

LADY MARY HEATH
FIRST SOLO FLIGHT CAPETOWN/CROYDON VIA CAIRO 1928

Lady Mary Heath, 1896–1939

Peg Woffington, c.1718–1760

Sara Allgood,
1883–1950

Siobhán McKenna,
1923–1986

Lily Yeats (second from right), *1866–1949*

Grace Gifford, 1888–1955

repentant old woman, Margaret calls this the 'hand of Providence ... wisely and mercifully' taking the children away from a life of vice. She admits that her own 'love of pleasure and want of reflection' played too major a role in her life. In a classic case of denial, she also claims that her 'heart was naturally good', but that this natural good was perverted by 'evil examples'.

After a long procession of evil examples had made their excuses and left – including one called Leeson – Margaret was financially comfortable and ready to become a full-time madam. In 1784, at the age of fifty-seven, she set up her own brothel in Pitt Street and employed handpicked young women from London's theatre world to service her high-class clientele. The 'men of fashion' who flocked to Pitt Street included none other than Charles Manners, the duke of Rutland and the lord lieutenant of Ireland. This house of ill-repute enjoyed enormous success for a decade and Margaret became notorious throughout the land. Of course, she failed to lay aside any money against the future, and one day found herself with nothing but pocketfuls of IOUs from her unprincipled customers. She closed the brothel and retired to Blackrock with a companion, Miss Collins.

Margaret then reformed and found religion. Ironically, her penitence made her poverty all the more biting since she felt unable to accept handouts from her rich but racy former acquaintances. Eventually, they stopped offering and Margaret got poorer and poorer. She started to write anecdotal and amusing memoirs, hoping they would produce an income – either from their sale or from their blackmail value to some of her more high-profile ex-clients. While waiting for this to happen, she was arrested for a debt of £15 she owed to a grocer in Grafton Street, and held in the Four Courts Marshalsea, a debtors' prison. She was bailed out by the governor of the prison – a previous client – and went back to living quietly with Miss Collins.

One night she and Miss Collins were out walking in Drumcondra when they were attacked and gang-raped. Shortly afterwards they both discovered they had contracted venereal disease, which, as Margaret sardonically noted, was an ailment she had managed to avoid all her professional life. Though cured of the disease, Margaret died shortly afterwards. She was sadly mourned by her friend, Miss Collins, who called the most famous brothel-keeper in Ireland an 'exemplary, pious, worthy, charitable woman.' Margaret is buried in St James's churchyard, Dublin.

Lady Betty
c.1750–1807

Public executioner

Born into a tenant farmer's family in County Kerry, the woman who came to be known as Lady Betty married another poor farmer, named Sugrue, and they had a family. On his death, Betty and her three children were left destitute.

She set out with her children on the long walk to Roscommon town to look for a better life. *En route* her two younger children died of starvation and exposure, leaving only her much-loved eldest son.

On reaching Roscommon, Betty and her son moved into an abandoned hovel and begged, borrowed and stole to eke out a sparse living. One day, unable to stand the grinding poverty any longer, Betty's son decided to go to America and seek his fortune. Maddened with grief, Betty begged him to stay but he would not be dissuaded. Promising he would return one day a rich man, he boarded a ship bound for Boston, leaving his distraught mother convinced she would never see him again.

Years passed, and Betty's miserable existence was punctuated only by the occasional letter from America. She supplemented her income by taking in desperate lodgers and travellers for a few pennies a night. One stormy night a traveller knocked on the door of Betty's cabin, looking for lodging. Betty took him in and treated him as usual, but then noticed something unusual about him. Unlike most of her guests, this young man was rich and had a purse full of gold.

The temptation was too much for Betty; years of deprivation, bereavement, heartbreak, bitterness, poverty and injustice bubbled to the surface. She may have been thinking she would use the money to go to America and be reunited with her son. Whatever her reasoning, she waited until the traveller was asleep, then stabbed him to death and took his money.

Tragically for Betty, it turned out that the man she had killed, unrecognisable after the long years apart and savouring the surprise he was about to spring, was in fact her own beloved son. Betty immediately gave herself up, was charged and tried for murder and sentenced to a murderer's death: public hanging by the neck until she was dead. She was imprisoned in Roscommon

Jail where, towards the end of the eighteenth century, the ranks of those waiting to be hanged were swelled by insurgents, such as United Irishmen and the Whiteboys. These political prisoners would be hanged in groups alongside the common criminals, like Betty.

The day eventually came when Betty, among others, had to mount the scaffold to be executed. However, possibly because of local loyalty to and respect for a number of rebels due to be hanged that day, no hangman could be found to carry out the bloody task. The prison authorities were in despair. Already overcrowded, the jails of Connacht couldn't possibly take any more rebels until the ones they had were despatched. But what would happen to law and order in the country if these people were not caught and sentenced in short order? A radical solution was needed.

This was when Betty made her mark on history. Unbelievably, the woman with apparently nothing to live for wanted to save her own skin so desperately that she volunteered to be that day's executioner. She killed several rebels that first day and, with the full support of the authorities, continued her 'work' thereafter in an official capacity right across the province.

Already beyond the pale of most human experience, 'Lady' Betty's cold-hearted actions meant she was universally feared, loathed and shunned. Eventually she was given lodgings inside the prison grounds for her own safety. In 1802 she received a pardon for her own horrific crime.

Lady Betty lived – and worked – until 1807, but by the time of her death a powerful myth had grown up around her and it was many years before mothers stopped telling children to watch out for the unnatural and evil Lady Betty. She is buried inside the grounds of Roscommon Jail – the scene of so much of her hideous handiwork.

Venerable Catherine McAuley
1787–1841

Founder of the Sisters of Mercy, one of the most widely distributed religious orders of nuns in Ireland

The nineteenth century saw a massive increase in the number of Irishwomen opting for the life of the religious. In 1800 there were only eleven religious houses across the country, containing about 120 nuns; by 1901 this had grown to 368 houses and more than 8,000 nuns. There were several reasons for this. Famine was endemic in rural areas, but the Great Famine in the mid-nineteenth century changed the very structure of land ownership. Firstly, it wiped out one whole class of people – the cottier, or poor subsistence farmer who rented his land from a slightly better-off smallholder. Secondly, the old custom among smallholders of dividing their land equally among sons gave way to the English custom of primogeniture, whereby the eldest son inherited every-thing. This meant younger sons got no land at all, which in turn meant they could not afford to marry. As well as this, there was increasing emigration, an option often preferred by young mar-riageable men. All of these factors resulted in more single, celibate women than ever before in the general population. To such women, living in a religious community, informal or otherwise, where there was support, status and intellectual stimulation, was a whole lot better than living in a society where they were the eternal daughter and drudge of the house, with the low status, huge responsibilities and lack of fulfillment that that entailed.

Catherine McAuley, the founder of one of the world's most successful religious congregations, did not quite fit into this category. For a start, she was not poor. Her father was a wealthy, charitable and devout self-made man named James McGauley. When he died, Catherine's mother, Elinor, perhaps mindful of the disadvantages of being a Catholic, abandoned her husband's religion in order to raise her three children as Protestants. She also changed the family name to McAuley because it sounded more fashionable.

When Catherine was eleven her mother died and the family went to live with a Protestant family, the Armstrongs. They persuaded Catherine's brother and sister to change religion, but were unable to budge the stubborn Catherine from her Catholicism. While she was living with the Armstrongs she met other wealthy relations, the Callaghans, who had just returned from India. Mrs Callaghan took a shine to the fair-haired, blue-eyed, nice-mannered girl and asked her to live with them. Around 1803 Catherine and the Callaghans moved into Coolock House in Coolock village, County Dublin.

Through the ups and downs of the family custody arrangements, Catherine had held fast to her religion, practising it alone and in secret. At Coolock, Mrs Callaghan was a Quaker while, on religious matters, Mr Callaghan did not care one way or the other. Though they both looked down on 'Romish superstition', as they called Catherine's religion, the Callaghans were more tolerant than the Armstrongs and Coolock House was not a bad place for a Catholic. Catherine was quietly able to receive religious instruction once again. In addition, Catherine also found herself deputising for Mrs Callaghan, a semi-invalid, in her charitable efforts in the village. This was Catherine's first real contact with the poor and she loved being able to help. She grew to admire and respect the villagers' innate courage and devotion to God in the midst of mass unemployment and poverty.

This was how Catherine lived over the next twenty years: enjoying a privileged though precarious position at Coolock House and stubbornly practising her religion alone. She taught catechism to the local children and needlework to young girls. She also attended to Mrs Callaghan's ever-worsening health with such love and devotion that, on her deathbed, Mrs Callaghan converted to Catholicism. Before Mr Callaghan died, three years later in 1822, he too converted. In his will he left Catherine his whole fortune – in today's money about £750,000. Relations tried and failed to contest the will.

Now Catherine could put her plan into action. Like her father, she wanted to give practical help to the poor so she came up with the idea of a 'house of mercy' where they could receive support. She consulted various priests, sold Coolock House and bought a site on the corner of Baggot Street and Herbert Street in Dublin's city centre. The site, right in the middle of that fashionable part of town, was not an accident – she did not want the poor to be invisible. The cornerstone was blessed in 1824 and the House of Our Blessed Lady of Mercy was officially opened in 1827.

Catherine gathered like-minded women around her in a lay community that had religious values. The women helped or taught the poor, lived in the house and dressed uniformly. Their central tenet was mercy to the poor and they were meant to deal with needs as they arose, be they educational or medicinal or spiritual. They fed the destitute every day, accommodated orphans, gave safe lodging to poor working girls and nursed victims during the cholera epidemic of 1825. Importantly, all the women were free to return home at any time. In addition to the responsibilities of running her institution, Catherine took on the rearing of her sister's five children after her sister's death in 1827.

The Baggot Street house was confusing to Catholic Dublin. Catherine insisted it was not a convent, despite appearances, because the women were free to leave. She faced great opposition from the priests of the parish. They not only found it difficult to pigeonhole this lay community with its outward religious appearance, but also found it slightly scandalous for a single woman to own and run an institution of any kind.

In 1829 Catholic emancipation was granted and Catholics were once again free to practice their religion openly. Catherine was given an ultimatum by the archbishop of Dublin: either she could abandon the religious appearance of the Baggot Street community or she could place it and herself under the clergy's jurisdiction. On condition that she would still be free to work outside among the poor, Catherine agreed to take orders so she could start her own congregation. She began her training at George's Hill Presentation Convent, Dublin, in 1830.

This was not an easy period in Catherine's life. At fifty years of age, she was used to her independence. She hated spending those fifteen months away from her work on Baggot Street, and nearly gave up. However, she persevered and in December 1831 she and two colleagues took their vows as the first Sisters of Mercy. Reinstated at Baggot Street, Catherine became Mother Superior and welcomed new novices. The following year her order gained papal approval.

The charismatic Mother Catherine was not above using her personality and social position to help her cause. Where she wasn't welcome as a nun, she made sure she was welcome as a gentle-woman; Daniel O'Connell described her as 'queenly'. Other accounts of her describe her as magnetic, with an abundance of charm and humour. Her social position meant that she found it easy to recruit among the well-to-do, and many of the novices of the Sisters of Mercy were, in fact, rich young heiresses. She insisted that if these heiresses were to convert comfortably into Mercy Sisters they had to be 'gentle, humble, patient, hard-working, obedient, charitable but, above all, simple and joyous'.

The Baggot Street premises flourished and a second Mercy convent soon opened in Dún Laoghaire. After this there was a demand for Mercy institutions all over Ireland, in places as far afield as Tullamore and Birr, County Offaly, Charleville, County Cork, Booterstown, County Dublin, County Carlow, County Limerick, County Galway and County Wexford. Two convents opened in England: Bermondsey in 1839 and Birmingham in 1840. The Irish bishops liked the scattered nature of the operation: the lack of centralisation and flexibility meant more autonomy to the local bishop.

Worn out by hard work, Mother Catherine died in November 1841, but her congregation has carried on to be the largest in the world. In 1990 Pope John Paul II declared Catherine McAuley 'Venerable', an important step on the road to sainthood.

Margaret Haugherey
c.1813–1882

A businesswoman and philanthropist, known as the 'Bread Woman of New Orleans'

Margaret Gaffney was born in Carrigallen, County Leitrim, the fifth of six children. Her parents, William Gaffney and Margaret O'Rourke, were of the poor labouring class, and when Margaret was a child she, her parents and several of her siblings emigrated to Baltimore, Maryland, USA. In about 1822, Margaret's parents and all except one of her siblings died in a yellow fever epidemic. The two siblings were separated and Margaret was reared by a kindly Welsh immigrant whom she had met on the ship on the way over. She was well cared for by her new guardian, but she never went to school and never learned to read or write.

In 1835, Margaret married an Irishman named Charles Haugherey. The couple moved south to New Orleans in Louisiana, a growing community with a vibrant mix of French, African-Americans, Irish and Germans. They lived in a slum area known as the Irish Channel, and Charles worked as a teacher. In 1836 Margaret gave birth to a daughter, Frances, but the baby died a few months later. Shortly after that, Margaret's sickly and grieving husband left her to go back to Ireland, where he too soon died.

Alone in the world, Margaret initially survived by taking in washing. From the pittance she earned she bought two cows and started to peddle milk, donating a percentage of her tiny profits to a ramshackle local orphanage known as the Poydras Asylum, which was run by the Sisters of Charity. Margaret built up her herd to about forty cows, and by 1840 she was in a position to help the Sisters financially to move their orphanage into a new building. There was a chronic shortage of food at the orphanage, so Margaret developed what she called her 'mendicant technique' for getting provisions for the children: she hitched herself to a cart and toured the shops begging for meat and vegetables that could be spared.

As well as running the dairy and begging for food, in the 1840s Margaret also worked in the St Charles Hotel in New Orleans, but her position there was essentially a cover to help her with her fund-raising activities. She would make friends with the well-to-do guests and then touch them for a donation to one of her causes, which included a fund for a new church, St Teresa's, and one for famine relief in her native Ireland.

New Orleans in the mid-nineteenth century was a lively but dangerous place, subject to periodic flooding from the great Mississippi River and rife with disease. In one of the bigger floods, Margaret piloted her own raft in order to reach and relieve stranded families. New Orleans was also prone to devastating outbreaks of yellow fever, or Black Jack as it was known. In 1852–1853 a particularly bad epidemic hit New Orleans, creating the need for a new orphanage. Margaret and the Sisters founded an establishment specifically for babies, named St Vincent's Asylum.

In the late 1850s Margaret sold the dairy business and bought shares in a failing bakery called D'Aquin's Bakery. When Mr D'Aquin retired soon afterwards, the other shareholders elected Margaret president of the company, largely as a courtesy. However, she took her position seriously and, against much opposition, insisted on updating the bakery to become the first steam-powered operation in the city.

Margaret's Steam and Mechanical Bakery prospered and she was able to buy a couple of foodstores, which grew to become one of the largest chains in the South. Meanwhile much of the bakery's produce was given free to charity, thus Margaret acquired her nickname: the Bread Woman of New Orleans.

During the American Civil War, Margaret continued to turn a healthy profit and used what influence she had to mediate between southern supporters of the Confederacy and northern supporters of the Union, which maintained a garrison in New Orleans until 1876. She widened her charitable interests to include adults, helping to build St Elizabeth's House of Industry for Young Women, and a home for the aged and infirm. During yet another yellow fever epidemic in 1878, the now-ageing Margaret personally visited and assisted the families of victims. Famous in her own lifetime, she was depicted in the newspapers as a local 'character'.

Margaret Haugherey amassed a considerable fortune, most of which she spent supporting her various charitable institutions. These institutions ranged across the racial and religious divide, and Margaret's will included bequests to the Widows' and Orphans' Jewish Home, the Seventh Street Protestant Orphanage and the German Catholic Asylum, among others. In 1884 New Orleans named Margaret Place after her and erected a statue in her honour – one of the first monuments to a woman in the whole of the United States. Since 1958, New Orleans has also honoured 9 February as Margaret Haugherey Day.

TOUGH COOKIES

'We're unsinkable.'

The Unsinkable Molly Brown

Queen Maeve of Connacht
Pre-Christian

Celtic queen/goddess

Queen Maeve (or Medb, or Meadhbh, or Maev) is known primarily as a mythological figure, although she did have a historical counterpart. The Maeve of legend was a warrior-queen and the main villain in the great seventh-century epic, *Táin Bó Cuailgne (The Cattle Raid of Cooley)*, which is part of the Ulster Cycle of stories and it centres mainly on the conflict between the greedy and ambitious Queen Maeve and the superhero Cú Chulainn.

According to the tale, Maeve and her husband, Ailill, are arguing one night in bed over who has the most wealth. Maeve is infuriated when she discovers that Ailill wins because he is the owner of a magnificent white bull. She determines to obtain an even better bull, known as '*an Donn*' (the Brown Bull), which is in Ulster. First she asks the Donn's owners nicely if she can have him, and then, when she is refused, she gathers a huge army, rampages across the country from her castle at Rathcroghan and takes the bull by force. The Ulster warriors were out of action after being cursed with labour pains for nine days, so the rest of the epic centres on the heroic efforts of Cú Chulainn to single-handedly rescue the bull and return it to its rightful owners.

In her legendary incarnation, Maeve's purpose was not only to inspire warriors but actually to participate in war as a fighter skilled in the use of spear and slingshot. This is a mythological interpretation of a common custom in prehistoric Ireland (and France and Britain), where women were often active participants in war (200 years after the introduction of Christianity in the fifth century, a law was passed imposing fines on men who allowed their womenfolk onto the battlefield).

The real Maeve seems to have been a rather ambitious woman. She was born in Rathcroghan, County Roscommon, possibly in the third century, the daughter of Eochaid, king of Connacht. When her sister, Clothra, became queen of Connacht after Eochaid's death (in ancient times royal women were not barred from becoming leaders of their people), the jealous Maeve was furious. She killed her pregnant sister and took her crown by force. The tales of her greed and acquisitiveness in the *Táin* probably stem from the frequency of Maeve's raids into neighbouring counties and her attempts to set up a matriarchy in Connacht.

It appears that the real Maeve was married several times and bore many sons and daughters. Her first husband was Conor, king of Ulster, whom she left. Her last husband was Ailill, the seventeen-year-old prince of Leinster who features in the *Táin* legend as her henpecked husband. Mythological Maeve was also known for her predatory sexual appetite – she was said to enjoy up to thirty lovers in a single night.

The Annals of the Four Masters claim the historical Maeve lived to be 120 years old. Even then she did not die a natural death – she was killed in a long-awaited revenge attack by her sister's son while taking a bath in the River Shannon. She is reputed to be buried at Knocknarea, a cairn in Sligo, but it's more likely she is buried near her old stomping ground at Rathcroghan.

Katherine FitzGerald, Old Countess of Desmond

c.1464–1604

Blessed with a unique longevity

Incredible though it may seem, there are several contemporary accounts supporting the Old Countess's major claim to fame – that she lived until she was about 140 years of age.

Katherine was probably born in Dromana Castle, County Waterford, the daughter of Sir John FitzGerald, lord of Decies. She became the wife of Thomas Maol FitzGerald (who was to become the twelfth earl of Desmond in 1529, when he was in his seventies), around 1483. At her wedding, which took place in London, the bride danced with the future King Richard III. Her wedding gift from her husband was the castle at Inchiquin, County Cork.

When her husband died an old man *c.*1534, his aged widow was allowed to live on at Inchiquin Castle until her own death, when the estate would revert to the earl's heirs. Since Katherine was already pretty elderly, the heirs expected to come into their inheritance sooner rather than later, but forty years on, in the mid-1570s, they were still waiting. Katherine finally signed over the land to Garrett FitzGerald, the fifteenth and last earl of Desmond, who later lost it to English settlers in the failed Desmond rebellion of 1583.

In 1589 Sir Walter Raleigh obtained the land as part of the plantation of Munster, and recorded that the Old Countess was still resident in the castle. He allowed her to remain, expecting, not unreasonably, that she would soon die, but in the event she saw him off. He sold the estate to Richard Boyle, earl of Cork, who was determined not to make the mistake of his chivalrous predecessor and promptly tried to evict the Old Countess.

Katherine had no choice but to take the problem directly to the court of James I. In 1604 she and her daughter – who was then over ninety years old – made the long and dangerous journey from Youghal, County Cork, via Bristol, to London. According to Sir Robert Sydney, second earl of Leicester, the Countess made the journey from Bristol on foot while her daughter rode in a 'little cart'. In yet another story, the Old Countess carried the ailing daughter on her back until the cart was obtained! Either way, they were desperately poor and the king seems to have taken pity on them. He paid for the Old Countess's expenses in London, and even had her portrait painted while she was there. Then the Old Countess was allowed to return home and take up residence once again at Inchiquin.

Not long after her return, the apparently indestructible Countess finally met her end. Sir Robert Sydney's account claims she was up tree, picking either cherries or nuts, when she fell off her ladder. She broke her hip and died shortly afterwards. She is probably buried at the site of the Franciscan Friary in Youghal, next to her husband who had died some eighty years earlier.

Grace O'Malley

c.1530–1603

Sea trader, pirate and clan leader

In the sixteenth century the Gaelic aristocracy in County Mayo was represented by four clans: the O'Malleys, the O'Flaherties, the Joyces and the Burkes. Grace O'Malley, also known as Granuaile, was a daughter of the house of Uí Máille (O'Malley), the hereditary lords of a region that, at its greatest extent, stretched from Connemara in County Galway to Westport in County Mayo.

Grace's father, Dubhdarra (Black Oak), was a very powerful chief. He traded and fished with a sizeable fleet of traditional curraghs, fast galleys and spacious caravels. He also sold licences to any foreigners – including the English – who wanted to fish in 'his' waters. Grace, his only daughter, took after him: she was bold, she was used to giving orders and she loved the rough sea.

In 1546, at the age of sixteen, Grace's father arranged her marriage to Dónal O'Flaherty (also called Dónal an Chogaidh or Donal of the Battles). He was the scion and subsequently head of the great clan of O'Flaherty, the pirating southern neighbours of the O'Malleys. The wedding was held in the chapel of one of the O'Malleys' own imposing abbeys at Murrisk, built nearly a century before and located at the foot of Croagh Patrick in County Mayo. The ruins of the abbey can still be seen today.

After her marriage, Grace lived mainly in the coastal strongholds of Bunowen and Ballinahinch, in the shadow of Benlettery in County Mayo. But as the pirate raids for which the O'Flaherties were famous continued, Dónal proved himself somewhat inept at managing them. The opportunistic Grace, a natural leader, gradually took over his role and captained the ships herself. She was still only in her twenties. She also organised more peaceful trade missions as far north as Scotland and as far south as Spain and Portugal. Consequently, she became the *de facto* leader of the O'Flaherty clan.

In the 1560s, as part of ongoing tribal warfare between Dónal O'Flaherty and the Joyce clan, Dónal was murdered. Grace was left a widow with three children, Margaret, Owen and Murrough, to raise on her own. She retreated to Clare Island, from where she continued to run the O'Flaherty fleet.

In 1566 Grace stayed on land long enough to make a strategic marriage with Richard Burke (also called Risteard an Iarainn or Richard-in-Iron), whose gaelicised Norman clan held the territory north of Clew Bay. It was a traditional marriage, contracted according to the ancient law of Ireland, the Brehon law, by which Grace and her people had lived for 1,500 years. According to Brehon law, women could fight on the battlefield, keep their own name and property after marriage, drink alcohol, be elected head of their clan – and divorce their husbands with no repercussions.

One of the reasons the acquisitive Grace had married Richard was to own the impressive castle of Rockfleet (Carraig an Chabhlaigh or Carrickahooley), on the north shore of Clew Bay by Westport. Once it was in her possession, she established herself here and bore a son, Tibbot-na-Long. One of the best and most unlikely Granuaile legends maintains that Tibbot, or Theobald, was born at sea as his mother was captaining a ship fighting Turkish pirates.

In due course, after a year and a day, Grace divorced Richard –

but made sure she kept possession of Rockfleet. (Since Richard crops up in accounts of her for many years after this separation, it can be assumed that their political alliance remained intact even if their marriage did not.)

Meanwhile, Elizabeth I of England had turned her attention to western Ireland and the resources it could provide for Tudor expansion. Having already gained a foothold in most of the rest of country through the efforts of her father, King Henry VIII, she now sent in administrators to infiltrate the old Gaelic families of the west and usurp their power – by fair means or foul.

One by one the clan leaders were forced to capitulate and soon it was Grace's turn. The English navy sailed to Mayo and on to Lough Corrib, where they besieged her in one of her late husband's hard-won forts, known as the Cock's Castle because of the fierce tenacity that Richard had shown while fighting for it. Tradition has it that Grace avoided capture by melting the lead on the roof of the Cock's Castle and pouring it onto the intruders below. She then escaped to the mainland and lit beacons to alert her allies. Reinforcements arrived and the English were driven back. Afterwards, in deference to Grace's own fierce tenacity, the castle was renamed the Hen's Castle.

After this adventure, a furious Grace sailed to the old O'Malley territory at Clew Bay, County Mayo. There she gathered support from both the O'Malley and the O'Flaherty clans and threw herself into revenge. She carried out a series of daring raids, plundering English and 'loyal' Irish ships which refused to pay protection money for safe passage along the coast, and generally flouting Her Majesty's authority.

In 1574 Galway merchants were so enraged by Grace's piratical attacks on their trade, they conspired with the English to send a force to lay siege to Rockfleet. But once again the sea queen turned the tables. By unexpectedly attacking the superior force and skilfully outmanoeuvring them, she succeeded in forcing them to flee.

In 1576 Her Majesty's representative, Sir Henry Sidney, arrived in Connacht to demand submission from the Gaelic chieftains of the region. Grace was among those who appeared before him. For the sake of political expediency, it would appear she came voluntarily and submissively. Grace was a smart operator, and she was more interested in local power structures than in whatever seismic reorganisation the English were up to. She wanted to ensure that Richard Burke, her erstwhile husband and Tibbot-na-Long's father, became The MacWilliam, that is, the acknowledged head of his clan, so that their son could inherit the title from him.

After the meeting, Sidney wrote: 'There came to me also a famous feminine sea captain called Grany Imallye, and offered her services unto me, wheresoever I would command her, with three galleys and 200 fighting men, either in Scotland or Ireland ... This was a notorious woman in all the coasts of Ireland.'

Grace recognised political reality when she saw it. Keen as she was to save face, English power was beginning to appear unassailable. If she could not save Ireland's autonomy, she certainly intended to retain her own as far as possible.

This turned out to be not as far as she would have liked. In 1577, while plundering the earl of Desmond's lands, Grace was caught. The earl, Garrett FitzGerald, was anxious to have Queen Elizabeth believe him loyal, so he showily had Grace imprisoned in Limerick Jail and then in the dungeons at Dublin Castle for eighteen months. Lord Justice Drury, the then president of Munster, to whom she was delivered, called her 'a woman that hath impudently passed the part of womanhood and been a great spoiler and chief commander and director of thieves and murderers at sea to spoil this province.' However, he grudgingly conceded that her reputation was widespread and that she was: '... famous for her stoutness of courage and person, and for sundry exploits done by her at sea.'

On her release, Grace returned to Connacht and, in 1581, gleefully witnessed her ex-husband and ally, Richard Burke, become The MacWilliam. There was a gathering of the nobility after the investiture at which the president of Connacht, Sir Nicholas Malby, noticed that a delighted Grace '[thought] herself to be no small lady'. When Richard died in 1583, Grace ruled his followers as well as her own from Rockfleet. By now, at the height of her powers, aged fifty-three, she was regarded as nothing less than a *bean rí* – a she-king.

In 1584 Sir Richard Bingham was appointed governor of Connacht. In a life filled with confrontation and conflict, Bingham was to prove Grace's greatest opponent – with his arrival everything changed for the worse. She had enjoyed what amounted to a working relationship with Bingham's predecessors, but Bingham himself was on a mission: he wanted to subdue Connacht and everyone in it. To Bingham, Grace, in particular, was an anomaly that had to be stamped out. Over the next ten years he made a special target of the woman he called a 'nurse to all rebellions'.

She was troublesome to him on many different levels. She had been indulging in insubordinate, piratical behaviour for nearly twenty years. Plus she was a woman and under English law was not entitled to any property (though under Brehon law she was entitled to a third of both her husbands' properties). Plus she was causing trouble in the province over who was going to succeed to The MacWilliam's title (in the end, no one did). All of this was too much for Bingham and he instructed his brother, Captain John Bingham, to confiscate Grace's property, capture her and hang her. Captain Bingham succeeded in confiscating her lands, but her life was saved when she was vouched for by one of her most loyal allies, her son-in-law, the picturesquely nicknamed Devil's Hook (a mistranslation of *Deamhan an Chorrain*, meaning Devil of the Hook).

Following the confiscation of her lands and the murder of her eldest son, Owen, by the Joyces in 1586, Grace was shaken and forced to fall back on what she called 'maintenance by sea'. However, Bingham's constant surveillance and intervention made this impossible, and Grace and her remaining family became destitute. At this point, aware that a rising was afoot, the 'nurse of all rebellions' spent three months in Ulster enjoying the hospitality of The O'Donnell and The O'Neill.

At this low point in her life, Grace was forced to write directly to Elizabeth I, disingenuously expressing regret that it had been necessary 'to take arms and by force to maintain [herself and her people] by sea and by land', and asking for 'reasonable maintenance' to which she was entitled from both her husbands' estates. The response from the royal court was the issue, by Lord Burghley, of eighteen articles of interrogatory, which included such questions as: 'If she [Grace] were to be allowed her dower, or thirds of her husband's living, of what value the same might be of.' Grace answered all the questions, but while she was awaiting an answer, Bingham arrested her youngest child, Tibbot-na-Long.

Grace had already lost one son and did not want to lose a second. On hearing the news of Tibbot's incarceration, she ordered a ship, sailed around Ireland, through hostile English and Spanish ships, around the south coast of England, up the Thames estuary and right into London. She was determined to plead for her son's life face-to-face with Elizabeth. She was granted an audience at Greenwich Castle in September 1593.

Even 400 years later, it is hard not to draw comparisons as these two women faced each other. The weather-beaten Irish chieftain remained standing, grey hair tied back, wearing a simple woollen cloak over a smooth linen dress, her only ornament an Irish silver pin; the English queen remained seated, sumptuously dressed in silks and sporting a jewel-encrusted red wig against a livid-white face and a black-toothed smile. They were contemporaries; both were acquisitive and astute; both were charismatic leaders, unused to taking orders from anyone; both enjoyed unprecedented success in predominantly male occupations. However, the differences between the women were greater than the similarities: their respective customs and beliefs made their values almost incomprehensible to each other. Above all, one woman's destiny was very much in the hands of the other.

Despite what legend would have us believe, it is unlikely that Granuaile was haughty or arrogant in the presence of Elizabeth I, and unthinkable that she should have treated the vision in front of her as an equal. She was politically shrewd, like the queen herself, and would have been very aware that many an Irish chieftain had had a long-awaited audience with the most powerful monarch in Europe, only to find themselves shortly afterwards cooling their heels in the Tower of London at Her Majesty's pleasure.

But Grace was wilier than that. Having conversed for some time with the queen in Latin – the only language they had in common – she managed to come away from the meeting with everything she wanted and more – not only her son's life but also the restitution of her property. To Bingham's fury, the fickle Elizabeth had granted Grace's petition: her family members were released, she was pardoned for her past activities and, even better, she was again allowed to 'support herself' at sea. Grace jubilantly sailed home to Ireland.

After this unparalleled coup, Grace's status as a leader was enhanced and she re-launched her trade – and even some piracy – under the guise of being a 'dutiful subject' of Her Majesty. But once again the vindictive Bingham stopped her, this time by quartering her troops and breaking her financially one more time. The relationship between them deteriorated to an all-time low. So poisonous were her feelings that Grace attacked her own son, Murrough, for having supported Bingham in the past. Unable to vent her spleen on Bingham, Grace went for Murrough instead, 'with a navy of galleys ... and burned his town [at Bunowen, County Donegal] and spoiled his people of cattle and goods and murdered three of four of his men ...' Grace needed to show *somebody* who was boss.

Luckily for Grace this unpleasant situation resolved itself when a conspiracy against Bingham emerged. In 1595 he fled to England to defend his reputation there, only to find himself imprisoned in the Fleet, a prison in London. In his absence, Grace's galleys sailed freely once more.

From 1597 to 1601 rebellion against the English raged in the shape of The O'Donnell and The O'Neill and their supporters. The 'nurse of all rebellions' had spent three months with the chiefs as their guest when she had first encountered trouble with Bingham, but after being seriously offended by The O'Donnell on a clan matter, the politically flexible O'Malleys withdrew their support from the rebellious earls. Grace's two sons, Murrough and Tibbot-na-Long, had no qualms about becoming captains on the English side and fighting against their countrymen and one-time allies under the new governor of Connacht, Sir Conyers Clifford.

At one point it looked very much as if the rebellion would be a success and the Ulster chieftains would finally drive the English from Ireland. As it turned out, the defection of the O'Malleys was an astute if cynical move: the rebellion went awry, the insurgents were brutally suppressed in 1601 – and Grace's youngest son, Tibbot-na-Long, was made a baronet for services rendered.

Grace lived long enough to see the crushing defeat of the last of the Gaelic aristocracy into which she was born, and the elevation of her line to the new order: Tibbot-na-Long was made first viscount Mayo. Perhaps such status was what she wanted all along. Ironically, Grace has stepped into legend and song as a symbol of freedom in an oppressed time.

It is said that Grace died peacefully at Rockfleet Castle around 1603 – the same year that Elizabeth I died. On Clare Island, off the coast of Galway, in a thirteenth-century abbey built by the O'Malleys, there is a tomb. It is said that Grace O'Malley is buried here. The inscription reads: *Terra Marique Potens O'Maille* (O'Malley: Strong on Land and Sea).

Iníon Dubh

b. c.1555

The mother of Red Hugh O'Donnell and key player in sixteenth-century politics

In the sixteenth century, Ulster was being colonised by the English and Scottish. The 'planters' were deeply suspicious of the native Irish and their ways, and especially of their ancient system of law, known as Brehon law, which actually listed women's rights. This was unheard of under English law and was deeply unsettling to the colonists, especially when the women in question – who had, after all, the power to participate in war councils – were of the stature of Iníon Dubh.

Iníon Dubh (Dark Daughter) was the nickname of Fionnghuala MacDonnell, an ambitious political mover and shaker. She was the daughter of James MacDonnell, lord of the isles. His territory comprised parts of County Antrim and some Irish and Scottish islands, such as Rathlin and Islay. As part of an ongoing feud between the MacDonnells and the O'Neills, James was killed by Shane O'Neill, his main rival and the most powerful chief in Ulster. It was politically expedient for his widow, Iníon Dubh's

Scottish mother, Agnes Campbell, to marry Shane's successor, Turlough Luineach O'Neill, and move to County Tyrone in Northern Ireland.

Sometime around 1570, Iníon Dubh was married off to Aodh Dubh O'Donnell, known as The O'Donnell, lord of Tyrconnell (Donegal) and the chief of her kinspeople, the O'Donnell clan. Iníon Dubh brought to the alliance 1,000 Antrim-Scots soldiers, known as gallowglasses. As was usual in Brehon law, goods brought to the marriage by the bride remained her property and could be deployed as and when she chose; in the sixteenth century, soldiers qualified as 'goods'.

Iníon Dubh was ambitious and it was not long before she was openly acknowledged as the 'head of advice and counsel' to her ageing husband. After The O'Donnell became senile, she not only controlled the territory and finances of Tyrconnell, but, as she was entitled to in law, negotiated with The O'Neill and other chieftains instead of and on behalf of The O'Donnell. Meanwhile, Iníon Dubh was also busy raising her four children: Red Hugh (Aodh Rua), Nuala, Rory and Cathbharr.

In 1587 the seventeen-year-old Red Hugh was captured along with his two friends, Donal Gorm MacSweeney and Eoghan mac Toole O'Gallagher, and held hostage in Dublin Castle by lord deputy Sir John Perrot. His mother spent the next five years trying to get him out of the Castle, while at the same time managing her husband's territory. Next to securing Red Hugh's release, her main concern was to defend her son's claim to the chieftaincy of the O'Donnell clan, and in this she was prepared to do all that was necessary.

In 1588 Hugh Gavelach O'Neill (Aodh Ó Gallchuabhair), her husband's nephew and her son's main rival for the chieftainship, attempted a coup to take the O'Donnell lands by force. Iníon Dubh had him killed by her own loyal gallowglasses. Two years later her stepson, Donnell O'Donnell, incited and bribed by the English, tried the same thing. Iníon Dubh had him killed as well.

Meanwhile, in December 1591, Red Hugh, along with his friend, cousin and fellow prisoner Art O'Neill, escaped from Dublin Castle's dungeons. After a horrendous winter journey across the mountains, Red Hugh reached home, but he was suffering from severe frostbite, which resulted in the amputation of his toes. Art did not make it home – he died of exposure in the mountains.

By 1592 Red Hugh was fully recovered and ready to take on his new role. Having got rid of the rest of the opposition, Red Hugh's only real remaining rival for the chieftaincy was Niall Garbh O'Donnell, his father's grand-nephew. Iníon Dubh was worried about the ambitious Niall Garbh and effectively got rid of him too when, in an astute political move, she gave him her only daughter, Nuala, in marriage. Iníon Dubh persuaded her husband to abdicate, whereupon she at last saw her son inaugurated as The O'Donnell, chief of the clan.

Over the next nine years, Red Hugh O'Donnell joined forces with The O'Neill, earl of Tyrone, and Ireland came closer to driving the English out than it ever had before. But on a freezing Christmas Eve in 1601, at Kinsale in County Cork, all was lost. The decisive battle was played out between the English forces, led by Charles Blount, Lord Mountjoy, the lord deputy of Ireland,

and the Irish O'Donnell–O'Neill forces joined by the troops of their Spanish ally, Del Águila. Things did not go well for the Irish: some of the Spanish troops refused to come to the battlefield; The O'Neill and his men became disorientated in the foul, misty weather conditions; key players, such as Iníon Dubh's erstwhile son-in-law, Niall Garbh, went over to the English side.

The crushing, bloody defeat of the Irish took just three hours to accomplish. After the rout, the cream of the Irish nobility were forced to flee to the Continent – an event that has since been commemorated in story and song as the Flight of the Earls – robbing Ireland of its leaders and ending any hope of overthrowing the English invaders.

All of Iníon Dubh's sons were dead by 1608: Red Hugh in 1602 of poisoning; Rory in 1608; and Cathbharr in 1608. Her daughter, Nuala, spent her life defending her young nephew. The boy, also called Hugh, was the son of Cathbharr O'Donnell and his wife, Rosa O'Doherty, and was therefore Red Hugh's nephew and the heir to the chieftaincy. In 1608 too, the treacherous Niall Garbh was sent to the Tower of London, accused of treason – the vengeful Iníon Dubh had implicated him in a rising of the O'Doherty clan in County Derry. He died a broken man, in prison, eighteen years later.

As for the Dark One herself, she retired to Kilmacrenan, once the heartland of the ancient O'Donnell territory, where she lived out the rest of her life in relative peace and quiet. The title of The O'Donnell, leader of the clan, which Iníon Dubh had fought so hard to protect, still exists and is held by a descendant of Niall Garbh.

Máire Rua O'Brien

1615–1686

Landowner

The Máire Rua of legend was quite a woman: tyrannical, power-hungry and as strong as a man, she is also described as being so lustful that she took a different soldier to bed every night, then had him killed in the morning. She also devised a cruel test for her many suitors. They had to stay in the saddle on her wild white stallion as it galloped towards the Cliffs of Moher. The story goes that when one suitor managed it and galloped back to claim his prize, Máire closed her castle gates against him. The stallion leapt the gates in desperation, dying horribly in the attempt. The stallion's loyalty is remembered in the name of the castle, which is called Leamaneh, or, in Irish, *Léim an Eich*, which means Horse's Leap.

The story of the real Máire Rua differs, in most respects. She was an ancestor of the barons of Inchiquin, County Clare, the senior branch of the important O'Brien clan. The real Máire probably became mixed up with the man-eating legend because she was indeed married several times, and each marriage was profitable. Tall and red-haired, Máire was also assertive and politically fickle, even for the notoriously flexible seventeenth century.

Máire Rua was born into affluence at Bunratty Castle, County Limerick. Her mother was the daughter of the third earl of Thomond and her father was Torlach MacMahon, lord of Clonderlaw, a barony midway between Kildysert and Kilrush in County Clare. When she reached marriageable age – about fifteen years old – a good match was made for her with a local landowning gentleman, Daniel Neylon. Daniel died when Máire Rua was still only in her twenties, leaving her with four children and total control of his estate at Dysert O'Dea, north County Clare.

This sort of wealthy independence was unusual and made Márie Rua a woman to be envied far and wide. But within the year, Máire had married again and this time it was for love. The bridegroom was a cousin of hers, Conor O'Brien. The couple lived on the O'Brien estate at Leamaneh, on the edge of the Burren, County Clare, where they rebuilt the family's old tower house in modern (some said ostentatious) style. Between them they owned vast tracts of land, but they were greedy and wanted more – especially the fertile land that had recently been settled by the English planters.

As Oliver Cromwell's reign of destruction gathered momentum in the 1640s, the opportunistic O'Briens took part in local skirmishes against recently settled English tenants. Máire Rua herself rode out in ambush gangs alongside Conor and killed men with her own hands. As Cromwell's campaign of terror continued, they persisted in attacking and ambushing Cromwellian soldiers. However, one night a Cromwellian soldier managed to shoot Conor. After a happy twelve-year marriage, which had produced eight children, Máire Rua was a widow once more.

Within two years of Conor's death, Cromwell had subjugated the Irish and the wily Máire Rua realised she was on the losing side. In order to protect Leamaneh and the inheritance of her O'Brien children, she switched allegiance. Around 1553 she married a low-ranking Cromwellian soldier, John Cooper, thereby making an Englishman the legal owner of Leamaneh. The

Coopers had one son.

Once again Máire Rua had chosen a mate as greedy as herself, and she and John became very wealthy through clever land deals. Máire Rua lived in comfort for the next decade, but with the death of Cromwell and the Restoration of King Charles II in 1660, she found herself on the wrong side yet again. Worse still, murder charges relating to the ambush parties she had taken part in twenty years earlier came back to haunt her. Her neck was saved when the easygoing Charles II granted her a pardon in 1664.

Máire Rua separated from John Cooper, who then lost all their money. Despite all her efforts of the previous decades, she was forced to sell up and leave Leamaneh. She took up residence at Dromoland Castle, County Clare. Through one of Máire's sons, Donough O'Brien, who was created a baron by King James II, Dromoland eventually became the official seat of the barons of Inchiquin. Máire Rua died there peacefully in 1686 and was buried in Ennis Abbey beside Conor O'Brien, the love of her life.

Biddy Early
1798–1874

Healer

The mysterious powers of the wise woman, or *bean feasa*, Biddy Early were renowned throughout the province of Munster. She could cure animals of ailments, commune with 'the little people' (fairies) and predict the future. WB Yeats called her 'the wisest of wise women' and Lady Augusta Gregory went to her house in person to collect stories about her. She is still remembered in story and song.

The facts of Biddy's life have become confused in the telling and retelling. It seems she was born on a farm in Faha, near Feakle, County Clare, to Thomas O'Connor and his wife, Ellen Early. It is said she married six times, once to her own stepson, and had three children, but she always retained her mother's name as it was through her mother that she had received her gifts.

When she was only sixteen, Biddy's parents died and she went into a hellish workhouse in Ennis. To get out of it, she started travelling the roads and visiting fairs. On her travels she met her first husband, a widower named Malley or O'Malley from Feakle way. Her husband was elderly and Biddy was widowed quite soon, whereupon she promptly married her husband's son.

It was in the 1820s that Biddy's reputation as a wise woman began to spread. She knew how to use wild herbs to treat people and cattle. The well-being of livestock could often mean the difference between life and death for a poor family in the southwest, so Biddy's skill was invaluable, and people came to her from far and wide. It was at this point that Biddy also came into possession of her famous blue bottle. This charmed object was variously said to have come either from the Sídhe (fairies) or from a baby son of hers who had died. By gazing into this bottle she could see the future. Such was her fame that, in 1828, no less than 'the Liberator' himself, Daniel O'Connell, came to visit her cottage – no doubt wondering how he would do in the forthcoming Clare by-election. (He won.)

In 1840 Biddy married yet again and settled in Kilbarron, County Clare, the place that today is most associated with her memory. Here she continued with her treatments and mediated between the locals and 'the little people'.

Although devoutly Catholic, most country people believed in the Otherworld and went out of their way to placate the fairies. Biddy would look into her magical bottle and proffer advice: for example, do not allow animals to graze near a fairy fort; leave out food for the fairies; cut back bushes from a fairy path, and so on. Biddy's reward for predicting the future, lifting curses and curing animals usually took the form of food or, better still, a jug of *poitín*, to which she was rather partial.

This sort of behaviour made Biddy unpopular with the local clergy, who tried to ban her neighbours from consulting her and even denounced her from the pulpit. One apocryphal story relates how a priest came to rebuke Biddy, whereupon she cast a spell on his horse, making it incapable of movement. After a few minutes of beating the horse, the priest had to return to Biddy's house and ask her to lift the spell he didn't believe in.

In 1865 the combination of severe clerical disapproval, the efficacy of her cures and a minor role she played in protecting local rebels, landed Biddy in court in Ennis, accused of witchcraft under a 300-year-old Elizabethan law. She was luckier than many others before her who had gone to the stake for similar 'crimes' – her case was dropped due to 'lack of evidence', in other words, none of the locals would testify against her.

Widowed again in 1868, Biddy managed to bribe a final husband into marrying her when she was in her seventies. He was a sickly young man who had come to her looking for help. Biddy promised to cure his illness on condition that he marry her. The young man agreed, but he passed away shortly after the wedding. Clearly, Biddy's powers were on the wane.

Biddy Early spent her final years living quietly in her cottage in Kilbarron and saying her rosary. She died after a short illness in April 1874, aged seventy-six. Before her death she made her neighbours promise to throw the supernatural blue bottle into the middle of Kilbarron Lough, where people continue to look for it to this day. A reconstruction of her little cottage has been built, overlooking the lake, and is open to visitors.

Molly Brown
1867–1932
Society figure and philanthropist

Mrs Molly Brown – the 'unsinkable', as she famously dubbed herself – was a raconteur and teller of tall tales, an energetic society hostess and charity worker, and a survivor of the *Titanic* disaster of 1912. She managed to embellish her rags-to-riches story until she became a legend in her own lifetime.

Molly Brown was born Margaret Tobin in Hannibal, Missouri, to Johanna Collins and John Tobin, a manual labourer and survivor of the Great Famine. She was the second of the family's four children, born in a dirt-poor shack in the Irish shanty town area of the fledgling city. Maggie – she was never called Molly –

was barely educated when she started working full-time in her early teens.

At nineteen she married the thirty-one-year-old John James Brown (known as JJ), another Irish-American and an engineer of some renown. The two moved into JJ's basic log cabin in the mining town of Leadville, Colorado, where Maggie bore two children, a boy and a girl.

In 1894 JJ Brown discovered one of the largest silver lodes in the USA and became a millionaire overnight. The delighted Maggie immediately started scheming to have the kind of life she had always dreamed of. Step one was to move into a great mansion in one of the best areas of Denver, Colorado. Once established there, Maggie threw lavish parties, went to the opera and got her clothes made in Paris. Yet in spite of her extravagant hospitality, she was not welcome in the best houses in Denver and was not accepted by the social élite. The determined Maggie redoubled her efforts. She posed for photographs dripping in jewels, learned foreign languages and invented wild stories about her own childhood and the origins of the Brown wealth. This immoderate behaviour only served to make her even more of an outcast in Denver society. The Browns were regarded by the 'old' Denver families as hopelessly *nouveau riche* – vulgar savages who needed to be kept firmly in their place.

Over time, Maggie and JJ became estranged and eventually he left her, but she continued to live life to the full with her parties and her travelling. In April 1912 she took the most fateful trip of her life when she boarded the *Titanic* to visit her sick grandson in the USA (she was visiting Ireland at the time). When the great ship went down, Maggie was flung into a lifeboat with more than a dozen other women and two men who were supposed to be in charge.

According to her own version, one of the men was panicking and she quickly seized control of the little boat, organised the women to row and shared around her warm clothing. When the survivors were picked up by *Carpathia*, Maggie immediately started fund-raising efforts and obtained nearly $10,000 worth of pledges for the worst-off victims of the disaster. On reaching New York, she grandly announced to the press that her luck was typical of the Browns: 'We're unsinkable,' she proclaimed. On the other side of the country, JJ Brown was heard muttering bitterly that his wife was 'too mean to sink'. It was at this point that the press gave Maggie her famous nickname, the Unsinkable Molly Brown.

Back in Denver, the snobbish set now welcomed Maggie with open arms and, for a time, she was the queen of society as well as the darling of the newspapers. But despite using her influence to campaign on behalf of those left destitute by the tragedy, Maggie did not make herself popular. Addicted to her fame, she became ever more blunt, ever more outspoken and her stories became ever more wild – all of which made her enemies.

In World War I, the ageing Maggie reinvented herself as an entertainer for the troops and received a *Légion d'honneur* from the French government. After the war she became active as a suffragette and joined the National Women's Party, at one point haranguing president Calvin Coolidge on the subject of equal rights.

In 1922 Maggie's estranged husband died intestate, leaving

Maggie penniless. She spent the next five years alienating both her children by fighting with them for a share of their father's money, which, because of her extravagance, was now a very depleted fortune. She got just about enough money to last her to the end of her days, as she became older, frailer and more friendless. In October 1932, in a small hotel frequented by young, poor actresses, the Unsinkable Molly Brown died of a stroke. The legend she built around herself lives on.

Kathleen Behan
1889–1984
Republican and mother of Brendan and Dominic Behan

The mother of writer, Brendan, and singer-songwriter, Dominic, Kathleen was herself renowned as a wit and regarded as one of Dublin's many 'characters'. She was born Kathleen Kearney into a poor Catholic family in Capel Street's tenement slums. As a result of her father's inability to handle money, the family fell into hardship. Her father died when she was nine years old and she was sent to an orphanage in Goldenbridge where she stayed until the age of fifteen.

Kathleen's family were steeped in republicanism – in 1907 her brother, Peader Kearney, co-wrote the lyrics to the future Irish national anthem, 'Amhrán na bhFiann' ('A Soldier's Song'). Kathleen was only a teenager herself when she became active in the turbulent politics of early twentieth-century Dublin, joining

Cumann na mBan and couriering despatches to Patrick Pearse and James Connolly during the 1916 Rising.

Kathleen married Jack Furlong in 1916. Her husband had fought in and survived the Easter Rising, but he subsequently died in the great 'flu epidemic of 1918, leaving her a widow with two small children. She asked Constance Markievicz to find her work, and Constance suggested employment in the home of Maud Gonne. Kathleen stayed there as receptionist/ housekeeper for nearly a year. After this she worked for Dublin Corporation and became active in the White Cross. In this milieu she became well-known throughout Dublin for her wit and forthright views.

Kathleen married a second time in 1922 to republican Stephen Behan. Just weeks after the wedding, he started a two-year sentence in Kilmainham Jail for his political activities. After his release, the couple went on to have five children, including Brendan and Dominic, and the whole family lived in one room in a tenement building in Russell Street.

Despite their humble surroundings there was plenty of culture in the house: Stephen read the classics to his children and Kathleen sang light opera to them. Their tenement building was condemned in 1935, and in 1939 the Behans moved to a modern housing estate in Crumlin, which Kathleen hated because she was lonely and missed the inner-city life and people she knew so well.

Kathleen was crucial in forming the political and cultural characters of all her children and she encouraged them towards republicanism, even when it resulted in Brendan's seven-year prison sentence for IRA activities in 1939. Two of her children, including

Brendan, and her husband died before her and her other five children emigrated to England.

Kathleen broke into the limelight again in her eighties with her memories and her marbles intact. She appeared on RTÉ and BBC television in 1970, made a folk album in 1981 and published her autobiography in 1984 – all while in her nineties. She died, aged almost ninety-five, in the Dublin nursing home where she had been living for many years.

INTREPID TRAVELLERS

'Flying is really absurdly easy.'
Lady Mary Heath

Lola Montez

c. 1820–1861

Dancer and courtesan

'Shameless devil', 'fraud', 'sorceress' and 'concubine' were just some of the epithets applied to Lola Montez, the most notorious woman of her day.

Lola was born Eliza Rosana Gilbert in Limerick around 1820. Her father, Edward Gilbert, was an English ensign stationed in Cork City where he met, seduced and quickly impregnated a fourteen-year-old milliner's assistant, Eliza Oliver, the youngest of the four illegitimate children of a County Cork squire. After Eliza's baby was born, the pair married quietly and the young father continued with his army career in Sligo and Roscommon.

When Lola was three years old the family was posted to India. Near Patna, on the last leg of their long journey, Edward Gilbert died of cholera. A widow before she was twenty, and with a small daughter to support, Mrs Gilbert's objective was simple: she had to remarry as soon as was decently possible. This she did in 1824, the summer after her husband's death, giving Lola as a stepfather the kind and caring lieutenant Craigie from Scotland.

Lola was left pretty much to her own devices over the next two years as her shallow and stupid mother concentrated on dazzling the expat community in northern India. When Lola was six, Mama decided she was a burden and should go to school in a country she'd only ever heard of, in the care of a step-grandfather she'd never seen. Mrs Craigie packed Lola onto a ship bound for freezing eastern Scotland; they didn't meet again for eleven years.

Little Lola lodged with various associates of her stepfather, who paid for a good education. By the time she was sixteen and at school in Bath, Lola could speak French, play the piano and dance, but she was already exhibiting her two defining characteristics: the unfortunate combination of extreme prettiness and excessive wilfulness. Curvaceous, black-haired and blue-eyed, she was unsettlingly gorgeous to those around her, but she was also considered vain, dishonest, extravagant, wayward and mischievous.

When Lola was seventeen the lackadaisical Mrs Craigie was finally persuaded to come to Bath and take control. The plan was to prepare Lola for life as a respectable married woman in India. But Lola had other ideas. After her mother's arrival, she took one look at the young 'gallant friend' who was accompanying her, a lieutenant Thomas James from County Wexford, and promptly eloped with him.

This was the first in a long list of scandals in Lola's short life. She was a minor and lieutenant James was practically the first man she had ever met. But the scandal of their elopement was hushed up and the pair were married quietly in Dublin. Afterwards they visited the James's family home in Ballycrystal, which, with its hunting and 'innumerable cups of tea', Lola hated with a passion. The following year they set sail for India.

Lola had rushed into 'a runaway match', as she called it, in her quest for freedom and adventure, but she quickly realised she had saddled herself with a master, and a mean-spirited one at that. The Jameses cut a handsome figure at his posting in northern India, but underneath it all Lola was bored, James was bitter and they both regretted the marriage. When James started to hit Lola, she left him and sought refuge with her mother. Mrs Craigie was horrified by the prospect of having to be responsible for Lola again, and instead made her choose between returning home to her abusive husband or returning alone to England. Lola chose England and set sail in autumn 1840.

Early Victorian England could cope with old maids, wives or widows, but nothing in between. There was no place for a woman who had left her husband. Lola had enough money to just about survive upon her arrival in England. If she wanted to supplement her income respectably, she could be either a governess or a lady's companion, and that was it. Faced with this situation, Lola chose an entirely different life: she took up with an attractive and aristocratic lieutenant, George Lennox, and by the time the ship docked in England, they were lovers. Lola was on the road to ruin.

Pleas from her stepfamily to save her reputation by going to live quietly in Scotland fell on deaf ears. Lola was in love with Lennox and lived happily as his mistress in London, naïvely believing that he would one day marry her. But by her actions, Lola had become the sort of woman Victorian gentlemen didn't marry, and eventually Lennox took himself back to the bosom of his well-bred family.

Shortly afterwards, lieutenant James divorced her – not in the polite, gentlemanly way of most middle-class divorces but as meanly and as vindictively as he could. He cited Lola's adultery with Lennox, destroying any chance she might have had of redeeming herself in society and depriving her of the possibility of remarriage.

After her divorce, the twenty-two-year-old Lola quickly went to the bad, entertaining a string of lovers at her London lodgings and allowing herself to be squired around town by a series of well-heeled bachelors. Always an exhibitionist, she decided that life on the stage was for her, so she took basic Spanish dancing lessons and then travelled to Spain. By the time she returned, she had reinvented herself: no longer Eliza James, disgraced wife and deserted lover, she was now Donna Lola Montez, exotic *artiste* of the dance and tragic Spanish war widow.

In 1843 Lola made her début at Her Majesty's Theatre, Haymarket. Throughout her career her dancing received a very mixed reception – some found her exciting, dazzling, exotic, even gifted, while others found her vulgar, unorthodox and totally without rhythm. Most, however, admitted she had nice legs.

While Lola was not entirely talent-free, she had started too late in life to become really good. She was certainly somewhat limited: she had just three dances in her repertoire, but these included the risqué Spider Dance in which she searched her skirts for tarantulas in a suggestive manner. She devised this dance herself, basing it on a half-remembered Spanish country dance. She wore relatively short skirts for the performance and took the whole thing terribly seriously, even as the members of the audience was splitting their sides laughing. As she perfected the routine it became more suggestive – she lifted up her skirts in her search for the elusive spiders.

After the London stage had grown tired of Lola and her three dances, she travelled to Europe. She spent the next eight years travelling, looking for work and letting her volcanic temper get the better of her wherever she went. She visited a principality in southeast Germany and was asked to leave by the prince after only a few days. She then visited Dresden and Berlin, and was asked to leave the latter after slashing a policeman with her horsewhip. Then it was on to Warsaw where she managed to make an enemy of the director of the city's biggest theatre; then to St Petersburg where she performed only once before leaving under the cloud of her by now noisome reputation.

Then, *en route* to the Paris Opéra – a Mecca for all performers – Lola met and managed to attach herself, limpet-like, to the celebrated composer Franz Liszt. Lola followed Liszt to Dresden where, according to him, they spent a passionate week together in a hotel room. But once again Lola disgraced herself. She got involved in a violent late-night fracas, and slapped the face of an Italian operatic tenor. Liszt had her locked in their hotel room, paid the hotel manager damages in advance for the destruction he knew she would cause – and made good his escape.

In 1844 Lola finally hit Paris. She got the inevitable mixed reviews at the Paris Opéra, but her love life improved. She was taken under the wing of a powerful and influential lover, Henri Dujarier, a journalist and the editor of the influential *La Presse*. Dujarier financially supported his 'dear little girl', raised her profile in the press and got her more engagements; for her part, Lola really seemed to love him. Then the first genuine tragedy of Lola's life struck. Dujarier was killed in 1845 in a dawn duel over a card game, and Lola was once again alone.

At twenty-four years old, Lola was at the height of her beauty but penniless. She managed to keep up appearances by 'borrowing' money from friends and lovers. Continually in need of funds due to the patchiness of her dancing engagements and her extravagant lifestyle, Lola tended to attach herself to men who were able to pay her way. However, she was not a gold-digger – she did not trade sexual favours for cash and she would generously pay her own and everyone else's costs when she had money, though this was rarely the case.

Lola travelled incessantly: fashionable Baden-Baden (from where she was expelled after throwing her leg over the shoulder of a man in public), back to Paris (which she quickly escaped to avoid her creditors), then on to Brussels, Heidelberg, Homburg, Stuttgart and Munich. In Munich, Lola met the man who was to be her most famous and exalted lover: sixty-year-old King Ludwig of Bavaria.

The next two years saw the meteoric rise and catastrophic fall of Lola Montez. Within weeks, Ludwig was bewitched by the raven-haired exotic dancer. He gave her a house, jewellery and money. He made her the countess of Landsfeld. She could do no wrong in his eyes and she exercised huge influence over the besotted old king. Lola had never been political, but she hated authority and was, essentially, a free-thinker. She turned Ludwig against the conservative elements of the government – especially the powerful Jesuits in the court. She formed what amounted to a private army of politically active students, whose motto was 'Lola and Liberty'. This 'army' was known as the Allemania and was a sort of student bodyguard for Lola. The members kept themselves aloof from the student body and were rather disreputable.

Lola became so dangerously unpopular with ordinary people that mobs used to descend on her in the street. Finally, in 1848 – the year of revolution in Europe – the once-beloved King Ludwig was forced to abdicate in favour of his son, the Crown Prince Maximilian, who became King Maximilian II of Bavaria. One hour after the abdication the government banished Lola from Bavaria forever.

Following Lola's banishment and Ludwig's abdication, their relationship limped on by letter, but out-of-sight proved to be out-of-mind and soon there was another husband in the offing for Lola. In the summer of 1850, thirty-year-old Lola married a handsome twenty-one-year-old English army officer, George Heald, in London – bigamously, of course, since the terms of her divorce did not allow for remarriage. The couple honeymooned in Spain, Lola's supposed 'homeland'. Due to her murky marital status, Lola risked jail if she returned to England so the couple lived the high life in Paris. And it was in Paris, after less than a year of marriage, that George Heald, sick of continual squabbling, money worries, scandal and house moves, abandoned his wife and went home.

Alone once again, it was time for Lola to assess her situation. She was now thirty-one – rather old for a not-very-good dancer. Nevertheless, she still had to live. She wrote her autobiography, danced frenziedly all over France and Belgium to earn and save some money and then packed her bags once again and headed for the USA.

In December 1851 a new chapter opened in the chequered career of Lola Montez as she landed in New York City. Lola had begun to realise she could capitalise on the only thing that was indisputably hers: the story of her life. Within weeks of her arrival she was was on Broadway starring in a stage play named *Lola*

Montez in Bavaria, in which history was cavalierly rewritten to make Lola the heroic innocent at the centre of the Bavarian revolution. For once she got good reviews. Her acting turned out to be vastly superior to her dancing, and in New York, Philadelphia and other cities she made a lot of money.

More plays followed and Lola performed in the south and all along the eastern seaboard. But the increased prosperity and success did not seem to have improved her infamous temper. In New Orleans she was arrested for assaulting her maid and had to fake a suicide attempt to get the charges dropped. In St Louis there was a further fracas and a court appearance when Lola kicked and punched a prompter.

In 1853 Lola sailed for San Francisco, California. She was a huge success in the west, starring in humorous plays and resurrecting the infamous Spider Dance. That same year, in a Catholic ceremony, she married a thirty-two-year-old journalist, PP Hull. She apparently believed a report she had heard that husband number two, Heald, had drunk himself to death, and by now she seems to have genuinely believed that her marriage to husband number one, lieutenant James, was somehow invalid. Bigamous or not, the marriage was less than three months old when Hull left, never to return. (He died shortly afterwards of a stroke.)

In 1855, on foot of her successes in America, Lola departed on an Australian tour. Again, in the more liberal atmosphere of a young country she met with less censure and more full houses, but her personal life was still troubled. She fell in love with her married acting partner, twenty-seven-year-old Frank Folland. Their tempestuous affair continued for the duration of the whole tour, from

Sydney to Melbourne and on to Adelaide, but tragedy struck Lola once again on the return voyage in 1856. After a night's drinking session, Frank disappeared from the deck of the ship. It was never established whether he fell over by accident, committed suicide, or was pushed by person or persons unknown.

Lola was devastated and held herself responsible for Folland's death. Now thirty-six, losing her looks and in increasingly poor health, this latest loss seemed to change her. She began to think about life after death and took to reading religious tracts. Back in the States her personal life went quiet. She no longer had pressing money problems so she sold all her jewellery at auction and sent the proceeds to Folland's stepmother to be held in trust for his two children. She even moved to New York City to be nearer all of Folland's dependants – his mother, sister, two children and ex-wife.

Lola's last acting tour, in 1857 – Albany, Providence, Pittsburgh, St Louis, Cincinnati, Chicago – was a success. Amazingly, Lola was now becoming known more for her good works than her bad behaviour. Her interest in matters of the soul had led her into spiritualism. She attended meetings, visited sick actors and spent a lot of time in study.

Lola knew she was coming to the end of her stage career and cast about for another means of support. She realised that her stage experience, her articulacy and her fame, combined with her love of being in the public eye, meant that she could carve out a career as a lecturer. Engaging the help of an associate of hers, Charles Chauncey Burr, she organised and embarked upon a lecture tour of Canada. She wrote and edited all her own lectures, the subject matter ranging from 'How to Stay Beautiful', 'The Role of the

Catholic Church', 'America and its People', 'Slavery in America', 'Heroines of History' and 'Comic Aspects of Love'. She delivered the pieces like the old pro she now was and the tour was a success.

But Lola still had one last disastrous romantic liaison in her. Some years before coming to America she had met an Austrian aristocrat by the name of prince Ludwig Johann Sulkowski. The two renewed their acquaintance in New York and Lola was left with the quite definite impression that she was to be a princess. In late 1857, she duly sold all her goods and sailed to Paris to meet her prince and marry him. But once in Paris, there was no prince. He did not show up. Lola soon learned that, as he had a wife and several children back in Austria, he was never going to.

She had put all her financial eggs in one basket and was now poor once again, but Lola seems to have been fairly philosophical about this last matrimonial setback, and apart from diligently saving face in the press by claiming that she herself had broken her engagement, she forgot about the prince and went on with her lecturing. She re-made her fortune yet again by publishing her lectures and a surprisingly commonsensical beauty manual, one of the earliest of its kind.

In November 1858, Lola returned to Ireland for the first time in more than twenty years. She lectured in Galway, Dublin, Cork and Limerick and then sailed to Scotland and England. In 1859 she completed her final lecture tour in the States: Philadelphia, Pennsylvania, Ohio, Indiana, Chicago, Toronto and back to New York City.

Wealthy enough to take a break, she became involved in supporting the Magdalen Society in New York, a charitable institution for fallen women. But if the racy Lola Montez was getting ready for a middle age filled with philanthropic deeds, her ambitions were to remain unfulfilled. In June 1860 she had a massive stroke and nearly died. Against all the odds, and no doubt utilising her famous wilfulness, she clawed back to mobility and was walking again, slowly, by the Christmas of that year. But in the New Year, in her weakened state, she came down with pneumonia. She died on 17 January 1861, at the age of forty-one. She is buried in Brooklyn, New York.

Daisy Bates
1862–1951
Anthropologist

Daisy Bates was one of the great Irish eccentrics. She struck out alone in middle age to live the hard life of the Australian Aboriginal. Distrustful of her own kind and ferociously independent, Daisy was also a snob who constantly lied about her background and exaggerated her own importance. Yet her life was a story of unconditional love for the most powerless and vulnerable of peoples – the black outcasts of white Australia – and she was uniquely knowledgeable about the southern and western Australian people with whom she lived for nearly forty years.

Daisy's birthplace could not have been more different from the place she was to spend most of her long life. She was born in the green and fertile townland of Kilnamanagh, near Roscrea, in

County Tipperary, on 16 October 1862. Her family name was O'Dwyer, a family of the old Gaelic order. Daisy fancifully claimed that by the time of her birth her family had become absorbed into the Protestant middle class. According to her own wildly contradictory accounts, her rich parents died and she was reared by her grandmother, a fine old lady. In reality, this is an unlikely story. Daisy probably came from a poor, Catholic background, was raised in an orphanage and educated in a charity school.

Wherever she was raised, what is certain is that Daisy was bright, ambitious and could not wait to get out of Ireland. In 1883, after training as a governess, she embarked on the first of her many long journeys: she headed for a remote sheep station in northern Queensland, Australia.

Daisy was happy working at the station, but the following year she made a mistake. After a whirlwind romance, she married a dashing and unreliable horse-breaker called Murrant, who left her just five weeks later and was never seen again. She covered up this indiscretion by moving to New South Wales and starting afresh. In 1885 she (bigamously) married a station-owner called John Bates, and in 1887 they had a son, Arnold.

Already craving freedom, it seemed Daisy was not the marrying – or even the maternal – kind. In 1894 she left her little boy and husband and sailed to England 'for a holiday'. Once there she found work on a magazine, the *Review of Reviews*, owned by the well-known journalist and feminist WT Stead. She then worked for the London *Times* and found there was a lot of interest in what was happening to the natives of Australia. In 1899, five years after her departure, Daisy returned to Australia with a brief to report on the mistreatment of the Aboriginals. For Daisy it would become more than a job – it would be her vocation.

In her late thirties, after a half-hearted attempt to reconcile with her husband and son, Daisy moved to Western Australia on her own. She had made the acquaintance of a priest on her last sea voyage and now she accompanied him from Perth to Broome to camp near a religious mission in Beagle Bay and research the local tribes. She spent the next few years in different camps in the west, learning Aboriginal languages, customs, rites and legends. Daisy kept copious notes on everything and by 1905 she was considered enough of an authority to be given a grant by the Western Australian government to continue her research.

In 1910 the government asked her to assist a Cambridge anthropologist, Professor AR Radcliffe-Brown, with his research into Aboriginal kinship systems. With mind-boggling inhumanity, the government seemed to be legislating against the Aboriginals to the point of extinction, while at the same time collecting data against the day when there might not be any Aboriginals to legislate against. The Aboriginal population was being decimated by diseases carried by settlers, especially venereal disease, which Aboriginals called 'white-fella sickness'.

Daisy and Radcliffe-Brown spent most of their time together working in the euphemistically named 'hospital islands'. These were two small uninhabited islands that were used by the government to ghettoise sick and dying Aboriginal people. Daisy translated for Radcliffe-Brown, mediated between him and the tribal people, gave him access to her notes and even lent him money. It was after her time at the hospital islands that she acquired the affectionate Aboriginal name of Kabbarli, or Grandmother.

In 1912 the vigorous fifty-year-old Daisy travelled to the tiny settlement of Eucla on the vast, inhospitable Nullarbor Plain, which stretches across Western Australia and South Australia. Here she started a new phase of her outback life. She lived in a tent, surviving largely on tea, bread and bush tucker – wombat, emu, grubs and lizards. She spent her time caring for what she had come to regard as 'her people'.

Two years after moving to Eucla, she was asked to speak at a conference in Adelaide. To the amazement of the other conferees, she got to Adelaide by camel buggy across more than 200 miles (390 km) of the unforgiving Nullarbor Plain, accompanied by two friends.

But once in Adelaide it seemed Daisy Bates had already out-lived her usefulness. She spoke but no one listened. Those in power had ceased to take her seriously and now considered her a harmless, slightly batty, middle-aged woman. Some felt that her work among the Aboriginals actually damaged their cause in the long run because she wanted to keep them separate and 'wild' rather than assimilated on reservations. Dispirited after the conference, Daisy left Eucla and set up a new camp further inland and east along the great Australian Bight, at a spot called Yalata. Surrounded by Aboriginal friends who had followed her from Eucla, she lived here for three years.

In 1918 Daisy had a nervous breakdown and was confined to a hospital in Adelaide. When she emerged it was into a world changed beyond belief by World War I. She responded to the outward transformation and her own inward cataclysm by retreating once again to the Nullarbor Plain, this time more than 400 miles (645 km) inland, at the very edge of the desert, to Ooldea.

By the time Daisy got to Ooldea in 1919 it was a dreary railway siding with a transient population. Originally a meeting place for nomadic Aboriginals, it had an ancient, life-sustaining waterhole, which had sustained them for millennia. But when the railway came it used so much water that it changed the water table and then polluted what was left. Whites would work on the railway line and move on, and they were not impressed with the little Irish lady in Edwardian clothes who let the side down by living among 'the blacks'. The Aboriginals were mainly transient too. They would emerge, naked, from the desert and camp with Kabbarli for a while at Ooldea. Then, irresistibly drawn to the promise of plenty 'further down the line', they would disappear, only to return later, exploited, disillusioned and sick.

Surrounded by a small group of permanent friends who lived alongside her camp and treated her as one of their own, Daisy would nurse her 'poor children' when she could and bury them when she had to. All the time she wrote incessantly about their culture and movements, and she lived on the little income forthcoming from articles published in magazines such as *The Australasian*. Daisy saw herself not as a bridge but as a barrier between the Aboriginals and the 'white fellas' – she wanted to protect her loved ones from what she called 'the contamination of civilisation'. Lasting fourteen years, Ooldea was to be her longest stay in one place.

In 1932, at the age of seventy, Daisy left the sand dune she had called home for so long. She wanted to go to the big city and write her book, *The Passing of the Aborigines.* The book was published in the UK in 1938 and in Australia in 1946. Un-PC though it certainly is, it is an absorbing account of the life and culture of the dying tribes of the Nyool-Nyool, Bibbulmun, Baduwonga, Kaalurwonga and Baadu, among others. It shows very clearly that Daisy Bates loved and respected the 'lost people', and that she knew what she was talking about.

Daisy could not settle in the city. Despite the recognition she had received – she had been made South Australia's first woman justice of the peace in 1920 and she was awarded a CBE in 1934 – she just was not prepared to give in and be an old lady. In 1941, aged nearly eighty and still wearing the high collars, hats and long skirts of her youth, Daisy set off into the desert once again, this time to a spot called Wynbring, east of Ooldea, looking perhaps to relive the happy days she had spent at Ooldea.

It was not to be. Things were too difficult. Her sight was poor, most of the old-style Aboriginal people she had known were dead and gone, and she found some of the up-and-coming generation had serious social problems which she simply was not equipped to deal with. In addition, the local whites hated her for encouraging Aboriginals to come and camp near the settlement, and they made life even more difficult for her whenever they could.

Finally, in 1948, after persevering in a tent for four years at Wynbring and living another three years in a hotel at Streaky Bay on the south coast, age and infirmity drove Daisy back to Adelaide. Losing her mental faculties but still sprightly enough to make a run for it, she had to be watched constantly by a female acquaintance, the journalist Ernestine Hill.

Daisy lasted three years like this, attended all the while by Ernestine. She died in a nursing home on 18 April 1951. She is buried in Adelaide, but there is a plaque to her memory in the tiny settlement of Ooldea.

Beatrice Grimshaw
1871–1953
Travel writer and record-breaking sportswoman

Ethel Beatrice Grimshaw was born into a wealthy, middle-class, Protestant family in Cloona, County Antrim. She had a financially secure upbringing and a good education, and as a young woman in her twenties she found herself with an abundance, as she said, of the '"beans" that goes with a good muscular system'. Bright, stubborn and fiercely independent, Beatrice considered herself a 'Careerist', and as soon as she decently could she left home and went to Dublin to look for work.

While living at 6 Fitzgibbon Street in the city centre, she took up cycling seriously and, in 1892, attempted to break the women's twenty-four-hour world cycling record. Breaking records or no, in late nineteenth-century Dublin the proprieties still had to be observed. Therefore, during the attempt, no man could accompany Beatrice to pace her through the 'improper twelve hours' of the night. Instead, she had to carry her own provisions and cycle alone to a police barracks out in the country to be paced.

In any event, she broke the record by five miles. This

achievement led to her being offered the position of sub-editor on a sporting newspaper – an unusual post for a woman even today – and subsequently she became the editor of a society journal called the *Social Review*.

After four years, Beatrice was bored out of her mind by Dublin, which, she complained, was 'infested by the givers and takers of *loathsome* parties'. She moved to London, seeking variety and a more exciting job. While there, she published *Breakaway* (1897), the first of her thirty-odd novels. The title proved prophetic, for Beatrice's heart's desire was to travel just about as far from home as possible. She approached shipping companies to employ her as a travel writer in return for free passage, and in this unusual manner she wangled a trip that was to last for the rest of her life.

In 1906 Beatrice boarded a Cunard liner at Liverpool and sailed for Tahiti, never to return. In one fell swoop she leapt free from the confines of her tightly buttoned Edwardian world, where young women were watched and chaperoned to within an inch of their lives, to a world where she could roam completely unhindered and, more often than not, enjoy male status while she was at it. She travelled 'alone', which is to say that on the islands she visited she would often have been the only European and certainly the only European woman. Her guides – invariably men – were usually what she called 'mission natives', that is, Christianised locals.

Over the next three decades, Beatrice travelled all over the Eastern and Western Pacific Islands, including the Torres Straits, Fiji, the Moluccas, Tonga, Samoa, the Cook Islands, New Zealand, the New Hebrides, the Solomon Islands and Papua New Guinea. She enjoyed what she called the 'pungent taste of danger', which was just as well since her travels brought her into contact with head-hunting, cannibalism, wild animals and natural disasters. Beatrice was a cool customer. On one boat trip through the rainforest, she realised that she and the crew were very close to witnessing an actual act of cannibalism taking place on the shore. At the same moment she realised they had run aground – and that they were lost. It should have felt like an adventure, she wrote, but it did not. Instead of 'fortifying the ship against attack and ... preparing to sell our lives and our beads and our tomahawks as dearly as possible ... we were complaining about the quality of the coffee and wondering if the rain was going to stop.'

In her later travel books she heartily recommended the Eastern Pacific Islands where cannibalism had been extinct for 'at least two generations'. However, she did not recommend the Western Islands of the New Hebrides or the Solomon Islands because, she claimed, 'the natives' were generally dangerous and almost all cannibals.

Beatrice slept with a revolver under her pillow, ready at all times to thrash any man who tried anything funny. She seems to have had a similarly combative attitude towards Mother Nature, which she saw as beautiful but treacherous. Beatrice took natural phenomena personally, describing an active volcano as 'alive and powerful and infinitely wicked', and a mini-typhoon she witnessed at sea as 'something blind, but mad and cruel'. She dealt well with minor irritations, however, such as sharing her quarters with centipedes as big as sausages, cockroaches who ate her hair while she slept and hermit crabs who fought noisily in the night over who was to occupy an abandoned sardine tin.

At a time when most women worked within the home, Beatrice designed and built her own homes. Her first house was on a tiny island called Sariba, which was a boat-ride away from the nearest 'town' on Samarai Island, off the coast of Papua New Guinea. The house was made of sago palm and bush timber and decorated with pearl shells; after two years there she sold the house to a missionary group and moved on to Papua New Guinea.

She settled in Papua New Guinea for eighteen years, clearing 300 acres of native forest and running coffee and tobacco plantations. It was the longest time she had ever spent in one place, and later she described the 'five stages in solitary bush existence'. Firstly, she admits to loneliness and fear of the night falling, when she would look for people to visit and no one would come. Then she describes resignation, when she would no longer look for company but was also no longer afraid of the dark solitude. Then comes what she calls a 'secret delight', when she describes herself positively revelling in her singular way of life – with the animals, rare orchids and unparalleled scenery, who needed people anyway? Beatrice felt she herself stopped at this stage, but looking at other European settlers she identified two more stages: a determination to remain independent no matter what, followed finally by an active dislike and avoidance of one's own race.

Beatrice became an acknowledged authority on the resources and settlement of the Pacific region, and on the different customs of the many islands she visited. She noted many of these in her travel guides, such as the idea of communal ownership practised by the Samoans, and the Rarotongan tradition of keeping one house for show and one to live in. She wrote incessantly and successfully: thirty-three romantic novels, ten travel books, countless articles for *National Geographic* and *Wide World* and her own autobiography, *Isles of Adventure* (1930).

Her articles and books are super-descriptive and even today give a real taste of life in the South Seas, such as her description of the Kuni, a tribe from a mountainous region who were so used to their hilly homeland that they felt quite uncomfortable on flat land and walked with 'an odd, high-stepping gait'. She offers details of day-to-day living, includes the eating, sleeping and washing habits of all the tribal people she encounters, as well as more lurid descriptions of 5ft (1.5m) birds, deadly snakes and bone-crunching crabs.

She also relates some anecdotes about the ingenuity of the indigenous peoples, such as the tribe whose custom it was, when their local river was in flood, to cross it safely by weighting themselves down with stones and walking underwater across the riverbed to the other side. Finally, Beatrice wrote of her own explorations: she was one of the first European women to explore the Sepik and Fly rivers in Papua New Guinea, and possibly the very first to climb to the top of the 9,000ft (3,000m) mountain on Raratonga.

Much of Beatrice's writing sounds downright racist by today's standards – her superiority complex was certainly as robust as her constitution must have been – but these were the first common-sensical guides to exotic travel written by a woman. Aimed at 'The Man Who Could Not Go', or what we would nowadays call armchair travellers, they are nevertheless recognisable as travel guides, being full of practical details on travel to the South Seas, including the various modes of transport, expenses, what to pack and what to see on the way.

Despite her love affair with the rougher side of island life, Beatrice Grimshaw spent her last thirteen years in retirement, living on her royalties in the relative comfort of Australia.

Lady Mary Heath
1896–1939

A campaigner in women's athletics and a record-breaking aviator

Sophie Mary Pierce-Evans was born into a privileged Protestant background in Newcastle West, County Limerick, and attended a boarding school in Dublin. She was a classic high achiever with a low boredom threshold, and her speciality was performing apparently unfeminine physical feats of derring-do. Thus Mary, as she was known, was a despatch rider in World War I, a graduate in agricultural studies, a university lecturer, an author, a champion high-jumper and javelin-thrower and a pioneering aviator – all before she was thirty years of age.

As an all-round athlete herself, Mary was interested in the lot of women in sport; she co-founded and became vice-president of the British Women's Amateur Athletic Association (BWAAA) in 1922. At the World Championships in England in 1923, she competed in the long jump, shot putt, discus and 100m hurdles, and broke the women's world high-jump record and British javelin record. Her 100m hurdle time of sixteen seconds stood, in effect, as an all-Ireland record for forty-one years. Becoming more and more high-profile in sport, she addressed the Olympic Committee in Prague in 1925 and successfully campaigned for women to be allowed to compete in the 1928 Olympics. She also wrote a very successful coaching manual, *Athletics for Women and Girls*.

Meanwhile, Mary's personal life was turbulent. In her early twenties, she married an army officer, William Elliott-Lynn, and went to live on a coffee plantation in Kenya. But life out there was too quiet for Mary – a loud character with a big personality, she had become addicted to being a celebrity. After a couple of years she left her husband and took up residence in England.

Like many Bright Young Things of the inter-war years, Mary was continually looking for the next new craze – and the world's latest high-risk activity for the filthy rich was aviation. In 1925 Mary became the first woman in Britain to qualify for a pilot's licence. However, her licence was theoretical because in 1924 the International Commission for Air Navigation had bluntly stated that the first requirement for the physical part of the test was 'being a man'.

At nearly 6ft (1.85m) and eleven stone (70kg), Mary was hugely insulted by the Commission's assumption that women were too frail to fly. She campaigned vigorously to overturn this injustice by pointing to her own steely nerves and excellent physical condition – aside from her sporting exploits, she was the first woman in Britain to make a parachute jump – and by repeatedly demonstrating her impeccable landing technique. In 1926 the Commission lifted its ban on women and Mary started earning money as a commercial pilot.

But Mary's competitive streak was still very much to the fore. In 1927 alone she entered and won several races, set an altitude record of 16,000ft (4,880m) and performed aerial stunts. She also lectured on aviation all over Britain. In November she married her second husband, Sir James Heath, who was wealthy enough to keep her in planes. The attraction of commercial flying palled, but Mary already had her sights set on another goal.

She wanted to make the first solo flight from Cape Town to London, a trip of more than 8,000 miles (12,870km). She could not be the first to do the London–Cape Town route because this record had already been set, in 1927, by a lieutenant Dick Bentley. However, Bentley had taken his new wife with him on the return trip, thus disqualifying himself from achieving the solo flight record. In early 1928 it was still wide open for Mary, and she wanted to go for it.

At the same time, there was yet another rich, titled Irishwoman who was challenging Mary's position as queen of the sky: Lady Mary Bailey. The friendly rivalry between the two had started a few years earlier at the London aerodrome at Stag Lane when Mary had helped teach Lady Bailey to fly. Since then they had been competing in races and taking turns in holding the altitude record. Now Lady Bailey decided that she too wanted to fly the distance between England and South Africa.

They settled it amicably. In her book, *Woman and Flying* (1929), Mary Heath wrote that she wanted to do the Cape Town–London route not just to set a record but also to prove that it was possible to organise such a trip from 'the colonies'. A shocking and patronising imperialist, Mary was very keen to develop commercial flying in Africa. 'We in England,' she wrote grandly, 'do not realise that the greater part [of Africa] is ours and that her … wealth is ours if we like to take it and use it.' In a contemporary newspaper interview, Mary Bailey claimed she was not even trying to set a record, but just wanted to have a 'rest cure' and 'blaze a trail' from London for commercial use at the same time. Neither lady was being honest: Heath was desperate to be a pioneer aviatrix and be the first person to fly Cape Town–London solo; Bailey was more than happy to outshine this achievement the following year by being the first person to fly the round-trip solo.

'Flying is really absurdly easy,' chirrups Mary Heath in *Woman and Flying,* her own personal love poem to the skies. 'And then flying is so safe,' she claims, somewhat disingenuously, before going on to make unfavourable comparisons with driving. And then, finally, with the customary nonchalance of the very rich, 'flying is so cheap,' – she had worked out that travelling expenses were less than tuppence a mile, though she admits that this, of course, was only if you had the wherewithal to run your own 'little machine'.

For her journey from Cape Town to Croydon, Mary's little machine was a Mark III Avian, which she had taught herself to fix and maintain (later, in the USA, she would qualify as a ground engineer). Unfortunately, Dick Bentley had lost his invaluable maps and notes, so Mary had to start from scratch and work out her route from borrowed atlases. She checked climate patterns, ground conditions and the fuel situation, but her main problem was insurmountable: while flying, she would have no radio contact with the ground. Such lack of communication was downright dangerous – it meant she knew nothing about the location of other aeroplanes in her vicinity, nor about the quality of the landing surface, nor about any new local features, such as potentially lethal telegraph lines. But there was no help for it; Mary had to push on.

Mary started out from Cape Town on 12 February 1928, flying a zigzag route. As well as the usual aircraft paraphernalia – spare wheel, shock absorbers, sandbags and so on – her luggage included a fur coat, a silk evening dress, six pairs of silk stockings, one white flannel skirt, one pair of black satin shoes, a tennis racket and tennis shoes. To someone of Mary's background, one could not possibly fly the length of Africa without stopping *en route* for dinner and the odd spot of tennis at the local manor.

Mary touched down in Zimbabwe, Zambia, Tanzania, Kenya, Uganda, Sudan, Egypt, Libya and Tunisia. Not all of her stopovers were intentional. On one leg of the trip over Central Africa, she realised, at 8,000ft (2,440m), that she was suffering from sunstroke. Just before passing out she managed to crash-land in the bush. She awoke in the harem of a native kraal, being washed and nursed by tribal villagers and fed on boiled chicken and milk. The following day, as she wandered about deliriously, she was spotted by a woman in a passing car who sensed all was not as it should be, picked her up and brought her to the local hospital.

On another occasion, when taking off from Nairobi, Mary realised she had to take prompt action if she did not want to crash into some unexpected hills, so she was forced, while in the air, to jettison some cargo – including most of her famously beautiful clothes and the precious tennis racket.

When Mary got as far as Uganda at the end of March, she heard that the governor general of Sudan, Sir John Maffey, had forbidden her to fly across the troubled southern part of Sudan without a chaperone. Maffey was nothing if not consistent in this matter – he had also forbidden Lady Bailey, who was coming in the opposite direction, from crossing the territory alone. The obliging Dick Bentley came to the rescue. He and his wife chaperoned Lady Heath from Uganda as far as Khartoum in central Sudan where they all waited for Lady Bailey to fly in from Egypt. Lady Bailey was late – she had spent hours stranded in the Nubian desert trying to fix her engine, and Lady Heath was full of praise for her friend and rival's 'gallant and plucky attitude'. The four aviators spent a few days partying, and then the Bentleys chaperoned Lady Bailey over southern Sudan, while Lady Heath continued north to Egypt.

Mary had been forbidden to fly across the Mediterranean alone, but this time she ignored the authorities and did it anyway. She had stopovers in Malta, Italy (which she particularly enjoyed owing to her admiration of Mussolini) and France, before successfully reaching Croydon Aerodrome on 17 May 1928. After a 10,000 miles (16,000km), three-and-a-half-month journey, Lady Mary Heath had become the first person to fly solo from Cape Town to Croydon.

Unfortunately, the rest of Mary's life did not live up to the glory of this achievement. The following year she claimed an altitude record that she could not verify and this damaged her reputation in Britain. She successfully toured and lectured in the USA, but in August 1929, while giving a flying demonstration in Cleveland, Ohio, she had a serious accident, which destroyed both her health and her flying career at the age of thirty-four. At this point her second marriage failed.

Mary returned to Ireland in 1931 and, still fascinated by aviation though she could no longer fly, she bought Iona National Airways. The airline went bankrupt within four years and Mary lost all her money. By now, she was estranged from her third husband, a professional aviator, and looking for work in London, where she gradually sank into obscurity, ill-health and alcoholism. In spring 1939, aged forty-two, Lady Mary Heath fell over in a London bus and died as a result of her injuries.

Maura 'Soshin' O'Halloran
1955–1982

Zen Buddhist monk

Maura O'Halloran was born, the eldest of six children, in Boston, Massachusetts. Her mother was from nearby Maine, her father was from County Kerry. When Maura was four years old the family moved to the Dublin area where Maura was educated at Loreto convent schools. The O'Hallorans returned to the USA when Maura was eleven years old because of her father's job, but when he was killed in a car crash shortly afterwards the family returned once again to Dublin.

Maura was academically bright and entered Trinity College in 1973, winning a scholarship that paid for her education. She graduated in 1977 with a joint degree in mathematical economics/statistics and sociology. Maura displayed a well-developed social conscience from early on in her life. During term-time she assisted organisations helping drug addicts in the city and she spent a summer break teaching autistic children in Northern Ireland. Other summers were spent indulging her great passion: foreign travel. She visited Europe and, after graduating, she worked her way around the USA and Canada, learning Spanish as she went.

Early in 1978 she took off for South America and again got involved in voluntary social work, this time with street children in Cuzco, Peru. In late 1978 it was back to Boston to earn some money for her next big trip. Late the following year, Maura set off for Japan, a country that had long fascinated her.

Maura, a naturally spiritual person, had been studying meditation and wanted to go deeper into the practice. In the winter of 1979, aged only twenty-four, she arrived at the Buddhist Toshoji Temple in Tokyo and asked to be admitted as a trainee monk. She was to spend three gruelling years in training there and at the associated Kannonji Temple, north of the city – the only woman and the only foreigner.

Reaching enlightenment through the study of Zen involves deep contemplation: one must exclude the superficialities of one's life and surroundings to know one's essential nature. Maura's training included rising at dawn for the daily practice of meditation and chanting. She did manual work within the temple and its grounds, which had to be performed with exacting care, especially the more menial tasks. She joined in the time-honoured practice of begging – in the -20C winter of central Japan – and she survived on the minimum of sleep and food.

Maura embraced this strict régime wholeheartedly. She developed a deep love for her Japanese fellow-monks, felt privileged to be in the temple and, as she recorded in her journal, very 'conscious of life'. The monks gave her the name Soshin, which means 'enlightened, warm heart'. It was a name she liked it because it rhymed with Oisín (*pron*. Ush-een), and reminded her of her Irish roots.

Maura achieved the enviable state known as enlightenment the spring after her arrival. The head monk was so impressed with her self-discipline and hard work that he felt she could succeed him as the head of the temple in due course – an unheard-of idea in Japan. As time went on, Maura achieved almost saint-like status within the community. In one of her self-imposed disciplines she emulated a past Zen master, Dogen, by performing the practice known as prostration thousands of times per week, increasing her working day to twenty hours and reducing her sleep to three hours a night, which she took sitting up. In August 1982 she graduated as a Tenzo monk – the second position in the temple to the head monk.

Maura planned to found a temple and teach Zen in Ireland, but first she wanted to take a short break to explore Southeast Asia. One night, *en route* from Bangkok, Thailand, to the ancient northern capital of Chiang Mai, the bus she was travelling in crashed and Maura was one of the two passengers killed. She was twenty-seven years old.

Outside her beloved temple in Tokyo, there is a statue dedicated to her. Its inscription describes Maura as having the same heart and mind as the great teacher, Buddha.

STARS OF STAGE AND SCREEN

'Oh, wouldn't I just love to be in the
Abbey once more!'
Sara Allgood

Peg Woffington

c.1718–1760

An acting legend of the eighteenth century known for her beauty and professionalism

Peg Woffington was born, possibly under the name of Murphy, in the narrow, vermin-infested slum area of George's Court, off Dame Street, Dublin. Her father, a bricklayer, died around 1720 and was buried as a pauper, leaving nothing for young Peg, her mother and her baby sister, Polly. Peg's mother took in washing and tried to run a small grocery shop, but failed, and the little family edged closer and closer to destitution. Eventually, the bare-footed Peg and her mother were reduced to scraping a living by selling watercress from a basket in the streets around Trinity College.

This was Peg's situation when her big break came at the age of about twelve. While fetching water from the River Liffey one evening, she was spotted by Madame Violante, a popular acrobatic performer from Europe. When Madame was not performing her own bizarre act, which involved walking a tightrope with a live baby hanging from each foot, she was scouting for talent for her children's acting troupe. She wanted looks and she wanted talent – and in Peg Woffington she struck lucky on both counts.

Peg was undoubtedly a beauty. Amazingly, despite being the most vulnerable of slum children, she had managed to avoid the usual malnutrition, rickets and smallpox, and she was blessed with a creamy complexion, perfect white teeth, dark, expressive eyes and thick, black hair. As for her talent, Madame quickly realised that Peg was an acting natural and gave her the female lead as Polly Peachum in a pirated version of *The Beggar's Opera* by John Gay. Peg's vivacity, wit and humour, phenomenal memory and versatility were apparent from the off (although, as she herself admitted, her speaking voice not terribly strong and this was, of course, in an age without microphones). In addition, Peg was a genuine trouper who became renowned for staggering on, even when ill. She never missed an opportunity to learn her trade and would take small parts if it meant learning something new or was for the benefit of the play. Though beautiful, she often played old or disfigured characters and was always willing to step into the breach at the last minute.

After this promising start, Peg was in demand. The playwright Charles Coffey gave her the lead in his comedy, *The Devil to Pay*, at the Theatre Royal, Aungier Street, which was the main Dublin theatre and the one patronised by the Dublin Castle set. During intervals, Peg also provided the song-and-dance routines that were *de rigeur* in eighteenth-century theatre. But soon, these light pieces were not enough for Peg. She wanted more – and in the true theatre tradition of *A Star is Born,* she got it.

In 1737 *Hamlet, Prince of Denmark* was just about to open at the Smock Alley Theatre, but the actress playing Ophelia suddenly fell ill. The manager, Mr Elrington, was about to cancel the production when Peg seized her moment. She had just two days in which to learn the lines and stage directions to a sell-out production of Shakespeare's finest tragedy, but she persuaded Elrington to give her a chance. When the curtain rose on her first night, Peg performed flawlessly. When the curtain fell, the applause was deafening and Peg was a star. She was nineteen years old.

After that, the tall, beautiful, comic, tragic, singing, dancing Peg could do whatever she wanted. She toured London and Paris, always in lead parts. In 1739 she started in 'breeches' roles, a mildly titillating piece of theatrical cross-dressing whereby an actress with exceptional legs would wear knee-high breeches and play a male part. Peg loved doing this and made the role of Sir Harry Wildair in George Farquahar's *The Constant Couple* a mainstay of her repertoire for the next twenty years.

Despite the on-stage breeches, offstage Peg frequently demonstrated she was all woman. The stage was not entirely respectable and neither was Peg – but respectability was not at that time the Holy Grail it was later to become. Unlike the dull, tightly corseted Victorian era, the liberated 1700s were characterised by a love of life. Beautiful Peg from the slums was nothing if not a woman of her times. She indulged herself with many lovers and did not waste energy worrying about the proprieties.

Then Peg fell in love. His name was Taafe, and he was a thoroughly bad lot from a good family. In 1740 Mr Taafe persuaded Peg to leave her beloved Dublin, took to her to London, promised marriage – and then abandoned her for an heiress. Peg hid her broken heart to exact revenge in an impressive and appropriately theatrical manner. Getting back into her breeches and posing as a young man, she befriended Taafe's new *amour*. Once she had gained the girl's confidence, and sparing no detail, Peg informed her of Taafe's penchant for Dublin actresses and his desire to marry money, whereupon the sensible young woman dumped him.

After this, Peg, all alone in the big city, picked herself up and presented herself to the renowned and deeply eccentric theatre manager John Rich of Covent Garden. Rich took her on immediately and Peg made a hugely successful début in November 1740. She acquired her soon-to-be-universal nickname, 'The Woffington', and became immensely popular with London theatregoers who loved her looks, loved her liveliness and loved the gossip surrounding her.

Her reputation as a sensual woman who was free with her favours caused her to be the butt of many a joke: one night she came offstage having played a particularly successful Sir Harry Wildair. 'Lord,' she exclaimed delightedly, 'but I have played the part so often that half the town believes me to be a man!' 'Aye, madam,' retorted a nearby wag named Quin, 'but the other half *knows* you to be a woman!'

In 1741 Peg defected to the Drury Lane Theatre and met the failed wine merchant who was to become the greatest actor of his day, David Garrick. The Woffington was greatly instrumental in Garrick's rise to superstardom, which later became known as 'Garrick fever', and in 1742 they became lovers. They set up an unconventional *ménage à trois* with another actor, named Macklin, in Bow Street, London, and then alone together in Southampton Street, but their relationship was tempestuous at best.

One of the problems was that, all her life, Peg had been generous to a fault – she lent her costumes to struggling young actresses, gave lavishly to charity and supported her mother and sister as soon as she was earning. In contrast, Garrick was notorious for his meanness. In spite of the fact that he earned three times as much as Peg, he made her take turns paying for the monthly upkeep of their home.

It was soon a standing joke among the big names they entertained – Dr Samuel Johnson, James Boswell and Henry Fielding – that the hospitality was much more lavish when it was Peg's month to pay. Garrick even complained that she was extravagant with tea-making, brewing it so strong it was 'as red as blood'. He hated this financial aspect of life with Peg, and also probably felt that her magnetic attraction to and for other men would not make her a good wife – he always had doubts about what he called in a love poem her 'wavering heart'. In 1745, Peg received an insultingly half-hearted proposal of marriage from Garrick. Shortly afterwards he either retracted the offer or she rejected him on other grounds, either way the two fell out.

Peg went to live in the healthier moral climate of Udney Hall, Teddington, thirteen miles upriver from London. When her younger sister, Polly, returned from her expensive convent education abroad, she came to live with her. Peg's social ambitions for her sister were fulfilled when Polly made a match with the Honourable Captain Robert Cholmondeley, the somewhat chinless son of an earl. Peg was very robust when dealing with her aristocratic future in-laws. She received a visit from the earl one day, complaining about the match. 'My lord, I have more reason to be offended with it than you have,' Peg responded in a typically spirited manner, 'for before I had only one beggar to support and now I have two.' Polly later went on to become a successful hostess in English high society, and an out-and-out snob who looked down on the big sister to whom she owed everything.

Peg had a good heart and a loyal one, but, with the exception of her beloved mother and sister, she saw other women as rivals. Then, as now, there was savage competition in the theatre for the same roles, and actresses would routinely block each other. In Peg's case, London rivals would refer slightingly to her 'brogue', which she kept all her life. Peg had a hot temper and had a tendency to throw tantrums – on occasion coming to blows with the actresses at Drury Lane. Eventually it got so bad she left and returned to Covent Garden.

However, at Covent Garden, Peg ran into the worst of them all, her one-time protegée, George Anne Bellamy. George Anne was the illegitimate daughter of an Irish peer, and was at least ten years younger than Peg, a fact she never failed to mention during a row. She was a nasty piece of work, who had conveniently forgotten that it was Peg who had helped her get started in the theatre. One memorable night, her taunting drove Peg to grab a knife and try to stab her, nearly within sight of the audience. George Anne saved her own neck by running away, 'to live,' as she quipped, 'to fight another day'. After this incident, Peg deemed it politic to leave Covent Garden.

In 1751, Peg returned to Dublin to work for Thomas Sheridan (Richard Brinsley Sheridan's father) in the Smock Alley Theatre. She found her appeal had increased in all her old roles as well as some new ones she had created, and she made a record-breaking fortune for Sheridan.

In her spare time she associated with the cream of society, as she had in London. Finally, she was elected the president of a society called the Beefsteak Club, which was a social club for the Dublin Castle set. She was the only female ever to have been admitted to the club and, no doubt, regarded it the pinnacle of social achievement for a woman from her background. However, Peg's fans were not pleased. Among all the harmless high jinks that took place at the club, there were some that were not so harmless. Bad enough that Peg was entertaining William Cavendish, third duke of Devonshire and lord lieutenant of Ireland, but soon rumours hit the streets of anti-Irish toasts being drunk by the Castle oppressors, and The Woffington herself drinking to the health of the king of England. To make matters worse, there were also rumours – true as it turned out – that Peg had converted to Protestantism. She felt she had sound financial reasons for this. The Penal Laws forbade Catholics from inheriting property, and an old actor named Owen Swiney wanted to leave his property to Peg. Ever the pragmatist, Peg simply threw off her religion like an old role and converted in order to claim the inheritance.

This was too much for The Woffington's Irish public. She was one of their own and was expected to remember where she came from. One night, Peg was performing in *Mahomet* by Voltaire, a play containing incendiary passages about touchy subjects, such as court favouritism and tyranny. The mob inside and outside the theatre, outraged at what they perceived as Peg's traitorous behaviour and inflamed by Voltaire's text, stormed the Smock Alley Theatre during her performance and wrecked it.

That was enough for Peg. After a three-year absence she returned, with relief, to Covent Garden, and there, in October 1754, yet again brought the house down with her first performance. She continued to appear in tragic roles, Shakespearean plays and contemporary comedies and never lost her popular appeal again.

Sadly, just as it appeared Peg was attaining the position of *grande dame* of the theatre, her career was actually nearing its end. In May 1757, at the end of her fourth successful season back in Covent Garden, she was playing Rosalind in Shakespeare's *As You Like It*. In between acts, Peg complained of feeling ill. The play was a 'benefit' for a fellow actor – this was a custom whereby actors were allowed to supplement their income by claiming the ticket money for a single performance. A true professional, and conscious of the fact that her non-appearance would make things difficult for her fellow actors, she tottered on to finish the Epilogue – and collapsed with a scream.

Peg had had a massive stroke. Everyone thought she would die, but she lingered on for another three years, crippled but with her mind in perfect working order. Her last lover, a Colonel Caeser, took care of her. Peg flirted once more with Protestantism, but she had never been religious and died as irreverently as she had lived on 26 March 1760. She is buried near her home in Teddington, Middlesex.

George Anne Bellamy
c.1727–1788

Popular eighteenth-century comic actress and rival of Peg Woffington

George Anne Bellamy was born in County Dublin, the illegitimate daughter of Lord Tyrawley and a Quaker schoolgirl named Miss Seal. The impoverished Lord Tyrawley and Miss Seal had already produced a son, after whose birth Lord Tyrawley disappeared in search of a rich wife. Meanwhile, Miss Seal took to the stage but proved merely average as an actress. So when Lord Tyrawley sent for her to join him in Lisbon as his mistress, she went.

In Lisbon, Miss Seal quickly realised Lord Tyrawley was continuing his hunt for an heiress and would never marry her. Pregnant again, she returned to Dublin and, in a fit of pique, married a sea captain named Bellamy. When a daughter was born suspiciously close to the wedding, Bellamy returned to sea and was never heard of again.

From the captain George Anne acquired her surname, but she got her unusual first name when an elderly priest officiating at her christening misheard the name Georgiana. Lord Tyrawley acknowledged little George Anne as his own, obtained custody and paid for her to have a good education at a convent school in Bolougne, France. She stayed there until she was eleven years old and then joined her father and his wealthy Portuguese wife (he had finally nabbed an heiress) in Hertfordshire, with at least three half-sisters – all of whom had different mothers. When Lord Tyrawley was made ambassador to Russia, George Anne was left alone with a sum of money and instructions not to contact her mother.

But contact her she did. When Mrs Bellamy wrote – possibly realising her pretty, educated girl could be a major asset – and begged George Anne to come to her, George Anne immediately left for London. Before long, the money left by Lord Tyrawley had run out. One day, while out walking, George Anne and her mother ran into the famous actress Peg Woffington. Since they were all Irishwomen and the Bellamys were obviously down on their luck, the charitable Woffington immediately invited them to stay with her at her house in Teddington, thirteen miles outside London. While there, George Anne managed to meet and ingratiate herself with the manager of Covent Garden Theatre, John Rich. She made her début at Covent Garden in 1744, claiming to be thirteen years old (she was about seventeen). When Lord Tyrawley found out about George Anne's career move, he was so angry he cut off all financial support.

'Beautiful, arrogant and extravagant,' as one contemporary described her, George Anne was an immediate hit and soon defected to Drury Lane Theatre. Drury Lane's diminutive leading actor, David Garrick, liked appearing opposite her because she was one of the few actresses shorter than himself. Between 1745 and 1747 'blue-eyed Bellamy', as she was known, toured in Dublin and reigned supreme in Aungier Street Theatre under Thomas Sheridan. In 1748 she returned to Covent Garden.

There then ensued her famous rivalry with Peg Woffington, her one-time benefactor. George Anne was lazy, unreliable, fickle, extravagant, vain and impulsive. The Woffington was conscientious, talented, affable, reliable and honest, and she was not impressed with the younger actress's attitude. So vicious was the ungrateful George Anne to the older actress that, in 1751, The Woffington left London for Dublin to get away from Bellamy and another compatriot actress, Kitty Clive. George Anne stepped into The Woffington's shoes and became the toast of London town.

But George Anne was always more notorious for her love life than celebrated for her acting ability, and she caused scandal with her numerous love affairs. Eventually she went to live in York with a lover named Metham. She had a son by him and begged him for marriage, and when he refused she left him. On the rebound she married a Mr Calcraft, whom she soon grew to loathe. This unfortunate experience did not stop her marrying a second time – bigamously – to a Mr Digges.

George Anne's success on the stage continued for a number of years until her looks declined. In 1760 she tried Dublin again, but this time was a resounding failure. Back in London she was briefly arrested for debts outstanding and she spent the rest of her life being bailed out by rich friends. From 1780 work dried up altogether and George Anne retired from the stage. A benefit performance was given for her in 1785, but George Anne had not aged well; after the show she was reported as being too decrepit even to stand and say a few words of thanks.

George Anne's adventures formed the basis of her shameless but popular six-volume memoirs, *Apology* (1785). Despite earnings from the book and proceeds from her benefit, she died in poverty in London in February 1788.

Sara Allgood
1883–1950

One of Ireland's greatest tragic actresses

Sara Allgood was born in Drumcondra, north Dublin, into a large, downwardly mobile family. Sara's father was a strict Protestant and Orangeman, her mother a feisty Dublin Catholic. Not surprisingly, home was not a harmonious place and Sara and her seven siblings, though nominally Protestants by order of their father, were secretly reared in the Catholic faith by their mother.

After her father's death, Sara trained as an upholsterer. She and her younger brothers and sisters (including the actress Molly, alias Máire O'Neill) became involved in pre-independence politics. In about 1902 she joined Inghínidhe na hÉireann, the nationalist women's organisation founded by Maud Gonne. It was here that she developed a reputation as a singer, a reciter of poetry and a promising amateur actress. When she met Willie Fay, a future director of the famous Abbey Theatre, Fay recognised a certain quality about Sara and persuaded her to get more involved in Irish drama.

In 1903, in Dublin's modest Molesworth Hall on Molesworth Street, Sara had a walk-on part in one of Lady Augusta Gregory's plays, followed by a small speaking part in one of WB Yeats' plays, followed by another slightly more substantial role in one of JM Synge's plays. Not a bad beginning for a nobody, but it was the following year it all happened for Sara. In 1904 the Abbey Theatre opened, and Sara Allgood made her successful début at the opening night of Lady Gregory's *Spreading the News*.

Physically, Sara was the opposite of a willowy tragedienne, but was somehow a natural in tragic roles (though in the early days she played comic roles too). She may have been a dumpy little figure, but she had the true actor's trick of being able to transform herself on stage. Her rival, and the actress she displaced as leading lady in the Abbey, Máire nic Shiubhlaigh, graciously called her 'the wonderfully gifted Sara' – according to nic Shiubhlaigh, Sarah's sad, expressive, dark eyes and her 'magnificent contralto voice' rivalled those of the great Sarah Bernhardt.

She was known to be a hard worker, which endeared her to the two most lofty directors of the Abbey: Lady Gregory and WB Yeats. This rather snobby pair eventually became unlikely friends of the working-class actress. Yeats felt that Sara alone could convey his difficult lines in a manner satisfying to himself. As for Lady Gregory, she recognised a fellow workaholic when she saw one, and Sara Allgood was the only Abbey actress regularly invited to sample elegant living at Lady Gregory's elegant residence, Coole Park in Galway.

After 1904 Sara quickly became the Abbey's leading lady and spent the next ten years carving out her reputation and touring with the company in the USA and Britain. She embodied the ideal of Ireland and heroic Irishwomen in plays, such as *Cathleen ni Houlihan* by Yeats and Lady Gregory, and the riot-inducing *Playboy of the Western World* and *Riders to the Sea* by JM Synge. Meanwhile, Sara's sister, Molly Allgood, had also joined the Abbey. She opted to use the name of Máire O'Neill so as not to live in the ever-lengthening shadow of her older sister. The two sisters were rivals throughout their careers – Molly possessed a not-inconsiderable talent herself, though Lady Gregory thought her too flighty to make anything of it. In 1907 Molly became engaged to Synge, but tragically the gifted dramatist died of cancer in 1909.

Although a nationalist all her life, Sara was not involved in the Easter Rising of 1916. Two of her brothers had joined the British Army and had lost their lives in World War I the previous year; it is highly likely she had had enough of bloodshed. Instead, she decided once again to try her hand at comedy and took the lead opposite a handsome young actor, Gerald Henson, in a successful comedy called *Peg o' my Heart* by J Hartley Manners. While touring the play in New Zealand, Sara fell in love with her co-star. In the autumn of 1916, at the age of thirty-three, she married Gerald in Melbourne. Safely away from the horrific war and the turbulent events at home, the two toured the country, blissfully happy, and enjoyed their professional and domestic success. Soon they had something else to celebrate: Sara was pregnant.

Poor Sara's happiness was short-lived. In early 1918 she gave birth to her much-wanted baby girl, but the baby lived only one hour. Then, in the autumn of that same year, her darling husband was struck down in the prime of his life in what was to become known as the Spanish 'flu epidemic. At just thirty-five years of age, Sara would never know marriage or motherhood again.

Characteristically, Sara carried on working for another eighteen months in Australia and New Zealand, and then she returned to Ireland to a warm welcome from Dublin and the Abbey Theatre. Her next major roles were studies in tragedy. With her own tragedies behind her and those of Ireland all around her, Sara was now able to bring a new dimension to her work. It is for her audience-stunning performances as the heartbreaking female leads in Sean O'Casey's classic plays *Juno and the Paycock* (1924) and *The Plough and the Stars* (1926) that she acquired legendary status as an actress. She toured with O'Casey's plays throughout Britain and the USA.

While in America on one of the tours, Sara appeared in the first British talkie, a thriller directed by Alfred Hitchcock called *Blackmail* (1929). The following year saw the first Hollywood production of *Juno and the Paycock* in which Sara, of course, played the lead.

By now, Sara was finding Abbey work rather limiting so she opted to stay in Hollywood. Here, she is generally regarded as having slid into a decline since, in common with most actresses over the age of about twenty-one, she was offered only small 'character' roles – battleaxe barmaids and cooks, mainly. However, the actress liked to keep active and it is worth noting that, except for 1939, she worked every year for the rest of her life – sometimes appearing in three or four movies in one year.

In all she appeared in forty-eight movies in the last twenty years of her life. Always financially pressed, at the very end she ventured into what she called the 'frightful' medium of television. She was granted American citizenship in 1945.

Sara Allgood died of a heart attack on 13 September 1950 and is buried in the Holy Cross cemetery in Culver City, California. Molly Allgood survived her sister by two years.

Dame Ninette de Valois
1898–2001

Ballet dancer and choreographer

Ninette de Valois was born Edris Stannus in Baltyboys House, Blessington, County Wicklow, the second daughter of a British army officer and a distinguished glassmaker, Lillith Graydon-Smith. So disappointed was her father that she was not a boy, he refused to light the celebratory bonfires which the estate tenants had prepared to mark the birth.

Edris showed an early interest in dance. The first dance she learned was an Irish jig, which she picked up from the family cook when she was seven. Soon afterwards her parents sent her to live in Kent with her grandmother, who sent her to ballet lessons.

In 1914 Edris started as principal dancer in a Christmas pantomime at the Lyceum Theatre in London's West End. This winter engagement continued throughout World War I and was supplemented by summer engagements in variety shows. She continued to study dance, and in 1921 embarked on a European tour that culminated in a meeting with the famous Russian impresario, Sergei Diaghilev. In 1923 Diaghilev engaged Edris, by now working under her more exotic professional name of Ninette de Valois, for his company, Les Ballets Russe. She stayed with the company for two years.

In 1926 Ninette was invited to London's Old Vic Theatre as a choreographer. The following year WB Yeats persuaded her to do the same job at Dublin's Abbey Theatre. While in Dublin she also performed in *Plays for Dancers* by WB Yeats.

She returned to London again in 1931 to work on a new project with the Old Vic's manager, Lilian Baylis, who had just opened Sadler's Wells Theatre. The project was to set up a resident ballet company; Ninette would be the director. The company was established, originally under the name of the Vic-Wells Ballet, then later the Sadler's Wells Ballet. A strong disciplinarian, Ninette was renowned for her imperious manner, phenomenal memory and ability to throw a tantrum.

In 1935 Ninette underwent a serious operation, which was performed by the Irish surgeon Dr Arthur Connell, who was based in London. The two fell in love and were married later the same year. She retired from dancing two years later, concentrating instead on raising the profile of British ballet and introducing classic ballets into the British repertoire. In the inter-war period, Ninette discovered and trained the great Margot Fonteyn, and gave the legendary choreographer Frederick Ashton a job with her company. As a choreographer in her own right, she created 110 works, including forty complete ballets. In 1946 she moved the Sadler's Wells Ballet into the Royal Opera House in London's Covent Garden and started a second touring company, now known as the Birmingham Royal Ballet.

In 1947 Ninette received the first of a number of awards: a CBE from King George VI. Later she received the *Légion d'honneur* from the French government, the Erasmus prize from the Netherlands, and an Irish Community award. The British further honoured her by making her a Dame in 1951 and conferring a royal charter on her ballet company in 1955, thereby transforming it into the Royal Ballet.

Ninette handed over the directorship of the Royal Ballet School to Frederick Ashton in 1963, but remained a governor. She became patron of Irish National Ballet and is also credited with helping to establish ballet companies in Canada and western Asia. Her involvement declined over the years, but she remained interested and attended performances at Covent Garden as late as 1997. Dame Ninette de Valois died in 2001 in London, at the age of 102.

Greer Garson
c.1904–1996

Hollywood film legend

Eileen Evelyn Greer Garson was one of Hollywood's favourite screen goddesses whose dignified acting style earned her one Oscar and six Oscar nominations.

Greer always claimed she was born in County Down, Northern Ireland, in 1908, though it is quite likely she was born in London in 1904. However, after her father died when she was just two years old, she spent every summer at her grandparents' home in Ireland.

In 1921 Greer entered London University and graduated with a BA in 1926. She was a keen amateur actress and spent most of her free time performing small roles for a local company, while by day she worked in the research library of an advertising agency. In 1931 she was accepted into the Birmingham Repertory Company.

Six years and one ill-advised marriage later, the auburn-haired actress was spotted by movie mogul Louis B Mayer and he immediately signed her up for MGM – Greer was on her way to stardom. After a shaky start in Hollywood, Greer landed the part of Mrs Chips in the whimsical *Goodbye Mr Chips*. She did not think much of the role or of her own acting in it, but the film was released to glowing reviews and critical acclaim for herself. When she lost out in the Oscars to none other than Vivien Leigh in *Gone with the Wind*, Greer Garson knew she was playing in the big league.

More triumphs followed, including *Pride and Prejudice* (in which the thirty-six-year-old Greer had the cheek to play a twenty-year-old Elizabeth Bennett) and *Blossoms* (in which she was again nominated for an Oscar). But the crowning glory of Greer's acting career was her 1942 role as the eponymous heroine in *Mrs Miniver*, for which she walked away with an Academy Award for Best Actress. In 1943 there was a mini-scandal when, having initially objected to the character of Mrs Miniver being old enough to have a college-age son, Greer began to date the actor who played him, Richard Ney. The thirty-nine-year-old veteran married the mid-twenties rookie the same summer.

Greer carried on working throughout World War II. *Random Harvest, Madame Curie, Mrs Parkington* and *The Valley of Decision* (third, fourth and fifth Oscar nominations respectively) were released in quick succession. However, there were rumblings of discontent from the critics: Greer was becoming typecast as a dignified, classy matron. In 1945, despite relief at the war's end, things went bad for Greer. The studio system, which had been more than kind to her, gave way to a less 'star'-centred policy with smaller budgets and a penchant for gritty on-screen realism. Her young husband divorced her in 1946 and this was followed by two critical flops, *Adventure* and *Desire Me*. However, Greer managed to rehabilitate herself in a comedy, *Julia Misbehaves*, which was received with rave reviews.

During the filming of *Julia Misbehaves* (1948), Greer met a Texan oil and cattle millionaire named Elijah 'Buddy' Fogelson. In 1949, after completion of *That Forsythe Woman*, the unlikely pair were married in Santa Fe. Greer loved New Mexico and loved ranching – she even bought and entered her own steers in competitions.

Despite this idyllic domestic life, throughout the 1950s and 1960s Greer refused to retire from acting and hung grimly onto the remnants of her career. In a sea of mediocrity, there were some honourable exceptions: *Julius Caesar* in 1953; *Sunrise at Campobello* in 1960, which garnered her sixth and final Oscar nomination; *The Singing Nun* in 1966; and *The Happiest Millionaire* in 1967. Her spirited return to the stage in late 1957 in the hit musical *Auntie Mame* earned her lasting respect from audiences and critics.

By the 1960s Greer was immersing herself and Buddy's millions in charity work. In 1965, in recognition of this, the College of Santa Fe dedicated the Greer Garson Theatre to her, and later awarded her an honorary doctorate. It was in this theatre, in 1975, that she gave her last stage performance in *The Madwoman of Challiot*.

In December 1987, Buddy Fogelson died in Dallas, Texas, with Greer by his side. Although his widow still loved Santa Fe and continued with her charities both there and in Texas, she was advised, for health reasons, to move to Dallas. In 1992, after a particularly generous bequest from the Fogelson Estate, the Southern Methodist University in Dallas opened a second Greer Garson Theatre. The same year, Greer moved into a suite at the Dallas Presbyterian Hospital so her health could be monitored continually. She died there four years later, surrounded by flowers and fans – a Hollywood legend to the last.

Siobhán McKenna

1923–1986

One of the finest Irish actresses of the twentieth century

Siobhán McKenna (or Siobhán Nic Cionnait Aisteoir, as she was also known) was born 24 May 1923 in a house off the Falls Road in west Belfast, although her mother was originally from Longford and her father from Cork. The McKennas were an academic, cultured, middle-class family who were passionate about the Irish language and spoke nothing else at home. At the time of Siobhán's birth, her father was lecturing at Queen's University, Belfast, but when she was eight years old he moved the family to Galway where he became Professor of Mathematics at Galway University.

At convent school in Galway and later in Monaghan, Siobhán was a bright, athletic, high-achiever. Her childhood was steeped in Irish culture – holidays were spent in the Gaeltacht and at her grandmother's in Longford, where she picked up an abiding love of folklore and storytelling. In due course, Siobhán won a scholarship to Galway University.

Siobhán was a formidable young woman who immediately involved herself in what she called the 'Irish movement' in Galway. She became active in the local Irish language theatre, An Taibhdhearc, at the age of eighteen, translating Eugene O'Neill, Sean O'Casey and even Shakespeare into Irish for the company's productions. She then personally visited all the head teachers of as many boys' schools as she could and, cheekily using the leverage of her father's university position, told them they should be sending the boys to see plays at the Taibhdhearc instead of allowing them to go to the cinema. Siobhán's father allowed her to spend as much time as she wanted working for the Taibhdhearc because he approved of the cultural aspect and the language. Little did he know that this was not just a hobby: he was about to lose his daughter to the stage.

Buoyed by a lot of encouragement from university teachers, Siobhán started acting in the Taibhdhearc productions herself and slowly abandoned her original idea of becoming a nun in Monaghan. Although she was falling in love with the theatre, she postponed her plans of becoming an actress. Instead she played the dutiful daughter and won first-class honours in English, Irish and French. Then she took off for Dublin and the Abbey Theatre.

Siobhán's first experiences in the Abbey were inauspicious. Her first audition for the company went badly and she was not called back until late one night when she was finally contacted as an emergency understudy for a sick actress. She was needed the next evening so she sat up all night learning the lines. She actually got as far as putting on the costume and waiting in the wings, when the actress herself arrived, recovered enough to go on. Meanwhile, Siobhán was living in one room in digs and running out of money. Finally, she got a small part in a Molière play and slowly became an accepted part of the company.

In 1946 Siobhán married fellow actor and Abbey Theatre veteran, Denis O'Dea, who had known Lady Augusta Gregory and WB Yeats. They were each offered movie parts in Hollywood, but Siobhán disliked the idea of being too far from Ireland at that time. Instead, she made her London début with *The White Steed* (1947) and the following year gave birth to her only child, Donnacha.

In 1950 Siobhán starred in her own translation, into Irish, of George Bernard Shaw's *St Joan,* which was the part that would later make her internationally famous. Her other acclaimed role was Pegeen Mike in JM Synge's *The Playboy of the Western World* in 1951. The success of *St Joan* was repeated in London in 1954, where rave reviews hailed Siobhán McKenna as the 'greatest actress alive'.

In 1956 Siobhán and Denis starred in different shows on Broadway at the same time. Two years later she was voted Actress of the Year by the London paper, *The Evening Standard.* In 1959 Siobhán emulated that earlier great Irish actress, Peg Woffington, by crossing the gender divide and successfully tackling the role of Hamlet.

Significant highlights in a rather sparse film career included *King of Kings* (1961), *The Playboy of the Western World* (1962) and *Doctor Zhivago* (1965). But in 1970 it was back to her first love when she staged her one-woman show, *Here are Ladies.* The show, a medley of the best female characters written by Irish poets and playwrights, included the famous and then-controversial Molly Bloom soliloquy from James Joyce's *Ulysses.* This show massively boosted Siobhán's waning popularity and was an enormous success in Dublin, London and the USA. On her return from her four-year tour with the show in 1974, Siobhán McKenna was fêted across the nation.

The 1970s and early 1980s were spent touring with the Abbey Theatre Company in the USA and Europe. In 1984 Siobhán completed her last work for the Abbey company when she directed, produced and performed, in Irish, the classic eighteenth-century poem by Brian Merriman, *The Midnight Court (Cúirt an Mheán Oíche)*.

Fittingly, Siobhán's last stage triumph was back in Galway where her career had started more than forty years earlier. She starred in *Bailegangaire* by Tom Murphy, a play written especially for her. Her very last performance was in this play, on her sixty-third birthday, on 24 May 1986, at the Druid Theatre. Six months later, on 16 November, Siobhán died of complications arising from lung cancer.

Siobhán McKenna brought intelligence and sensitivity to her life as well as her craft. She never forgot her Northern Ireland connection: she was fiercely opposed to the ill-advised policy of internment in the 1970s, and in the 1980s she supported the stance of the ten hunger strikers who died of starvation in the Maze prison. She was pro-conservation (and vociferous in trying to save the Viking site at Wood Quay in Dublin from developers) and, in relation to the political situation in South Africa, anti-apartheid.

She was awarded honorary doctorates abroad, while at home, in 1975, she was appointed to the Council of State by president Cearbhall Ó Dálaigh – the first time an artist had been so honoured. She is buried in Rahoon cemetery in Galway.

ARTISTIC TEMPERAMENTS

*'If an Irish artist of the eighth or ninth
century were to meet a present-day Cubist or
non-representational painter, they would
understand one another.'*
Mainie Jellett

Sarah Purser

1848–1943

Painter and founder of An Túr Gloine

Sarah Henrietta Purser was born in Dún Laoghaire, County Dublin, and raised in Dungarvan, County Waterford, in a middle-class Protestant family. She was educated in Switzerland until 1863 and then trained at the Metropolitan School of Art in Dublin. Since she could not continue her training at the women-excluding Royal Hibernian Academy (RHA), she was forced to attend the Académie Julian in Paris.

When Sarah's father's flour-milling business went into debt in 1872 he left his wife and family to seek work in the USA, and Sarah found it necessary to start earning to support herself. Since she enjoyed having long philosophical discussions while she was working, portraiture suited her perfectly. Sarah was acid-tongued but funny, frank but benevolent, and popular though famously intolerant of fools, and her open manner ensured that her sitters often became her friends.

Sarah was a hard worker and approached her financial problems by networking furiously among her connections in the British aristocracy, through which she progressed, she said, like a dose of measles, looking for commissions. Her admiring colleague, John Butler Yeats, described her as a 'portrait-painting peddler moving from one magnificent castle to the other'.

By the 1880s Sarah's hard work was starting to pay off and she had become much respected in the Irish art world. She was exhibiting regularly at the RHA and had a busy studio in Harcourt

Terrace. The subjects who sat for her were often national figures and therefore famous and influential people, including Maud Gonne, WB Yeats, Edward Martyn and Douglas Hyde. She also co-founded the Dublin Arts Club, a new approach to exhibiting work by professional artists. In 1890 the RHA made her an honorary member and, after John Butler Yeats left for the USA in 1909, she enjoyed growing fame as Ireland's premier portraitist, although some of her finest works, such as *Le Petit Dejeuner* (1885) and *An Irish Idyll* (1894), are not strictly portraiture.

By the late 1890s, between her shrewd investments and her earnings, Sarah was wealthy and able to indulge her generous streak, for example, in 1901 she organised and helped finance a Jack Yeats–Nathaniel Hone exhibition. She supported a range of Irish cultural activities and was one of the main guarantors for the Irish Literary Theatre (later to become the Abbey).

Avidly interested in the flowering of arts and crafts that became known as the Gaelic Revival, she became aware that Irish church art was generally produced by English or European concerns. Along with the playwright Edward Martyn, who was a major figure of the Irish Literary Revival, Sarah felt strongly that Irish art should be home-produced. She began seriously researching stained glass, and went on tours around the factories of Europe to learn production techniques. She became, as she acknowledged, 'some judge of glass', and in 1903 founded An Túr Gloine (the Tower of Glass) – the inception of stained-glass production in Ireland.

An Túr Gloine was located at 24 Pembroke Street, Dublin, and was a co-operative enterprise. Despite being the main mover behind it and paying for the studio, Sarah was very democratic and insisted the workers were not 'under her direction'. The artists, who included Evie Hone and Wilhelmina Geddes, each worked alone on one commission at a time, and were responsible for both design and execution – a new idea in stained-glass manufacture. Sarah herself made windows for Loughrea Cathedral and the Abbey Theatre. An Túr Gloine was a major focus of Sarah's energies for the next forty years.

In 1911, when she was already in her sixties, Sarah decided to move from Harcourt Terrace. She and her unmarried brother leased Mespil House, a beautiful Georgian mansion (now demolished). There she held enormously popular salons on the second Tuesday of every month for the artistic, the literary and the intellectuals of the day, becoming ever more influential in Irish cultural affairs. In 1914 she accepted a seat on the Board of the National Gallery of Ireland.

Sarah was not in Dublin during the Easter Rising of 1916, but she lost eight of her paintings when a British gunboat bombed Academy House on Abbey Street during an RHA exhibition. Displaying admirable perseverance, she repainted her canvasses.

In 1923, at the age of seventy-five, Sarah held her first and only solo exhibition. It was a critical success, and the success was all the sweeter because, in the same year, the RHA finally dropped its ban on women. After fifty-two years exhibiting as an 'honorary member', Sarah became the first *bona fide* female associate member of the Academy. The following year she founded the Friends of the National Collections of Ireland.

Along with Lady Augusta Gregory, Sarah campaigned for years

for a Municipal Gallery of Modern Art. Eventually, in 1925, through her influence with WT Cosgrave's government, the gallery finally found a home in Charlemont House, Parnell Square, where it still resides. Sarah herself continued living in Mespil House and painting into her late eighties. She was active in An Túr Gloine until her death.

All those who knew how passionate she was about art joked that her long and fruitful life was finally brought to an end by a bad portrait. In 1943 a stamp was issued carrying what Sarah regarded as a very poor painting of president Douglas Hyde. When she saw it she was so incensed that she suffered a stroke and died. She was ninety-five years old.

Lily Yeats, 1866–1949
and Lolly Yeats, 1868–1940

Entrepreneurs and publishers

The Yeats sisters – Susan, known as Lily, and Elizabeth, known as Lolly – kept and supported their famous brother, William Butler Yeats, throughout his impecunious youth. Later they played an important part in the Gaelic Revival when they founded and ran their own publishing house. Lily also ran a successful embroidery business.

The family into which the Yeats sisters were born was dysfunctional by any standard. Their father, John B Yeats, a middle-class Protestant from County Sligo, rejected his bourgeois life as a barrister in order to follow his inclinations as an artist. Unfortunately, he was completely incapable of making or holding onto money, or even of completing his commissions on time. The girls' mother, Susan Pollexfen, was terminally disappointed in life and became a recluse. Her mental instability obsessed the whole family who worried in turn about going mad themselves. Their two brothers, Willie and Jack B, were obviously gifted, but not in areas likely to produce a regular income. Therefore, the burden of supporting the family fell on Lily and Lolly.

Arty, sensitive and apolitical, the Yeats sisters wanted nothing more than to be the submissive and cherished wives of successful Anglo-Irish men. But instead of making a début into society and finding husbands, they found they had to work for a living as soon as they had finished their less-than-adequate educations. They led what Lily called 'a man's life' of work and worry.

In the late 1880s and 1890s, when the family was living in London, Lily trained in embroidery under the famous designer William Morris, rising through the ranks to become an instructor. Lolly trained as a teacher, lectured in art, published two books on water-colouring and taught herself typesetting in her 'spare' time. Their salaries went towards supporting their father, mother, Willie and Jack. The burden lightened somewhat in 1895 when Willie started to receive royalties and moved out of the family home.

By the turn of the century, the sisters had a decade of working in London behind them and were desperate to get back to Ireland. They felt like outsiders in England and they were not meeting any potential mates. In addition, their brother seemed to be almost single-handedly orchestrating the Gaelic Revival at home, and the sisters knew that, with their skills and experience, they could make a contribution.

In 1902 the whole family moved to a house called Gurteen Dhas in Dundrum, Dublin. Soon after, along with their friend Evelyn Gleeson, they founded a cottage industry, the Dun Emer Guild, in Dundrum. The guild was named after Emer, wife of Cú Chulainn, and her image appeared on one of their press marks.

The guild was a home-grown arts and crafts co-operative that employed Irishwomen to produce high-quality Irish embroidery and books. Although successful, within a couple of years it was beset by cash-flow problems and destructive personality clashes between its three founders. The result was that the Yeats sisters broke away in 1908 and set up their own business in Churchtown, Dublin. Cuala Industries, as it was named, comprised both Lily's embroidery business and Lolly's Cuala Press. It retained the idea of using only women workers, Irish materials and producing only the highest-quality articles.

While Lily produced piece after piece of finely crafted embroidery, from large ornamental banners to dresses to small domestic items, Lolly ran the publishing arm alone. WB Yeats had no hands-on function at Cuala – he was the 'editor', which meant he decided what was published and roundly criticised any mistakes. Cuala Press published first editions of Yeats' own work as well as books by other 'suitable' authors, including Lady Augusta Gregory, JM Synge, Ezra Pound, George Bernard Shaw, Oliver St John Gogarty and Elizabeth Bowen. The responsibility for design, typesetting, proofing, production and quality fell to Lolly, who worked incredibly hard for thirty-two years to make Cuala Press the best-known literary press in Ireland.

Meanwhile the sisters still lived at Gurteen Dhas, the upkeep of which they paid for from their low salaries. But by 1909 they were living there alone: their remaining brother, Jack B Yeats, had married and moved away while their father, John B Yeats, had visited the USA on holiday, liked it and decided never to come back, leaving his daughters to get along as best they could. This was unfortunate because, as the sisters aged, their differences became more pronounced and there was constant tension between them. Lily was non-confrontational, maternal and languid, whereas Lolly was twitchy, blunt and something of a workaholic.

As time dragged on, they grew to hate living together. However, as single women with little cash the sisters had no choice but to stay manacled to each other until marriage or death released them. As for relations with their famous brother, Lily, who claimed to be psychic, was the only one in the family Willie had any time for, whereas Lolly, the one with whom he had to work most closely, irritated him beyond endurance.

Although deeply interested in Ireland's cultural life, the sisters were uninterested in its political struggles. The events of Easter 1916 left them frightened and they had little time for radical organisations, such as Sinn Féin. Neither had they time for politically minded women, and they strongly opposed the unfeminine undertakings of Constance Markievicz, Maud Gonne, Hanna Sheehy Skeffington, *et al*, with their marching and their prisons and their hunger strikes. However, after witnessing the behaviour of the Black and Tans during the War of Independence, the sisters both became supportive of Irish independence and Lolly even did some voluntary work for Sinn Féin.

This changed again during the Civil War. The Yeatses were a firmly pro-Treaty family and Willie was elected to the Dáil as a senator in 1922. When the republicans attacked Willie's houses in Galway and Dublin, the sisters withdrew any support they might once have given to republicanism and again became apolitical.

In 1925 the sisters moved Cuala, press and embroidery, to a larger premises at 133 Lower Baggot Street. A couple of years previously, Lily had survived tuberculosis, but her health remained delicate and she worked at her embroidery less and less. Instead she spent her time on the Yeats family history, which she had started as a labour of love some years before. In contrast to her sister, Lolly did more than ever. After supervising the move, she increased the output of Cuala Press, went on business trips and taught art twice a week. Her famous pupils included Mainie Jellett and her own niece, Anne Yeats. Ironically, she remained chronically short of money, even though some of her early books were now selling for large sums at auction.

In 1931 Lily's embroidery stopped altogether and she relied on Lolly and Willie to support her. By now in her sixties, Lolly had no intention of retiring and worked doggedly on, ignoring the economic climate, which fostered distrust and resentment of professional women. She had a last major spat with Willie in 1938 when he reorganised Cuala, bringing in new people to sit on a managing committee. A year later, Willie was dead, and a year after that, in 1940, Lolly herself died of a heart attack. Lily, despite being an invalid, proved the stronger of the two sisters and lived on at

Gurteen Dhas for another nine years. When she died at the age of eighty-three, she was buried beside her sister – still forced together, for eternity, whether they liked it or not.

Grace Gifford
1888–1955

Cartoonist, republican and Joseph Mary Plunkett's wife

Grace and her famous sisters were born to a Protestant unionist lawyer and his Catholic wife in the well-to-do suburb of Rathmines, south Dublin. Despite their parents' mixed marriage, all twelve Gifford children were reared as Protestants.

When Grace was sixteen years old she went to study at Dublin's Metropolitan School of Art, and later at the prestigious Slade School of Fine Art in London. As she grew older she became interested in politics, but she was not as proactive as her sister, Sydney, who, in 1906, joined the women's nationalist organisation Inghínidhe na hÉireann, and also wrote for the nationalist press under the name 'John Brennan'.

However, Grace's predilection for mixing with Dublin's arty types eventually led her into the orbit of Constance Markievicz. Inevitably, Grace was drawn into the independence movement and became a member of both Sinn Féin and Inghínidhe na hÉireann. By 1910, Grace, Sydney and another sister, Muriel, were serving daily hot meals to Dublin's poorest children as part of an action instigated by Inghínidhe na hÉireann and the Irish

Women's Franchise League (IWFL). All of the Gifford girls were active supporters of the League.

Grace met her future husband, the revolutionary Joseph Mary Plunkett, in late 1914 or early 1915. Joe, a respected published poet, was the son of a papal count and editor of *The Irish Review*. By Christmas 1915 Grace and Joe were engaged and, in deference to the Plunkett family, Grace converted to Catholicism. Grace and Joe's original plan was to marry on Easter Sunday 1916; it was and is unusual for Catholics to marry on a holy day, but Joe's sister (Eilís Dillon's mother) had set a precedent. However, as Joe was suffering from glandular tuberculosis and had to have an operation, the wedding was postponed.

Although Grace knew that Joe was a nationalist, she did not know that he was also on the military council of the IRB, nor did she know the extent of his involvement in the republican fight. As a founder member of the Volunteers, it was he, along with Eamonn Ceannt, who was largely responsible for the military strategy of the rebellion planned for Easter 1916. However, to protect the secrecy of the organisation, he was unable to divulge information to Grace about the Rising.

Grace first realised that something was afoot when she received a message from Joe on the night of Easter Sunday. He told her that he had written his will, leaving everything to her. He also sent her a gun. When the Rising started the following morning, Easter Monday, Joe immediately took himself from his sickbed and joined his comrades. He had been out of hospital for only two days and was not a particularly active participant. He was sincere in his commitment, however – taking part was essential, even if it meant lying miserably on a mattress in the GPO most of the time.

Grace kept a low profile during the Rising, anxiously waiting for news of her loved ones. Apart from her fiancé, she had family members to worry about. Yet another of her sisters, Nellie, was a member of the Irish Citizen Army (ICA), and was stationed with the regiment at Stephen's Green, working primarily as a cook and delivering food to command posts. Grace's brother-in-law was the poet, dramatist and scholar Thomas MacDonagh, who was married to Muriel. Thomas was in charge of the Second Battalion of the Volunteers, which had taken over Jacob's biscuit factory, located a few minutes south of Dublin Castle.

After the failure of the Rising, Joe was arrested along with the others and jailed in Kilmainham. He was court-martialled and found guilty of treason and sentenced to be shot at dawn on the morning of 4 May. When Grace heard the news she went out and bought a wedding ring and brought it round to Kilmainham. Somehow she managed to get permission to be married.

The ceremony took place in the prison chapel by the light of one candle, held by a soldier. Two other soldiers, both with fixed bayonets, acted as witnesses. There were no speeches and no time to talk – Grace was not allowed to spend time with her husband. Afterwards she went to stay in lodgings in Thomas Street.

Grace was awoken at two o'clock the following morning. She was taken back to Kilmainham and allowed to spend ten minutes with her husband in his cell. Joe was executed by a firing squad one hour later.

In the aftermath of the Rising, Grace was elected onto the Sinn Féin executive. In 1922 she was anti-Treaty, as her husband would have been, and during the Troubles that followed, Grace used her artistic talent to propagandise for Sinn Féin on banners and posters.

By the 1920s Grace was active in the Women's Prisoners' Defence League (WPDL), and this was enough to earn her a period of imprisonment in 1923, along with many other republican women, including Mary MacSwiney and Dr Kathleen Lynn. Before she was released (without charge), she painted a figure on the wall of her cell that became famous as the 'Kilmainham Madonna'. (A replica of Gifford's Madonna was made when the jail was refurbished and can be seen by visitors today.)

Grace published three collections of her satiric cartoons, but became less and less politically active. Under de Valera's government in the 1930s and 1940s, her life became slightly easier and she was able to live on a pension she received as 'a widow of the Rising'. She never remarried.

By the 1940s Grace was suffering from serious health problems and lived in almost complete retirement. At her funeral in 1955, which was attended by the president of Ireland, Seán T Ó Ceallaigh, she received full military honours. She is buried near the republican plot in Glasnevin cemetery, Dublin.

Mainie Jellett

1897–1944

Modern artist

Mary Harriet Jellett, known as Mainie, was born into a wealthy family living in Fitzwilliam Square, Dublin. Her father was a senior barrister, her mother was descended from a long line of scholars of Irish language and culture – the Stokes family. Mainie showed an early talent for art. Lolly Yeats and other private art tutors taught her and her friends (including the novelist Elizabeth Bowen) at the Jellett home in Fitzwilliam Square.

At sixteen years of age, Mainie attended the Metropolitan School of Art in Dublin, after which she transferred to the Westminster School of Art, London. At Westminster, Mainie met Evie Hone, who was later to become her close friend and one of Ireland's most prominent stained-glass artists. Mainie studied under Walter Sickert, a post-impressionist and pupil of JM Turner. She won a Taylor art scholarship from the Royal Dublin Society in 1917, and a Taylor prize the following year. In 1920 Mainie returned to Dublin. An extremely talented pianist, it was only at this stage that she decided to choose art over music as her career.

The beautiful Sickert-period oils that Mainie produced at this time were what she called the 'first revolution' or phase of her art. Her 'second revolution' started early in 1921 when she and Evie Hone travelled to Paris and enrolled under André Lhote, a disciple of Picasso. André ran a traditional teaching academy, combining Cubism (abstract art in which objects are represented as geometric shapes) with a study of the Old Masters. In Paris, Mainie fell in love with non-representational art and her life course was set.

Mainie was a fast learner. After a few months she came to feel that André's work was a 'compromise', that it did not go far enough into Cubism. She wanted to get down to what she called the 'essentials' of the art form. So, in late 1921, she and Evie tracked down a more extreme exponent of Cubism, Albert Gleizes, who underplayed realism in favour of pure form and colour in his art. Albert was initially unwilling to take on the two Irishwomen, but Mainie and Evie hounded him until he gave in. Every winter for the next decade, they spent six weeks with Albert and other students in his Paris studio, sometimes all working on the same painting. They would then return to Ireland to work out new ideas and develop their individual styles.

In 1924 Mainie and Evie held a joint exhibition of their abstract work in Dublin, which was largely met with derision, both from the Irish art world and from the general public. But Mainie was not going to allow Irish art to remain isolated from the modernist movement – in art, as in politics, she wanted to see less of a link to Britain and more of a link to the rest of Europe.

Around 1930 both Mainie and Evie returned to Ireland fulltime. While Evie turned to making mainly representational stained-glass pieces, Mainie channelled her energies into creating new art for what she saw as a new, young Ireland. She saw many similarities between Cubist art and early Christian Celtic art, for example, in the way that simple shapes often contain within them swirling and vibrant abstract forms. 'If an Irish artist of the eighth or ninth century,' she said in a 1942, 'were to meet a present-day

Cubist or non-representational painter, they would understand one another.'

According to her friend, the writer Elizabeth Bowen, Mainie's work fell into three main categories: non-representational art, which is born purely of the mind and based on experience or on nature; realistic landscapes treated in a manner inspired by Chinese art; and non-representational, Christian subjects. Mainie felt religious art was particularly important in Ireland because the lack of religious freedom of the preceding three centuries had led to a stagnation in this field.

In spite of a cold reception to the 1924 exhibition, Mainie felt she had a mission to make modern art more accessible to the public, and to this end she lectured, opened exhibitions, broadcast and wrote tirelessly. Her plea was that viewers should approach modernist works with an open mind – quite apart from the narrative ideas behind more traditional art, the viewer could also experience a strong initial response to colour and form that was valuable. Mainie always took in pupils and was remembered as being selfless and innovative with her time and techniques. If the students could not be in the studio with her, she would teach them by post; if the students did not wish to learn about Cubism, she would help them trace Old Masters. Her teaching style was unique – she often used music to illustrate a point.

Although her work was vocational, Mainie remained open-minded. Her attitude to art was unfussy and workmanlike; the artist was not, as she said, 'an exotic flower set apart from other people'. She believed art had a role to play in everyday life and in Irish industrial expansion, a belief reflected in the fact that she herself worked with textiles and carpets, made theatre sets, costumes and shop signs and was involved in town planning.

Mainie's work had a massive influence on modern Irish painting in the inter-war years. Her efforts were slowly recognised by the Irish government, which, in the late 1930s, commissioned her to produce works for industrial exhibitions in Glasgow and New York.

By the early 1940s Mainie was the leading figure of a circle of Dublin-based avant-garde artists, including Evie Hone, Nora McGuinness and Louis le Brocquy. In 1943 this group founded the Irish Exhibition of Living Art (IELA), of which Mainie was the first chairperson. True to Mainie's own style, the IELA believed in accessibility, for example, one of its functions was to show work that was considered too unconventional for the Royal Hibernian Academy (RHA).

Shortly after the establishment of the IELA, Mainie became painfully ill with cancer. She died in a Dublin nursing home the following year, at the young age of forty-seven.

GLOSSARY

Anglo-Irish Treaty – treaty between the Irish government and the British government that ratified partition of the Six Counties. The treaty was signed, reluctantly, on 6 December 1921 by Michael Collins, Arthur Griffith, Robert Barton, Eamon Duggan and George Gavan Duffy. The main terms were:

1. Ireland received Dominion status within the Commonwealth, that is, the same constitutional status as Canada.

2. A representative of the Crown, known as the governor general, would remain in Ireland.

3. All members of the Free State parliament would take an oath of allegiance to the British monarch.

4. Britain would retain control of the treaty ports, that is, Cobh and Berehaven in County Cork, and Lough Swilly in County Donegal.

5. Britain would be responsible for Ireland's coastal defence for five years.

6. Boundary Commission to be set up to determine the boundary between north and south.

7. Council of Ireland to be elected if and when the Northern Ireland parliament chose to enter the Free State.

Black and Tans – an armed force sent by the British government to Ireland during the War of Independence (1920–1921). They became notorious in Ireland and America for the brutality they used against the Irish, particularly against their main opponents, the members of Sinn Féin.

Brehon law – a pre-Christian legal code that was still in use until the conquest of Ireland in Tudor times. Under Brehon law many women had more rights than under English law, for example, they retained ownership of property they brought to a marriage.

Cat and Mouse Act – passed in 1913, it allowed hunger-striking prisoners in poor physical condition to be released, only to be re-arrested as soon as their health improved.

Civil War (1922–1923) – following the ratification of the Anglo-Irish Treaty in the Dáil by just seven votes, there was a split between republicans who were unhappy with such a compromise and wished to continue fighting for a fully independent republic, and Free Staters who accepted it because they saw the vague Dominion status of Ireland as a stepping-stone to a full republic in the future. This difference led to Eamon de Valera and his colleagues in Sinn Féin fighting against their one-time comrades in the Irish Free State. The republicans were defeated in 1923.

Cumann na mBan – translates as 'the league of women'. An auxiliary corps to the (all-male) Irish Volunteers. Set up in 1914, it was initially led by Agnes Farrelly, but after the Easter Rising of 1916 it was led by Constance Markievicz. Its subordination to the Volunteers meant it was not involved in decision-making, but its members were unanimously anti-Treaty in 1922. The organisation eventually fizzled out due to disagreements between itself and the IRA, which had taken over the militaristic role of the Volunteers.

Dáil Éireann – translates as 'the assembly of Ireland', that is, the Irish government. Members are called Teachta Dála (members of the house) or TDs or deputies. The prime minister is the Taoiseach, and the deputy prime minister is the Tánaiste. Dáil Éireann was first proclaimed in 1919 by Sinn Féin, in opposition to the British government at Westminster.

Fairy fort – features in the landscape, now known to be prehistoric tombs or fortifications, which were once widely believed to be home to the Sídhe, or fairies. These enchanted places were (and often still are) treated with respectful awe.

Fianna Éireann – founded in 1909 by Constance Markievicz as, what she called, a 'rebel Boy Scout organisation'. Its members were all young boys and its activities included training the boys to use real firearms. When they came of age the youngsters moved on to join the Irish Volunteers, fulfilling their commitment to fight for Irish independence.

Fianna Fáil – translates as 'Soldiers of Destiny'. The party was founded in 1926 by Eamon de Valera and comprised moderate members of Sinn Féin. De Valera led the party until 1959.

First Dáil – following a massive swing towards Sinn Féin in the 1918 general election, the seventy-three Sinn Féin elected representatives refused to take their seats at Westminster. Instead, in January 1919, they formed their own assembly, the Dáil Éireann, electing Eamon de Valera as president and issuing a Declaration of Independence. The Dáil was proscribed later the same year.

Free State government – see Irish Free State.

G-Men – a term that originated in the USA, but in Ireland referred to a 'spy' or 'Government man'.

Gaelic League – founded in 1893 by Douglas Hyde and Eoin MacNeill to revive the Irish language. Ostensibly non-political, it played a crucial role in the Gaelic Revival of the late nineteenth and early twentieth centuries.

'German Plot' – an attempt by the British government to incarcerate more than seventy people involved with Sinn Féin by accusing them of complicity with Germany during World War I.

Home Rule – a movement in the 1870s and 1880s that sought to re-establish the separate Irish parliament, which had been abolished by the Act of Union (1800). The first Home Rule Bill was defeated in 1886, and the second in 1893. After that the movement was overtaken by popular demand for a republic.

Inghínidhe na hÉireann – on Easter Sunday 1900, Maud Gonne founded a nationalist women's organisation and acted as its first president. The group was committed to fostering Irish culture and supporting Irish manufacture. It organised amateur dramatics, Irish classes and history lectures. It was also unashamedly political, with an agenda for Irish independence.

Irish Free State – comprised the twenty-six counties of Ireland, which were granted Dominion status within the British Empire by the 1921 Anglo-Irish Treaty. WT Cosgrave, first president of the State, held office until 1932. In 1937 the Free State was renamed Éire. In 1949 Éire left the Commonwealth and became the Republic of Ireland.

Irish Republican Brotherhood (IRB) – founded in 1858, the IRB was a secret organisation with links to the Fenians in America. Its aim was an independent Irish republic, by any means necessary. It fomented rebellion, funded by its sympathisers in the USA, and organised the failed 1867 Fenian rising. In 1916 the leader of the organisation was Patrick Pearse, and its members were often also members of other nationalist organisations, such as the Irish Volunteers. The Irish Republican Army (IRA) took over its role in modern times.

Irish Women's Franchise League – a militant suffrage organisation, founded in 1908 by Hanna Sheehy Skeffington and Margaret Cousins, which grew to have branches all over Ireland. Full suffrage was achieved in the Free State in 1923, five years ahead of Northern Ireland and Britain.

Kilmainham Treaty (1882) – an agreement between Charles Stewart Parnell, leader of the Irish Parliamentary Party and president of the Land League, and the British government. The treaty promised concessions to impoverished Irish tenants if Parnell called off violent agitation.

Ladies' Land League – a sister organisation to the Land League, it was the first official women's political organisation in Ireland to engage in a campaign of reform.

Land Act (1881) – this Land Law Act, passed by William Gladstone's government, granted the three Fs (fixity of tenure, fair rent and free sale), and authorised a commission to make loans to peasants trying to purchase their land.

Land League – founded by Michael Davitt in 1879, it worked to transfer ownership of land from landlords to the people who worked and lived on the land. William Gladstone's Land Act (1881) undermined the League, and Charles Stewart Parnell dismantled it in 1882.

Parnellites – after Kitty O'Shea's scandalous divorce case in 1890 the Irish Parliamentary Party was split, but Charles Stewart Parnell refused to relinquish leadership. Twenty-eight members, known as Parnellites, supported Parnell, while forty-six members did not and formed a separate Home Rule-seeking faction. The party eventually reunited in 1900 under Parnell's successor, John Redmond.

Royal Hibernian Academy (RHA) – founded in 1823, it was a forum for artists and ran its own art school. Women were not welcome to attend, however they could enter paintings for exhibition as 'honorary members'. The ban on women was lifted in 1923. The RHA is still a strong force in Irish art, promoting and exhibiting Irish artists from its premises at Ely Place, Dublin.

Royal University – founded in 1880 in Dublin in response to Catholic demands for university education. It was abolished in 1908 and replaced by the National University of Ireland (NUI).

Second Dáil – Sinn Féin members returned in the election of 1921 formed a larger assembly, including one representative from Northern Ireland. The Second Dáil disbanded in June 1922 in preparation for the general election of that year.

Sinn Féin – translates as 'ourselves alone'. The party was founded in 1905 by Arthur Griffith with the political aim of Irish independence. Sinn Féin was more nationalistic than the Home Rule movement and eventually replaced it. It supported the Easter Rising in 1916 and won a landslide victory at the polls in 1918. Its members' subsequent refusal to attend Westminster led to the establishment of the First Dáil. Most of its members joined Fianna Fáil in 1926 in protest against Sinn Féin's acceptance of the Anglo-Irish Treaty. The remaining members continued to be known as Sinn Féin, and they became the political wing of the IRA.

Submit and Regrant – an English policy of the sixteenth century whereby Irish noblemen who submitted to English rule and English law (such as primogeniture, whereby the first-born son inherited all the titles and power instead of the clan electing a new chieftain) would be given English titles and could lawfully retain their lands.

The Truce – in the summer of 1921, a truce between the IRA and the British Army ended the War of Independence.

White Cross – founded early 1921 after Irish-Americans raised funds for the civilian victims of warfare in Ireland. The White Cross was in charge of distributing the funds.

Women's International League for Peace and Freedom – a pacifist organisation formed in 1915, and originally called the Women's International League. It raised money for civilian war victims in Europe and lobbied for a reworking of the harsh terms of the Treaty of Versailles after World War I.

Women's Prisoners' Defence League – founded in 1922 by Charlotte Despard and Maud Gonne to help the families of republican prisoners and to protest against prison conditions for republicans during the Civil War.

Women's Social and Political Union – a suffrage organisation founded in Manchester in 1903 by Emmeline Pankhurst. Its tactics became more militant in 1912.

BIBLIOGRAPHY

Arnold, Bruce, Mainie Jellett and the Modern Movement in Ireland. USA: Yale University Press, 1992.

Bates, Daisy May, The Passing of the Aborigines: a lifetime spent among the natives of Australia. London: Panther, 1972.

Bence-Jones, Mark, Life in an Irish Country House. London: Constable and Co. Ltd, 1996.

Blackburn, Julia, Daisy Bates in the Desert. London: 1994.

Branca, Patricia, Women in Europe since 1750. London: Croom Helm,1978.

Byrne, Patrick, Witchcraft in Ireland. Cork: Mercier Press, 1967.

Campbell, Mary, Lady Morgan: The Life and Times of Sydney Owenson. London: Unwin Hyman Ltd, 1988.

Chambers, Anne, Eleanor, Countess of Desmond: c.1545–1638. Dublin: Wolfhound Press, 1986.

Chambers, Anne, Granuaile: The Life and Times of Grace O'Malley. Dublin: Wolfhound Press, 1979.

Chambers, John, 100 Irish Lives. Dublin: Gill & Macmillan, 1992.

Clarke, Kathleen, Revolutionary Woman: My Fight for Ireland's Freedom. Dublin: The O'Brien Press, 1997.

Connolly, SJ (ed.), The Oxford Companion to Irish History. Oxford: OUP, 1998.

Coxhead, Elizabeth, Daughters of Erin. London: Secker & Warburg, 1965.

Cullen, Mary and Luddy, Maria (eds), Women, Power and Consciousness in Nineteenth-century Ireland. Dublin: Attic Press, 1995.

de Breffny, Brian (ed.), Ireland: A Cultural Encyclopaedia. London: Thames & Hudson, 1983.

Defoe, Daniel, The Life and Adventures of Mrs Christian Davies, commonly called Mother Ross [introduction by the Hon. Sir John Fortescue]. London: Peter Davies Ltd, 1928.

Doherty, JE and Hickey, DJ, A Chronology of Irish History since 1500. Dublin: Gill & Macmillan, 1989.

Duncker, Patricia, *James Miranda Barry*. London: Serpent's Tail, 1999.

Dunne, Seán (ed.), *The Ireland Anthology*. Dublin: Gill & Macmillan, 1999.

Edgeworth, Maria, *Chosen Letters*, in FV Barry (ed.). London: Jonathan Cape, 1931.

Fallon, Charlotte H, *Soul of Fire: a Biography of Mary MacSwiney*. Cork: Mercier Press, 1986.

Field Parton, Mary (ed.), *The Autobiography of Mother Jones*. Chicago: 1990.

Flower, Robin, *The Western Island*. Oxford: OUP, 1978.

Frost, Stella (ed.), *A Tribute to Evie Hone and Mainie Jellett*. Dublin: Brown and Nolan Ltd, 1957.

Glazier, Michael (ed.), 'Margaret Haugherey' in *The Encyclopedia of the Irish in America*. Indiana: University of Notre Dame Press, 1999.

Grimshaw, Beatrice, *From Fiji to the Cannibal Islands*. London: Thos Nelson & Son Ltd, 1917.

Grimshaw, Beatrice, *In the Strange South Seas*. London: Hutchinson & Co, 1907.

Grimshaw, Beatrice, *Isles of Adventure*. London: Herbert Jenkins Ltd, 1930.

Hamilton, CJ, *Notable Irishwomen*. Dublin: Sealy, Bryers & Co., 1904.

Harbison, Peter, *Cooper's Ireland, Drawings and Notes from an Eighteenth-Century Gentleman*. Dublin: The O'Brien Press, 2000.

Hardwick, Joan, *The Yeats Sisters: A Biography of Susan and Elizabeth Yeats*. London: Pandora (an imprint of HarperCollins), 1996.

Henry, Noel, *From Sophie to Sonia: 75 Years of Irishwomen's Athletics*. Dublin: 1996.

Hughes, Mary, 'The Parnell Sisters' in *Dublin Historical Record*, (21.1), 14–27, Mar./May, 1966.

Irish Feminist Information Publications, *Missing Pieces: Women in Irish History*. Dublin: IFIP, 1983.

Jellett, Mainie, 'My Voyage of Discovery' in *The Artist's Vision*, Eileen MacCarvill (ed.), 1958.

Johnson, Captain Charles, *A General History of the Robberies and Murders of the Most Notorious Pirates from their First Rise and Settlement to the Present Year* in, Arthur L Hayward (ed.). London: Routledge, 1926.

Jordan, Anthony J, *Willie Yeats and the Gonne-MacBrides*. Dublin: privately printed, 1997.

Kelly, AA, *Wandering Women: Two Centuries of Travel Outside Ireland*. Dublin: 1995.

Keogh, Dáire and Furlong, Nicholas (eds), *Women of 1798*. Dublin: Four Courts Press, 1998.

Kohfeldt, Mary Lou, *Lady Gregory: The Woman Behind the Irish Renaissance*. London: Andrée Deutsch, 1984.

Lawless, Emily, *Maria Edgeworth*. New York: MacMillan, 1904.

Lennon, Mary, McAdam, Marie and O'Brien, Joanne, *Across the Water: Irish Women's Lives in Britain*. London: Virago Press, 1988.

Levenson, Leah and Natterstad, Jerry H, *Hanna Sheehy Skeffington: Irish Feminist*. New York: Syracuse University Press. 1986.

Lewis, Gifford, *Somerville and Ross: The World of the Irish RM*. Harmondsworth: Viking,1985.

Linklater, Andro, *An Unhusbanded Life: Charlotte Despard, Suffragette, Socialist and Sinn Féiner*. London: Hutchinson, 1980.

Lomax, Judy, *Women of the Air*. London: John Murray Ltd, 1986.

Lyons, Mary (ed.), *The Memoirs of Margaret Leeson, Madam, 1727–1797*. Dublin: Lilliput Press, 1995.

MacCurtain, Margaret and O'Dowd, Mary (eds), *Women in Early Modern Ireland*. Dublin: Wolfhound Press, 1991.

MacMahon, Bryan, *Peig: The Autobiography of Peig Sayers of the Great Blasket Island*. Dublin: Talbot Press, 1973.

MacMullen, Major-General HT, *The Voice of Sarah Cullen*, privately printed, Dublin, 1955.

Mac Neill, M, *Máire Rua, Lady of Leamaneh*. Ballinakella: 1990.

Maddox, Brenda, *Nora: A Biography of Nora Joyce*. London: Minerva, 1989.

McNeill, Mary, *The Life and Times of Mary Ann McCracken 1770–1866*. Dublin: Allen Figgis & Co. Ltd, 1960.

Newcomer, James, *Maria Edgeworth*. New Jersey: Bucknell University Press, 1973.

Norman, Diana, *Terrible Beauty: A Life of Constance Markievicz*. London: Hodder & Stoughton, 1987.

Ó Céirín Kit, and Ó Céirín, Cyril, *Women of Ireland: a Biographic Dictionary*. Galway: Tír Eolas, 1996.

Ó Dúlaing, Donncha, *Voices of Ireland*. Dublin: The O'Brien Press, 1984.

O'Grady, John, *The Life and Work of Sarah Purser*. Dublin: Four Courts Press, 1996.

O'Halloran, Maura, 'Soshin', *Pure Heart, Enlightened Mind*. 1995.

O'Neill, Maire, *Grace Gifford Plunkett and Irish Freedom*. Dublin: Irish Academic Press, 2000.

Perkin, Joan, *Victorian Women*. London: John Murray Publishers Ltd, 1993.

Peter, A, *The Magdalen Chapel*. Dublin: Hodges, Figgis & Co. Ltd, 1907.

Pritchard, Rev. J, *An Account of the Ladies of Llangollen*. Wales: H Jones, no date.

Robinson, Lennox (ed.), *Lady Gregory's Journals 1916–1930*. London: Putnam & Co., 1946.

Rose, June, *The Perfect Gentleman*. London: Hutchinson, 1977.

Russell, Mary, *The Blessings of a Good Thick Skirt*. London: Flamingo, 1994.

Salter, Elizabeth, *Daisy Bates: the Great White Queen of the Never-Never*. London: Corgi, 1973.

Seymour, Bruce, *Lola Montez: a Life*. Connecticut: Yale University Press, 1996.

Sheehy Skeffington, Andrée, 'A Coterie of Lively Suffragists' in *Writers, Raconteurs and Notable Feminists*. Dublin: National Library of Ireland Society, 1993.

Tomalin, Claire, *Mrs Jordan's Profession*. London: 1999.

Trowbridge, WRH, *Daughters of Eve*, London: Chapman and Hall Ltd, 1911.

Uglow, Jenny, *The Macmillan Dictionary of Women's Biography*. London: Macmillan, 1982.

Wallace, Martin, *100 Irish Lives*. New Jersey: Barnes & Noble Books, 1983.

Ward, Margaret, *In Their Own Voice: Women and Irish Nationalism*. Dublin: Attic Press, 1995.

Ward, Margaret, *Unmanageable Revolutionaries: Women and Irish Nationalism*. London: 1995.

Welch, Robert (ed.), *The Oxford Companion to Irish Literature*. Oxford: Clarendon Press, 1996.

Wilde, Lady Jane, *Social Studies*. London: Ward & Downey, 1893.

Women's Commemoration and Celebration Committee, *Ten Dublin Women*. Dublin: 1991.

Yeats, WB, *Dramatis Personae*. Dublin: Cuala Press, 1935.

Younger, Calton, *Arthur Griffith*. Dublin: Gill & Macmillan, 1981.